Exam Nation

Exam Nation

*Why Our Obsession with Grades Fails Everyone –
and a Better Way to Think About School*

SAMMY WRIGHT

THE BODLEY HEAD
LONDON

1 3 5 7 9 10 8 6 4 2

The Bodley Head, an imprint of Vintage, is part of the Penguin Random House group
of companies whose addresses can be found at global.penguinrandomhouse.com

First published by The Bodley Head in 2024

Copyright © Sammy Wright 2024

Sammy Wright has asserted his right to be identified as the author of this
Work in accordance with the Copyright, Designs and Patents Act 1988

penguin.co.uk/vintage

Typeset in 12/14.75pt Bembo Book MT Pro by Jouve (UK), Milton Keynes
Printed and bound in Great Britain by Clays Ltd, Elcograf S.p.A.

The authorised representative in the EEA is Penguin Random House Ireland,
Morrison Chambers, 32 Nassau Street, Dublin D02 YH68

A CIP catalogue record for this book is available from the British Library

ISBN 9781847927521

Contents

Author's note

This is not a technical book. It isn't a manual, or a textbook for teachers. I hope teachers read it, and parents read it, but I also hope people who are neither of these read it just to understand a little better what it means to be a child at school in Britain today – and what that tells us about the society we live in.

It is also, on a pretty fundamental level, personal. Personal to me, and reflective of my own experience – but also personal to the hundreds of kids (and their parents and teachers) to whom I've spoken during the writing of it. In trying to describe the landscape of schools in Britain today, I made a choice early on that I would prioritise the voices of those who live and work in schools, who grow up in schools, who love and hate them. But I also knew that I couldn't write without the weight of my own twenty-two years in the sector bearing down on me. I couldn't ignore what I've learned from the places I've taught in and the schools I've known. So while I've tried to visit a range of schools in my research and talk to a range of pupils, and while my own experience is pretty varied geographically and contextually, the book I wanted to write is one in which there is an inevitable bias – towards secondary, towards mainstream, towards the North-East.

What I hope, though, is that in paying attention to the particular, we can see the shape of the universal. And that in acknowledging and embracing the personal, subjective way that we perceive education, we might actually get a better understanding of the ways it can be made to serve us all.

A note on my methodology. Much of the data I've used is taken from pre-Covid datasets – simply because nothing from the pandemic years is easily comparable. All children have been interviewed with the permission of their parents or carers and are fully anonymised – by name, by description and by changing the name and location of their school. There are four schools that have been named, due to their position in the national discourse (William Ellis School, Michaela Community School, Reach Academy and XP School), but for this reason there are no extended interviews with children from those schools. Interviews from my own current school fall into two categories: those with students now over eighteen, and group or classroom-based interviews that don't touch on any personal issues. Some adults agreed not to be anonymised – you can tell this if I have used a full name. Everyone identified by first name only has been given a pseudonym. The process of anonymisation includes the scrambling of other details such as description, location and particular circumstances.

Where students have revealed difficult circumstances, I have indicated them only in rough outline. Please understand that when I make oblique reference to challenges, these are not of a minor character. Wherever this happened, I followed standard safeguarding procedure and passed concerns on to the school.

All quoted speech from interviews is verbatim – sometimes I have cut hesitations and phatic utterances to clarify the meaning. Where quotes are not given in the context of an interview, or are attributed to no named student, they are re-creations. Some passages and exchanges with students are anecdotal reframings of conversations that happened many years ago – as such, they are neither verbatim nor authoritative. Others are generic versions of responses that I have heard many times.

Introduction

I had an odd phase a few years ago. It sprang from the fact that I spent a lot of my time in the schoolyard during lunch break. This kind of thing sounds unimportant, but any teacher will tell you it's vital. By being in the yard you become visible, approachable, invested with a kind of permanence and omnipresence that goes beyond your own classroom.

It can be boring, though.

Personally, on lunch duty I always make time to talk to kids. I say 'always', but in my school, a carefully constructed wind-tunnel on the North Sea coast, where rows of seagulls perch malevolently and swoop down for discarded chips, some days it's enough just to last until period five without being shat upon. But I do try. Mostly it's normal stuff: what lesson have you got next?; what did you have for lunch?; look out, that seagull's got its eye on your chips. But, as I said, a few years ago I had an odd phase where I tried to go a bit deeper.

What's school for? I'd ask.

The kids certainly thought it was odd. One girl, Alice, looked at me with a weary scowl and said, 'It's prison.'

But in most cases, the answer was simple. What was school for? Why, exams, of course.

Sometimes being a teacher is the greatest job in the world, but sometimes I find myself sympathising with Alice. I've been doing this for twenty-two years – and I'd be lying if I said, after all that time, that I think I have unequivocally been a force for good. I'm not sure you can class yourself as a proper teacher until you've had a moment, facing down a recalcitrant kid, when you realise that you're at fault, that the rule might indeed be bullshit and that you're going to enforce it anyway, because you just want to bloody *win*.

That sounds negative. I don't want to be. I love teaching, but it's a strange mix. You have moments of wonder and joy, special moments of connection on a surprisingly regular basis. You have fun in class, then you walk out and someone calls you a fat cunt. You have amazing long holidays, stretching out in ways that people in other professions only dream of. And when you return, you lie awake all night, scared of stepping back in, scared of how exposed the whole thing is. You work at breakneck speed and yet time stands still, with each year following the rhythm of the last, and November creeping up on you like the ghost of Christmas never-to-come.

And you do make a difference. Of course you do. Only, every year you fail as much as you succeed, and sometimes even the successes feel like failures.

Sometimes I try to describe to new teachers the way school works. I say that a teacher is a sprinkler, not a hose. You're not just directing water into the one spot that needs it, you're spraying across as wide an area as possible, in the hope that some random drop of knowledge hits a seedling that you weren't even aware of. You're not in control – at least not as much as you think you are.

That's my more hopeful take. In the grimmer moments I think that, as teachers, we're agents of the status quo, trained to weed out those who don't fit into neat rows.

None of this is the singular truth, though. I'm a 'school leader' now and I see that my values in the classroom are probably at odds with my values as a Head. I see schools that work, and I know they are about systems and rules, about certainty and predictability, about consistency in uniform and effective teaching strategies, about HR and performance management. Only, ask me about my classroom and I'll say it's about trust and love and long, rambling discussions about free will. Both are right. It's right that schools should be places of routine and order, and that kids need qualifications; and that they need the motivation that qualifications provide. But it's also right to say that the moments you touch someone emotionally – the times you make them *feel* – are the ones that stick.

It is possible to see all this and to still want your Year 11s to get excellent grades in their GCSEs.

★

Or at least it was. For me, there came a point at which the contradictions of our system became so glaring that I could no longer ignore them.

It starts with August 2020 and the release of that year's A-level grades. Unlike the previous year, and every year before that, no exams had been sat. Covid had laid waste to the basic structures of our education system, closing schools and cancelling A levels, BTECs and GCSEs. But the grades still had to be awarded. Without the grades, how would students access jobs and university courses? How would we know how *good* they were? There was a huge amount of angst in the education sector – and amongst those poor students who were suddenly plunged into limbo.

I had a ringside seat for this debate. At the time, alongside my day-job, I was a member of the Social Mobility Commission (SMC), the government body tasked with monitoring and advising on how to promote equality of opportunity. I'd been appointed in 2018 – after applying on a whim – with a remit for schools and higher education. By the time the pandemic hit, I'd spent two years scratching my head at the impossibility of coming up with meaningful ways to impact the life-chances of young people amidst the sound and fury of the Brexit wars.

But here was something concrete. The way we responded to this moment would have a definable impact on every exam-age child in the country. So I spoke to Ofqual (the body that regulates the exam sector) and UCAS (the Universities and Colleges Admissions Service), and the government, and participated in consultations, and spoke on news outlets, making the case for a system that acknowledged the complexity of how we measure performance. And I waited.

I remember results day so well. Teachers had submitted their data – comprising both grades and a rank order of students, from best to worst – which was then moderated by Ofqual. After a mysterious process, their 'calculated grades' would be handed out in the normal way. It was all a little odd. We approached the big reveal feeling both far more confident than normal – after all, we already pretty much knew what grades the kids would get – and yet somehow far more worried.

We were right to worry. When the grades were released in the morning, the normal joyous hysteria was replaced by an atmosphere of stunned fury. I walked around the sixth form, trying desperately to say something meaningful to students who had ended up with Ds where we had given them Bs, and whose university places had been lost. The newspapers splashed headlines stating that 40 per cent of grades had been moved down. What had gone so wrong?

Put simply, the system was designed to make the grades fit the distribution of previous years. Schools were supposed to get roughly the same spread of grades in each subject that they'd had on average over the last three years.

On the face of it, this might seem fair enough. After all, in a cohort of students numbering in the hundreds of thousands there *should* be the same distribution of grades year-on-year. In fact that's quite literally the job of exams – to make sure that the standards of what makes an A or a B don't shift over time.

But in 2020 it wasn't about 'distribution' in that general sense, looking across the whole cohort of students in the country and tweaking the boundaries. Instead it was done on a school-by-school basis, using the rank order that we had provided to simply – and illogically – match students to the previous year's grades. If last year the top student got a B and the second student got a D, then this year, even if the first- and second-ranked students were *both* on an A, they were dropped to B and D. And if no one in a given school got an A★ last year, then this year, no matter how great a particular student was, they were barred from that grade.

So in schools and sixth forms where results had improved dramatically, or where unusually bright children had exceeded expectations, the grades the teachers had submitted were universally slashed. By definition, the kids whose achievements were most deserving of recognition – the ones who had beaten the odds to do well – were hit hardest.

It seems insane, looking back on it. But it was the underlying logic behind this system that was truly eye-opening. It's worth stating baldly: essentially, the DfE (Department for Education) had decided that it was more important there were the right numbers of As and Bs and Cs, grouped neatly into the right schools, than that each individual got the grade they merited. In other words, it was more important that the students were ranked and sorted – even erroneously – than that their actual abilities or achievements were quantified.

It would be easy to say this was an anomaly. After all, back in 2020 the egregious unfairness of this system made the headlines, the unions were up in arms, and by the next week there was an almighty U-turn and the 'calculated grades' had been revised back to the original teacher assessments. But sometimes you pull a thread and everything begins to unravel.

For me, that thread began with thinking about the precise ways in which the shock of that moment played out. Because we weren't shocked at the basic fact of some kids getting grades lower than they should. That's actually quite normal. They fail to revise, or break up with a girlfriend two weeks before the exam, or their gran dies the night before, or they simply have a bad day, or the examiner has a bad day. No – we were shocked that it felt so *arbitrary*.

But why exactly does that make it worse? After all, there are so many far more predictable reasons for underachievement. We all know that kids who are in care, or have grown up in poverty, or whose parents are addicts, or who just go to a shit school, are less likely to do well in exams. And somehow we all accept that's okay. It's okay to have your education blighted by the chance assignment of social privilege – but not for it to be held back by a 'rogue algorithm'.

I wasn't the only one in 2020 to be pulling at these threads. As that summer of chaos drew to a close, many of us in education seemed to feel like (even without the disruption of Covid) our exam system was suddenly appearing a little ragged. Everywhere I looked there were articles on how it was not fit for purpose – so I started to think more about the nature of what it actually measures.

In one sense, the answer is easy. Exams measure what you know and what you can do on a given day at a given time. But really what that means in practice is that they also measure the circumstances that led up to that day and that time. They measure how you revised, how you slept, how anxious you were, how well you had prepared yourself to deal with the pressure.

It's okay to ignore this circumstantial detail sometimes. If we are training someone to be a physicist, then the things they know about physics are the most important aspect that we need to measure. The context is irrelevant. It doesn't really matter to us whether they crammed with the aid of a £120-an-hour tutor or revised with flash-cards taped to the back of the counter while working their part-time job – they need to know their stuff. And in order to choose who goes on to become a physicist, it is reasonable to judge on the basis of an exam to test this, and a grade to rubber-stamp it.

Only, the big assumption that sits behind the education system in Britain is that we are all, metaphorically speaking, training to be physicists. Most of our exams – certainly the 'core' compulsory subjects – are geared inexorably towards preparing for specialised degree study. Qualifications like GCSE and A level are basically reverse-engineered to provide the knowledge and structures to prepare for the next level of education. And yet for many students, the actual subjects they take – certainly at GCSE, and often at A level – are irrelevant to their later education or their work environments. Instead of a measure of specific skills and knowledge (for example, the physicist's ability to explain the second law of thermodynamics), when an employer encounters a grade on a CV, it is mostly taken as an indicator of generalised aptitude: hard work, study skills, problem-solving, and so on.

And to judge this, context *does* matter. It is absolutely crucial in fact. What could be more relevant to a judgement of character and aptitude than to know the head-winds someone has had to battle to achieve their goal?

Of course it's not the only thing, either. Some knowledge is help-ful, whether or not we're going to follow a career in it – and some knowledge is a moral right and should be democratically owned. But what knowledge? How much of it? Is it different from skill, and how do we test it? The question of what exams measure – or what they *should* measure – inevitably rests on the deeper question of what school is for.

Alice says it's a prison. She's wrong, of course, even as she hits on something uncomfortable about roll calls, bare concrete yards and bad food. But the least contentious way of putting it is probably that – in the most general sense – school exists to prepare people to become func-tioning members of society. It ought, therefore, to produce people who are good: morally good. Compliant with the law, compassionate and caring, willing to think about others and to countenance other view-points. It ought also to produce people who are skilled – economically productive, intellectually curious and equipped with good judgement, accurate knowledge and the ability to think laterally.

The problem, though, is that school as it is currently set up also exists to ensure that some of us fail. That was what struck me with such force in 2020. I spent months talking to well-meaning people in the DfE and Ofqual – committed, principled people, who were hon-estly trying to find a fair way to administer the grades, in the teeth of a nightmarishly difficult situation. And ultimately they came up with a solution that prioritised the need to have the correct distribution of grades (the correct *ranking*, sorted into the right number of passes and fails) over the need for accuracy, because our education system demands failure with such persistence that it seemed better to them to be unfair than to be over-generous.

In a school, pupils are told, clearly and unmistakeably, that to get your GCSE grades will give you a better life. To not get them will impair your life. They are explicitly given the language of pass or fail,[1] and implicitly given a value system that says the cleverer you are, the better you are. And this is done in the full knowledge that not all of them are capable of a pass and that, generally, it is entirely pre-dictable who comprises that lucky 65 per cent. Of course not every kid should receive an A grade. But it seems to me that there is a kind of mass gaslighting going on, whereby we tell kids to try their hard-est, and that they can do it, and only afterwards do we admit that we only meant that for the top sets.

Not everyone can succeed in a narrowly defined academic system. Not everyone can be a physicist. But then we don't even *want* every-one to be a physicist. In fact if everyone *was* a physicist, we'd all die in dirty, unfurnished squalor.

There is an argument that the reason we have the system we have – this intense 'meritocratic' system designed around meeting academic norms – is that competition is the thing that makes us better. We need to be in some kind of Darwinian struggle to make us stronger. If, in the race of life, everyone got a prize, we'd all just saunter to the finish line at half-speed. We need to winnow out the chaff. And this could well be the case – *if* the race were fair. But it's not. For all the years we have measured the gap in educational attainment (the gap in the grades gained) between students who grow up in poverty and those who don't, it has not shifted by any significant amount. Yes, there have been percentage gains and percentage losses. But fundamentally it is true to say that poor children, even though the most elementary logic would tell us they have so much more to gain from education, do less well at school.

One of the biggest and most rarely stated issues we face, as an education establishment and as a country, is this mismatch between what we promise young people and what we offer them. It is no coincidence that the communities where schools have the greatest difficulties – those with the highest numbers of students failing to get a decent education – are also those where there are no jobs and no hope, where the glib promises of bright futures if you pass your French GCSE ring increasingly hollow.

So how have we arrived at such a state? And how might we do things differently? These are the questions that I want to answer in this book.

We talk about education constantly. There is an insistent churn of news stories about standards and grades and rankings – about deficits in skills, and inequalities in outcomes, and plucky inspirational kids, and nightmare feral teens. Recently that's been intensified by a rash of culture-war scare stories: woke teachers force-feeding cultural Marxism, sex-ed classes that teach nine-year-olds about butt plugs. But, like many of the matters that are closest to us, we rarely take the time to *actually* look at what schools really are. It's time we did exactly that.

Why don't we do it more? We teachers are partly to blame. One of my great frustrations with the profession is the way we have become trapped by a mindset (fuelled, to be fair, by the oppressive accountability system of Ofsted, the schools inspectorate, and its well-documented impact on the well-being of teachers) that demands we never admit weakness or uncertainty, that we have to tell a story of success – or lay the blame for failure at the door of factors beyond our control. Because it feels so risky to admit error and struggle and shades of grey, and because, for all the strides that educational research has made, it is still dogged by unreliability,[2] it can be tempting to take refuge in simplistic stories about school.

I don't want to do that. I don't want those easy platitudes about all teachers being wonderful – or about kids these days being little shits. But I do want to offer *some* answers, even if they are uncomfortable, and sometimes unexpected.

You might expect a book called *Exam Nation* to argue for or against exams. But the Exam Nation I describe is not one where the act of sitting in an exam hall and doing a test is the root of all evil. Exams are not bad. Far from it – they are a vital tool. But if they're a tool, they are one we're not using for the right purpose. And that's the problem. The Exam Nation I want to show you is one where a useful tool has become a distorting goal – where the means has become the end. Where the ranking and sorting of our pupils, the creation of winners out of a particular kind of pupil at the expense of everyone else, is not just an unfortunate but unavoidable by-product of school; it is the guiding principle. Where one kind of thinking – a competitive, marketised view of school, a transactional mindset exemplified by the prioritisation and proliferation of grades and the meritocratic ranking they feed – has eaten away at the basic moral purpose of education.

And yet the answer isn't simply to scrap exams. We need to go deeper than that. In this book I aim to demonstrate how muddled our thinking is around the *purpose* of school – and how addressing the values at the heart of education can save it.

I say 'save it', but let's be clear what that means, too. Education is peculiarly vulnerable to half-arsed messianic pronouncements on minor side-issues. I'm not going to declare whether or not kids should wear uniform, or whether they should sing the national anthem. The solution isn't going to be about more group work or less group work, or group work in odd numbers, or that we should simply scrap desks and sit in circles, talking about our feelings. The

last chapter of this book does contain concrete recommendations –
because there are things that can, and should, be done. But this is not
a quick-fix guidebook for teachers. Nor is it an ideological polemic.
Instead it is an attempt to cut to the heart of the big issues, to think
about structures and purpose and policy – and yet to keep the ambiguity and messiness of the real world firmly in sight. Because while
our understanding of the purpose of school is so conflicted, the ideal
system doesn't – and cannot – exist.

We are at a moment of inflection. Society and the world around us
are in the midst of radical change. We have experienced political
upheaval, economic decline and demographic shift. And now, in the
wake of the pandemic and in the midst of the rise in the cost of living,
we need to think carefully, not only about how to make schools
better, but how to re-evaluate what we ask of them, how to change
the terms by which we judge them and how to allow them to work
better as agents of fairness, cohesion and possibility.

To write this book, I've drawn on two decades in the classroom, in
London and in Sunderland. I've drawn on the wealth of educational
research and history out there. Most importantly, though, I've been
trying to look with fresh eyes on the actual experience of what it is
like to be at school in England today. I should be clear that it is England, rather than the UK, that I'm looking at – the Scottish, Welsh
and Northern Irish education systems differ in greater and lesser ways
and, despite growing up in Edinburgh, my professional life has been
in England. But while the specifics of the systems might differ, the
place that school occupies in our society is similar across the country,
and the challenges that educators face run in parallel.

So this book also documents a journey that I've taken through the
landscape of schools in England, from tiny first schools in rural
Cumbria to multi-ethnic secondaries in Birmingham; from Catholic
primaries to Special Schools. I visited twenty schools over the course
of a year – as well as spending the rest of the time in my own – and
wherever I've been, I've interviewed the children who attend them:
more than 100 of them in one-to-one interviews, and then
hundreds more in groups. I've asked how they feel, and what they
think they are doing in this place where they spend most of their

waking lives. And then we've talked – sometimes for hours – about those lives.

This book is going to follow the thread of that simple question I first asked Alice in the schoolyard: *What is school for?* I'll start with the official answer to that basic question. I'll show how modern schooling has been defined by the need to measure, and the impact this has on how and what we teach. I'll also look at *why* we teach – both by examining the history of schools and the contradictory purposes they've had, and by exploring the current debates about the curriculum. I'll tell the story of how our schools are designed to perform a meritocratic ranking of their pupils, even as I also show how flawed this design is.

Then I'll turn to the reality. Many people don't learn what they're supposed to at school – but everyone is changed by school, for good or ill. So now I'll ask: *What is school really like?* I'll go beneath the surface, looking at different types of school, different stages, and exploring how it really feels to fail there – as well as the price of success. This is where I'll let you listen at length to what the young people I talked to think about their lives.

The last question of the book will bring together all the experiences I've had, asking: *How can we do it differently?* The first stage is thinking differently – and here I'll lay out an alternative story that we can tell about school, and what it could mean for our society. But telling a new story about school isn't possible without changing it. So I'll finish the book by setting out five concrete actions and five new narratives about school they could create, and how that would allow us to start finding a better way.

Schools are places where many truths coincide. Any talk of 'schools' in general is a simplification, flattening into one entity an ecosystem as complex as the country it serves. I want to open this up: to think about early years *and* sixth form, about the academic *and* the social, to think about how it feels to be successful at school – and how it feels to be a failure. And yet I do want to arrive at some fundamental truths and to question the basics: why schools are the way they are, what their real function is and how they fit with the society they spring from. On the most basic level, we need to get to an understanding of school that enriches *all* students, not merely the winners, and that values the process, not just the endpoint. Because, ultimately, that process will shape our children for thirteen crucial years of their lives — and *how* they learned may prove to be more indelibly marked on their souls than *how much*.

Whether or not you agree with my diagnosis, I think it is worth a hard look at the complexity of this world — and worth listening to the kids who inhabit it. Not because they have all the answers. They are children, after all. But because doing so will reveal what lessons school is *really* teaching them.

PART ONE

What is school for?

1. 'You just need school'

Let's start in my office. It's on the bottom floor of the New Block in our school. The New Block is indistinguishable from the Old Block. Both are a bit shit. I've been in this office since September, but I'm still not unpacked. I have an exam desk by the window. I use it to sit kids at when they are catching up on work, being naughty or (sometimes) sobbing inconsolably. My desk has a litter of papers: minutes from meetings; essays to mark, creased from my pocket; small folded pieces of paper with badly written accounts of one kid swilling another with orange juice; sweet wrappers from when I had no lunch and had to raid the treats drawer.

On my walls are some slightly dog-eared posters. Every room in the school has these posters.

Ready, Respectful, Safe, says one.

Aspire, Achieve, Enjoy, says another.

These are your Designated Safeguarding Leads, says a third. A row of embarrassed-looking mugshots runs underneath.

I arrived this morning at 7.30. So far, I have marked some books, giving feedback to fifteen-year-olds about their understanding of the imagery of time in *Macbeth*. I have attended a pastoral briefing in which I've listened to a rundown of some of the issues of the day – who's on report, who's suspended, who needs careful attention because their stepdad put a brick through the window last night. I've delivered an assembly on Holocaust Memorial Day. I've taught a lesson on Milton to Year 13, then met with other senior leaders to discuss the balance of subjects we will offer at GCSE next year. I finished that meeting abruptly when I had to run to get to my duty post at the restaurant, where I supervised the queue, then wandered around reminding students to pick up their rubbish. At the end of break I had to nip to my office to record on our safeguarding system a concern about a student who I noticed had suicidal messages written on their hand.

And it's still only 11.15.

Schools are busy places. Mine is a secondary, which means that every hour 1,500 pupils and 120 staff shuffle themselves, pouring out of rooms and along corridors and across the windswept yard and down the clattering stairs in packed, giggling, shouting hordes, and then decanting themselves neatly back into other rooms. There are twenty-nine lessons in a week, twenty-four subjects taught, up to thirty-three children in a classroom, and so far today I've received fifty-nine notifications on our recording system about misbehaving kids.

When this is your daily experience – as a student or as a teacher – school just seems like a fact of life. It is your ecosystem, and it follows arcane patterns and rules that aren't so much to be understood as merely observed. If you're a student, you know that to wear a coat over your blazer in cold weather is basic common sense – but to wear it under your blazer, with the hood poking out at your neck, is to signal devil-may-care rebellion. To speak out of turn in Mrs Harris's lesson is impossible – but to pretend to the supply teacher that of course you're allowed your phones out is only natural. And to drink out of your bottle by unscrewing the top is lame – but to use your compass to puncture a hole in the lid and then suck on it, like a teat, is the ultimate sign of sophistication.

And if you're a teacher, you battle through the day, accepting that, no matter how unsuccessful you might feel, your basic job is simple: to 'teach' while your charges 'learn'. You know that of course there will be a bell, and a break, and a lesson – that of course school means these things, along with Formica desks and plastic moulded chairs and chewing-gum spots and whiteboard markers. Of course there will be holidays, and of course the summer will be long, punctuated only by the heart-stopping anxiety of results day. You know that by the end of the term you will be loaded up with flu and funny stories, that you'll listen to your friends describe their day at work and think, simultaneously, 'lucky fucker' and 'poor bastard'.

But today I've decided I won't merely accept the complexity of it all as a fact of life. I'm going to dig a little. So I have recruited a focus group.

On the comfy seats at one end of my office I have gathered five

Year 7 students. They are excited. I took them out of English. They probably like English, but they like this more. Anything different is good – but particularly anything different with comfy seats and friends to giggle with. I start with the question I intend to ask all the students I will meet: What is school for?

Paul is a small boy with a bright smile, kind eyes and a slow voice.

'Your future,' he says carefully. 'Like, so you can get money and a house, like, get a good job. So you don't have any problems like paying bills and that.'

His friend Tyler is about twice Paul's size. Year 7 is like that – wild disparities between kids, and they barely seem to notice.

'Like education.' He takes his time, too. 'So you don't end up in a bad place with a bad headset.' He stops, confused. 'Like – no, not headset, mindset.' The others giggle. Tyler doesn't really register that. Like Paul, his concerns are on the big picture. 'So like you can get a good job and not be on the streets, or something, begging for money.' His eyes are wide at the thought, and he adds, 'Nowadays people don't give money to people who are just on the streets, because sometimes they're not poor, they just make money off begging on the streets.'

The others nod. Talking to Year 7 is often like this. You get a strange mixture of the thoughtful and the random opinion that they've heard once. It gives an odd impression: of honesty and malleability at the same time, of people not quite formed yet.

Olivia, sitting in the middle of the five, is more direct.

'You can't not go to school, because you need knowledge to live, really, as in like, so, you . . .' She pauses helplessly. 'You just *need* school.'

Why, though?

By definition, teachers believe you need school. 'School leaders' – headteachers, deputies, CEOs – they *really* believe it. They're often 'passionate' about it. Schools nowadays tend to have 'visions', not in the freaky 'hermit seeing a seven-headed beast eat the sun' kind of way (although that might be a little more interesting). No, these visions tend towards the blandly political, peppered liberally with words like:

Aspiration
Potential
Future
Achievement
Outstanding

At the same time, under the surface is the more prosaic legal framework of it. You need to go to school because, frankly, you can be fined if you don't go. Technically you need to be in education or training up to the age of eighteen. You can be home-schooled, but then you might not have the chance to gain the qualifications, which, in various ways, you also 'need'.

You need Level 2 qualifications (GCSE or equivalent) to get on to a Level 3 course (A level or equivalent). You need English and Maths passes at GCSE to qualify as a nurse, a teacher or a police officer. You need Level 3 qualifications to access university – and a university degree is necessary for a whole host of other careers.

Of course, all of this isn't really why we need school. Rather we need the *education* that school provides – and the qualifications, laws and regulations are simply checks and balances to make sure we get the right amount of it. And yet those checks and balances, the ways that we scrutinise and measure schools to be sure they are providing the education we want them to, are far from neutral.

Take performance tables – often referred to as 'league tables' or, quite simply, 'results'. The equation is simple. The more good grades a school elicits from its pupils, the better it is. So, the thinking goes, if we put this together into a 'performance table' and introduce an element of healthy competition, schools can only get better.

The thing is, measuring how 'good' the grades actually are turns out to be a bit more complicated. And every way that's been tried has introduced another layer of perverse incentives for schools that seek to bolster their position in the table.

When performance tables were first introduced, back in 1992, they simply reported how many students passed GCSEs. So some canny schools focused on kids who were on the cusp of a pass and threw all their resources into getting them over the line – neglecting other, less marginal cases. Some pupils would also be entered for exams early, as soon as they could secure a pass, denying them the chance to really stretch themselves.

The answer to this was not only to count the passes and fails, but to start looking at the total *value* of all grades – with each grade given a numerical worth, and higher grades worth more. But now the temptation was to engineer as many different qualifications as possible. Early entry still happened – only now followed by re-sit after re-sit, to slowly boost the score. Kids did extra courses of dubious quality, building up to the point where some finished school with eighteen, nineteen or twenty assorted GCSEs and BTECs – with correspondingly vast point scores – even if none of the individual grades was especially high.

And then there was CVA: Contextual Value Added. This entered the mix in the mid noughties and was an attempt to show the 'Value' added by schools – measuring how well pupils did in comparison to the average for their socio-economic status. But if you did the right combination of courses at the (cough) less rigorous end of the scale, maybe involving coursework, that could be massaged pretty well, too.

By now it was pretty clear that performance tables were not quite the straightforward comparison they seemed to be. Rather than clarifying and exposing quality of education, they became something to manipulate to conceal failings. Even when schools behaved with strict ethical rigour (which many did), rather than a motivating competition, the tables often simply created a sense of weary unfairness.

At this point let's imagine Michael Gove, Secretary of State for Education from 2010, as Captain Renault in *Casablanca*, walking into Rick's Café ready to play poker – only to turn on a sixpence and say, 'I'm shocked! Shocked to find that gambling is going on in here.' Gove stayed at the DfE for four tumultuous years, and is probably the key figure in the recent history of education in England. He managed to combine a decent nose for bullshit, a willingness to piss off everyone and some fine raised eyebrows to match Claude Rains. He said, with some justification, that reporting CVA led to a lack of ambition for the most disadvantaged, and that the poor quality of the

qualifications offered meant that students were not academically prepared for the next stage – again, something that I and many other
teachers would be broadly in agreement with. Most of all, Gove was
shocked and appalled at the levels of gaming-the-system that went
on: the idea that when you call something a league table, people
would seek to climb it!

The big idea of the reforms he instigated – and that still form the
basis of the education system now – was that the woolly progressivism and 'everybody wins' grade inflation symbolised by those
ever-shifting league tables had resulted in a less-than-rigorous curriculum and had undermined 'standards'. Nothing was properly
comparable – you couldn't trust that exam scores meant what they
said they meant, what with re-sits and coursework and bogus qualifications. As far as Gove was concerned, traditional academic rigour
was the way forward. The way to level the playing field was to ensure
that all students – and all schools – were incentivised to follow a
content-heavy curriculum that prioritised recall and old-school 'subject knowledge'. With a curriculum like that, you could be sure that
a top grade was a top grade. The reformed GCSE and A-level courses
largely ditched the idea of both modularity (the ability to sit different units of a course separately, and hence retake only those with the
weakest score) and coursework, meaning that everything came down
to the final exam, and upped the challenge of the content. As for the
league tables that would measure this revolution, they were purged
of many of the 'Mickey Mouse' qualifications, retakes no longer
'counted' and a new concept – the English Baccalaureate (EBacc) –
was announced.

The EBacc is a strange beast: a kind of imaginary qualification
with no presence in the real world. It was based on the idea, fed down
from Russell Group universities (the most competitive and prestigious of our higher-education institutions), that some subjects are
better than others for preparing students for future academic success –
but really it was a way of reversing the trend towards students
entering multiple non-academic qualifications at sixteen, and instead
incentivising schools (without quite making it compulsory) to keep
the range of subjects within a narrow, 'academically rigorous' range

of core GCSEs. The EBacc consists of English, Maths, Science, one humanity (Geography or History) and a language. I have yet to encounter any university, educational institution or employer that specifies a pass in all EBacc subjects as being desirable. Nonetheless, schools that prioritised EBacc in their curriculums were considered 'ambitious', and so pass rates in EBacc were now reported in the league tables, as were entry rates – how many students sat the qualifications in the first place. A national target was even announced: that 75 per cent of all pupils would be entered for EBacc.

Now the pressures on schools became very different. Jobs in the Arts and PE teaching went down – and Humanities teachers became the flavour of the month. Kids went from a two- or three-year process of sitting and re-sitting modules and coursework tasks, to one where everything was decided in a four-week period over as many as twenty-eight academic exams.

At the same time, a fiendish new metric to measure and compare performance was introduced – Progress 8. It took SATs tests (Standard Assessment Tests, taken in Year 6, the last year of primary) as a benchmark and used them to calculate a progress score for sixteen-year-olds, based on the relationship between SAT scores and GCSE scores. A score of 0 meant expected progress, while a score of -1 indicated one grade lower than expected and +1 showed achievement of one grade higher than expected. It was calculated using individual grades, but was not reported for individuals – only for schools. And it amalgamated all subjects into one handy score (easy for direct comparability between schools), but weighted them differently, with English and Maths counting double, and EBacc worth more than 'Open Bucket' subjects like Art or Music or Sport.

If your brain hurts now, spare a thought for the school leaders and their achievement spreadsheets.

So did it work? Well, it would be fantastic to report that having refined how we measure schools, we have eradicated the gaming of league tables, improved the curriculum that students receive and now have a proper, statistically accurate assessment of how well schools provide their core service. The truth is, as ever, more nuanced. We are undoubtedly doing better than we were at one version of school.

Kids who sit the new GCSE come out of it better prepared for the world of A level and university study. And most schools, held to account by the new metrics, push their best and brightest towards this ideal, irrespective of their background. This is unequivocally a good thing.

At the same time, though, the 'progress gap' – the gap between the progress made from the end of primary to the age of sixteen by those who grow up in poverty and those who don't – has increased every year since these reforms landed in 2016.[1] And we're certainly nowhere near that target figure of 75 per cent EBacc entry.

Meanwhile, somewhere along the way, a conceptual shift has taken place. For all the traditionalist trappings of the Gove reforms, they responded to a very twenty-first-century environment – where rather than league tables being a snapshot of the state of schools, they have become one of the principles around which the school curriculum is built. They didn't try to take us back to a mythical golden age of education, as some (both critics of Gove and his supporters) had suggested. Instead they took us even further down the road to an Exam Nation – where ranking and comparability are assumed to be an automatic good. In fact their demand that we should be able to make direct comparison and equivalence between 'difficulty' in different subjects has changed the way we assess and teach.

One example shows this change perfectly. In the English Language GCSE – one of the central planks of the 'core' curriculum – Speaking and Listening used to make up 20 per cent of the final grade. But because it had to be assessed in school and was hard to do objectively, it was 'unfair'. It could be used by schools to provide much-needed extra marks. In the reforms, Speaking and Listening was therefore relegated to being a box that had to be ticked, without making any impact on the final grade at all.

I'd steer clear of any view that paints what came before as a perfect system. I know for a fact that some Speaking and Listening assessments were less than rigorous. The new exams and the tables they feed are much 'fairer' in one way – just as there is no doubt that if comparability is the aim, exams outperform coursework every time. But when it came to the teaching of English, the removal of

Speaking and Listening marks at one stroke stripped out the incentive to properly teach the part of the subject that will be most relevant to the widest range of kids – both those academically inclined and not.

The educational system we have now is a result of the tools we use to scrutinise and measure it, just as surely as the skills of a professional footballer are a product of the rules of the game they play. Performance tables have redefined how we think of success in schools, for better or worse. The same tendency is everywhere in the curriculum. If you can't measure it, you shouldn't do it – or at least, the better it fits with the demands of ranking and comparability, the better it is educationally. And if it's 'easy' for kids to get credit without being 'able', then it must be educationally worthless.

Sometimes, now, it can feel like the answer to that question 'What is school for?' is depressingly straightforward.

To get a good score at Progress 8.

That's not what the kids say.

'You learn a variety of subjects, you can find out which one you like more and then whichever one you like more, you can get different jobs for, and then you'd be happy with the job,' says Alisha firmly.

But is there stuff you just have to know? I ask, channelling Michael Gove. Specific things, like Geography?

'You have to learn about the various, like, "normal subjects",' says Paul uncertainly.

Shauna is the tallest of the five, and the most confident. She's clearly bright and is used to academic success. 'I think it's all about the learning, and all of that.' Her head dots about eagerly as she speaks. Her words fire out quickly. 'Like, knowing more things. Like you go to school and you can talk to people, and then you go and you can pass on more knowledge, and then you can go to someone else and they'll give you different experiences so you'll be able to, like, learn more and then you'll be able to tell people. Like you don't have to be a teacher to be able to teach someone.'

I like this. There's something there about education as a broader social good, not simply a method of advancement for the individual – even if it doesn't tell me much about which knowledge, and why. But what the older kids say leaves me with a nagging worry. When I ask the bright Year 11s, for example – the ones who seem to know what they are doing – their answer is pretty universal.

'If you get good grades, it'll help you get a job.'

'I need the grades to get into sixth form.'

'You need EBacc because the universities want you to have it.'

And when I ask the ones who are struggling, I get this:

'Why do I have to do French? I'm never going to France.'

'What's the point of History? I don't need it. I'm going to be an electrician.'

And, of course, the classic:

'Why do I need to study English? I can speak.'

Both of these sets of students see their education as transactional – get this knowledge, and get that result, and don't bother with it if you don't want the result anyway. And both seem to me to be the product of an educational landscape that has been shaped by league tables, one that has been defined by the need to label success neatly and numerically. This explains a third kind of response to the question, the one that makes me feel like dying inside, because it's both terribly unfair and horribly true.

'You just want us to get good grades so the school looks good.'

I wouldn't turn the clock back. The most recent round of reforms has done a lot of good, and the pressures of league tables have undoubtedly improved our educational offer. But it seems we might have become caught in a kind of tautological trap – that we need school because it allows us to get grades, and we need grades because they are the thing that shows we've succeeded at school.

As I wave goodbye to my five keen Year 7s and turn back to the day-job – the tracking of data, the checking of spreadsheets – I have a familiar sense of failure. A sense that there are missed opportunities, that I have lost the secret ingredient. That I have been sidetracked from my core purpose as a teacher.

Those words still ring in my ears: 'You just *need* school.'

But *why*?

I remember the day, at another school, when a Year 8 boy, twelve years old – let's call him Jack – came in after a twenty-minute break in the pouring rain. He was soaked to the skin. He went into my colleague's lesson and she said with sympathy, 'Jack, you're soaking wet!'

He replied, politely, 'Yes, Miss. Just like your pussyhole.'

We made him tell his mum what he'd said. Jack was very contrite. He said his mate (actually a kid who bullied him relentlessly) had dared him to do it. He sobbed his heart out in the meeting. He didn't stop being naughty, though.

A few months later I remember talking to Jack as he loitered outside in the yard, refusing to go into his lesson. He had a habit of not meeting your eyes, of letting a faint smile play over his face as he looked down to the left of your feet or at a spot on the wall beyond your right shoulder. I always felt it was an attempt at the kind of ironic detachment that a laconic action hero might have, a Bruce Willis or a Clint Eastwood. Only Jack was fat and spotty, and liked to rest his hand inside the front of his trousers, cupping his junk for security.

'You need to go into your lesson, Jack,' I said.

His eyes drifted. He smiled. 'There's no fucking point, sir.'

It always got me, that – the combination of needless obscenity with conscientious politeness. And there was a shift: one of those little moments where something that must have seemed defiant when it left his brain became desperately, heartbreakingly sad by the time it reached his lips.

He didn't turn it around. I wasn't the hero teacher who made him care. He stopped attending and managed maybe two GCSEs. If Olivia was right and you just *need* school, Jack was in trouble.

Six years later I was having a drink in a pub nearby – one of those North London Irish boozers with shamrocks, swirly carpets and dank back-rooms with sticky dance floors – when we saw Jack. There were a few of us, all teachers from the school. He came up, taller, leaner, the spots gone. He met my gaze as he shook my hand. He bought us a round and we had a chat. He said he was working as a scaffolder. His dad had been a scaffolder. He seemed happy, open and bright. He apologised again and again about his behaviour at school.

He might still have been a proper shit, of course. Just because some-one buys you a pint and looks you in the eye doesn't make them a decent person (although it helps). But it struck me then – and it has kept on striking me – that we often start any discussion of schools from the principle that of course you need it, that education (school) is an inherently good thing, because being good at school – somehow – makes you good at life.

That wasn't the case for Jack. Something more like the opposite was true for him: he was bad at school and yet had turned out to be pretty good at life.[2] But the assumption persists, and on top of it we layer others – that kids need classrooms, that grades mean goodness – despite the fact that for most of human history, school as we know it did not exist.

If we really want to understand the way schools work in Britain today, it's not a bad idea to start by looking at the ways they've grown and evolved over the last two millennia, because the history of our schools explains a lot of why they are the way they are.

2.   A history lesson

A full history of education in Britain is a mammoth undertaking –
but a quick journey through the ways in which the answer to that
question 'What is school for?' has changed is very revealing. Because
it *has* changed – far more than we might think.

Let's start in 597 CE. That year a boat landed on the Isle of Thanet
containing (one guesses) a damp and somewhat worried Christian
mission, sent to Britain on behalf of Pope Gregory and the Kingdom
of God. The mission's leader, Augustine, had been tasked with con-
verting the wild Anglo-Saxon tribes – and while I've never actually
taught on the Isle of Thanet, I like to think anyone who's had Year 9
on a Friday afternoon in November can sympathise.

Augustine had to have schools as well as churches, otherwise he
would have had no priests.[1] This was the start of the 'English' education system – even if much of it had its roots in Augustine's hometown
of Rome. Augustine created two types of school: 'Song' schools,
where the performance of church services was taught; and 'Grammar' schools, which prepared students for a life in the Church through
a diet of Latin grammar and literature. While the relevance of Latin
literature in the twenty-first century is almost aggressively esoteric,
it is important to remember that for Augustine, Latin grammar and
the Latin literature of the Church were, quite literally, vocational
learning. The skills being taught had a specific purpose for carrying
out the duties of a priest, but they were seen as inherently enriching,
too. This combination is perhaps only possible when the vocation in
question is a matter of, as they believed, the highest truth. The
eighth-century teacher Alcuin doesn't just say he wants to 'enable
young people to achieve excellent outcomes and destinations', like
my local college – he says that his school 'moistened thirsty hearts
with divers streams of teaching and varied dews of study'.[2]

Even so, it was not without controversy – Pope Gregory himself was guilty of some pearl-clutching over the prospect of students reading corrupt pagan literature in their study of Latin,[3] and this tension, between 'good knowledge' and 'bad knowledge', seems pretty familiar to anyone who follows modern educational debates. Learning seems to have a way of getting out of control – starting from a point of pure 'use', then straggling out in unruly offshoots, like a badly managed veg patch.

Education was going on outside school, too. Anglo-Saxon society produced sensational works of art and craft – all skills learned in apprenticeships.[4] But in terms of formal schooling, the next big development came with King Alfred's insistence on the teaching of English alongside the teaching of Latin. This single-handedly broadened the conception of why we learn, from a vocational Church-based project into an aspect of nation-building, an attempt to forge a unified culture in the face of the barbarian Danish invaders. Once broadened like this, the purposes of school kept on expanding. As Christianity spread a network of parish churches across the land, and looked for the priests needed to run them, education shifted subtly towards something that could be a vehicle for social mobility. There even developed an ill-defined requirement that the parish churches should provide education if asked, almost as if it were a right.[5]

When the Normans arrived, they added French to the curriculum, acknowledging (just as Alfred had done) the power of education to shape society. In the process they also formalised 'schools' as separate institutions in a way they had not previously been – instituted by legal 'charters'.[6] While cathedrals and churches still maintained their vocational schools, grammar schools became institutions more of the city than the Church, and wealthier merchants began increasingly to take for granted the necessity of some kind of schooling for their sons. But the nature of the schools they attended was hugely varied – and, as ever, there was a fascinating tension between the idea of educating the elite and allowing for limited social mobility. Eton is a great case in point: on its foundation by Henry VI, like many of the 'public' schools later famous for high fees, it offered free education to all. But some of those 'all' were sons of the nobility, who paid for their own living expenses – while the poorer 'all' worked as their servants to defray their costs. This was education as opportunity, but also as reinforcement of the social order.

At the same time, the apprenticeship system was increasing in complexity and sophistication – to the point where guilds of skilled trades would demand that apprentices were able to read and write.[7] This increased the demand for non-clerical education at exactly the time when the printed word and the Renaissance began to transform access to knowledge. Books were now *available* in ways they had never been previously. And, in England, with the Reformation and the dissolution of the monasteries came a new wave of 'grammar schools' and 'cathedral schools'. The end product of this sudden flowering of knowledge – 'humanist' education – encoded for the first time a belief in the benefit of learning for its own sake and was revolutionary. Education was *good*, not just because of what it did, but because of what it *was*. Like money or vegetables, the more you got of it, the better.

But as the Reformation gathered pace, with the translated Bible at its centre, *what* you taught became more and more politically significant. In the seventeenth century alongside the military convulsions of the Civil War were transformations in who read, and why. Two forces began to wrestle with each other: on the one hand, the state control of education, through royal endowment and standard textbooks, supporting the elite, with limited access to select deserving 'grammar school' boys; on the other there arose a dissenting impulse, self-educating through Bible study and the growing spread of cheaply produced pamphlets. By the time of the Restoration in 1660, the experiment in republican government might have been over, but the idea of education as a revolutionary tool was firmly established.

The year of 1660 was also the one in which the first school I taught in was established – the Henry Box School in Witney, Oxfordshire. Like many schools, it has changed in nature over the years, starting out as a grammar school for thirty boys funded by an endowment from Henry Box, and ending up as a mixed modern comprehensive with more than 1,000 pupils. That journey was fundamentally shaped by the next major social upheaval in British (and world) history: the Industrial Revolution.

Although the idea of educating the poor for their moral good was periodically pushed until the nineteenth century, no one, at any stage of British history, had suggested that schools were literally for everyone. They were exclusive by class, by wealth and by gender. And yet in 1870 that is exactly what happened – the British government legislated for the compulsory schooling of every child up to the age of ten (later thirteen). This unexpected move towards universal education happened hand-in-hand with the move towards universal suffrage and the dismantling of the pre-industrial social structures. What caused this transformation?

Images of Sir James Kay-Shuttleworth, the key figure in nineteenth-century educational reform, look much as you might expect them to: stiff black clothes, severe gaze directed thoughtfully off to the left, the general air of someone for whom the future existence of flip-flops as a legitimate sartorial choice is beyond all comprehension. But there is one, an engraving, where the angle is such that his set, lipless mouth turns up into the hint of an impish grin, and you start to wonder.

In fact Kay-Shuttleworth embodied the contradictions of his time. His life was beyond admirable: a doctor, a tireless worker for the poor, a public-health campaigner and the author of an 1832 pamphlet on social conditions in Manchester that raised the same issues as Engels did, thirteen years later. And yet he was far from revolutionary. Rather, he belonged to a tradition that saw education not as a route to individual empowerment or elevation of the masses, but as the glue that held society together. In campaigning for universal elementary education, he addressed the Tories directly, saying in 1839 that it was 'astonishing to us, that the party calling themselves Conservative, should not lead the van' – because, after all, the 'diffusion of . . . knowledge among the working classes' would 'promote the security of property and the maintenance of public order'.[8] Gladstone, the great Liberal prime minister who actually passed the bill, went further. On seeing the success of the Germans in defeating the French in 1870, he saw more than simply good generalship. 'Undoubtedly, the conduct of the campaign, on the German side, has given a marked triumph to the cause of systematic popular education.'[9]

It's worth highlighting this: far from being a scheme of simple generosity to those who couldn't pay for it, the universalisation of education was explicitly sold as a means of maintaining property and order, social hierarchy and stability, national strength and unity. After all, if the state didn't provide education, there was no telling who might step into the void. In the informal village schools of the early nineteenth century you might find Chartists and Wesleyans and other rabble-rousers who would do the very opposite of 'promote the maintenance of public order'. And Gladstone's link between military success and schooling was made again thirty years later, when the poor condition of soldiers in the Boer War led to the introduction of school meals in 1906.

And yet, inescapably, the provision of education for the masses *was* also a force for 'bettering' them. Ruskin College and Toynbee Hall were the most famous outposts of a new, secularised desire to educate the working classes, this time not only for the benefit of the national collective, but for the socially mobile individual.

This story, of transformation through learning, a counter-narrative to the ways in which school was co-opted for social control, was articulated brilliantly in George Bernard Shaw's *Pygmalion* (1913). In it, education becomes power and ends up disrupting the very structures (and people) that enabled it: Shaw's Eliza is plucked from a flower stall in Covent Garden and schooled in how to speak like a duchess by the professor of linguistics Henry Higgins, only to reject her teacher at the end.

But even though Shaw dramatises the transformational potential of learning, he also puts his finger on quite how large the spectre of class looms in British education. Eliza is defined by her accent, the marker that shows education to be not just what you know, but where you come from – and, in Britain, where you come from is inextricably linked to what school you go to. It's a striking symmetry that, at exactly the same time as universal schooling was introduced, the role of the 'public schools' became fixed in the popular imagination.

These public schools – so called to distinguish them from grammar schools, which only took in pupils from their local area, but practically defined as the poshest and oldest of the schools that had sprung up since the Middle Ages – shifted from their initially stated focus on educating the poor for free (as we saw with Eton in the fifteenth century) to taking in a greater and greater proportion of fee-paying students. By the end of the nineteenth century, when anyone could get the basics of an education for free, the benefit of the public schools began to be more to do with social connection and exclusivity than with academic advantage. In essence, they evolved to the point where they had become a testing ground for the elite, serving – and then served by – the ruling class. And the last thing the powerful inhabitants of this parallel educational system wanted was social mobility.

So the nineteenth century left Britain with a collective confusion over what education was for. It was possible to think that it might be a route to 'bettering' oneself (either by social advancement or moral enrichment), a dangerous breeding ground for radicalism, and the primary way in which we keep a tight lid on the existing social order, all at the same time. And with the introduction of school meals in 1906, it also became a vehicle for ensuring the welfare of the young.

These four ideas – school as a route to power, a site of transformation and revolution, a means of control and a provider of basic welfare needs – are still with us. And many of the conflicting ways in which we talk about schools stem from the fact that few people balance the four of them in exactly the same way. But there was one further shift in our understanding of the purpose of schools and education that explains our current dilemma.

In the wake of the trauma and heroism of the Second World War, Labour's landslide election victory of 1945 and subsequent wave of reform established the modern welfare state. This was an expression of a new conception of society, one in which everyone was entitled to a fair share. In the world of education, the overriding question became how schools could provide, even become engines for, equality of opportunity. The first answer, in 1944, was the three-tier system, governed by the 11+ exam. The logic was straightforward: sort kids into the settings that will allow them a chance to flourish, and do it by a fair, standard assessment at age eleven. The problem was that the settings weren't equal. The top of the pyramid, the grammar school, had (as we've seen) a long pedigree and a recognised role in the kind of limited, academic social mobility that had been going on for centuries. Grammar schools had identities, ways of teaching, institutional knowledge about the elite world and a curriculum recognised by that world. The other two types of school were new and somewhat ill defined. The technical schools were so ill defined that they barely existed, while the secondary moderns became the default dumping ground, the school for those who didn't follow the academic route, and yet which didn't really manage to articulate any alternative to it.

The post-war years were undoubtedly a huge improvement on any educational offer we had had before. But ultimately this three-tier system lasted barely more than two decades before being cast aside with a reasonable degree of consensus that it hadn't worked. There were two basic problems. One was that a system designed to be fair simply wasn't. The 11+ exam was too crude a measure, and for many kids came too early in their schooling, resulting in egregious mistakes that blighted lives. It also contained an arbitrary cut-off – not based on anything about the capacity of children to learn, but simply about the capacity of the different schools to take them. In some ways, whether you went to a grammar school didn't depend on ability; it depended on the size of the local school.

But the subtler and more fundamental problem was that for millions of children who didn't go to grammars, their education was the booby prize given to them for failing – effectively a space-filler until they could get on with their working lives.

I say there was a reasonable degree of consensus, but there has also always been a strong current of nostalgia for this moment as a high point of the English system. Mostly the defenders of three-tier education point to the huge increase in social mobility of the fifties and sixties – the grammar-school kids who came from working-class homes and made a new aspirant middle class. My dad was one of these, riding the wave to a degree at Oxford and a career as an academic. But this period was also marked by a massive expansion of white-collar 'middle-class' jobs, an expanding pool of opportunities that fuelled the social mobility that took place. When those opportunities started to dry up in the seventies and eighties, the pace of social mobility declined. These days, where the grammar-school system has survived, the proportion of disadvantaged students who actually gain access to it is tiny[10] – and that is without even taking into account the difference between types of disadvantage.[11]

The next attempt to make schools fair was the comprehensive system, in which grammar schools were largely abolished and where intake reflects the immediate area, with proximity to the school the key factor in admittance. And this, largely, is what we still have.

In my sixth year of teaching I took a job at Fortismere School. It was a great place to work and has a history as one of the testing grounds of comprehensive education. Creighton School, as it was at first, was formed by the amalgamation of two schools, a secondary modern and a grammar, in Muswell Hill, North London, in 1967 – and in the seventies it was led by Molly Hattersley, wife of the Labour big beast Roy. It was the subject of a book by the journalist Hunter Davies[12] and was seen as a beacon of success.

Only my experience of it, years later, showed up the big hole in the ideal of the comprehensive. By 2008, when I started, Muswell Hill was one of the most expensive areas in London to buy a house. So the school was loaded with kids who came from affluent educated backgrounds and brought all the cultural capital and family commitment that can imply. All this combined to make it a successful school, high in the league tables, outstanding according to Ofsted, and increasingly a reason for people to fork out more and more for houses in the ever-decreasing catchment area, creating a selective intake by default.

So now we get to the last stage of the development of the landscape of schools in Britain today: academisation. In response to so-called 'sink' schools, which were stuck in a trap of low aspiration, low achievement and then further low aspiration as the wealthier, aspirant middle classes abandoned them, Tony Blair's government introduced the idea of academies.

Initially academisation was simply a reform of school management. The idea was to take schools out of local-authority control and give them greater autonomy to make radical decisions. To allow 'superheads' free rein to 'turn failing schools around'. Academisation was a circuit breaker, not a blueprint. But when the Coalition Government of the early 2010s changed the nature of the academisation programme from one targeted at a few failing schools to one designed eventually to transform every school, a lot of other consequences were set in train.

Academies have an independent financial existence. They have to balance their books, and they do this through revenue from students – the per-head funding they get from government. This effectively turbo-boosts competition between schools, particularly when there are more school places than there are children in an area. Meanwhile the birth of academies led eventually to Multi-Academy Trusts (MATs). These were designed to enable expertise in one school to support others, and to allow for economies of scale. So in the case of my school – part of a small MAT of two – we can employ one finance department, one health-and-safety officer and one careers advisor instead of two.

In other words, there are financial incentives for academisation, and for schools taking on other schools. There are sweet spots in terms of those economies of scale, so that MATs have a momentum that pushes them to grow. There is pressure to develop a brandable identity that can be sold to prospective new schools. None of which is automatically bad, but like so many other parts of our system there can be downsides. One of the most obvious is that academies, far from being bastions of freedom and experimentation, are by design over-sensitive to the accountability measures that define our modern system. If your average school lives in fear of its performance in the league tables, then your average academy lives in existential terror of it. The very independence offered is tempered by a 'no-excuses' scrutiny and a jittery awareness of the market forces of education. Like the companies they have been designed to imitate, academies live in a world of takeovers, decapitated leadership and rebrokering. They have been given one freedom – the freedom of means – but the end has been very tightly defined by Ofsted and Progress 8, and for the vast majority of schools, under the pressure of tight scrutiny, that means a homogeneity in how they reach that end.

There is a tacit acknowledgement of this in the latest new type of school: the Free School. Here even more of the apparatus of outside control has been stripped away – even down to the fact that, in the first few years of the policy, Free Schools could be established irrespective of the local demand for places (and even now they only have to demonstrate a need for 50 per cent of the places they intend to create).[13] Some of these have been hugely innovative – as we will see. But others have been yet another part of the increasing, and often damaging, climate of competition that now pervades the sector. The direction of travel is inescapable: the number-one solution to the problems in schools over the last decade has been to turn to the idea of the marketplace.

Crucially, though, every single type of school we have developed in this long history is still with us. The landscape of education today is like the landscape of our cities: ancient monuments cheek-by-jowl with shining modernist towers, palatial mock-Tudor just streets away from cramped brick terraces. And it is precisely this diversity and this history that account for the many conflicting answers we now have about what school is for – whether it is a source of moral enrichment, a route to power, a basic meeting of a welfare need, a means to create a compliant population, a revolutionary agent of change or the ultimate tool of fairness and social mobility. In a very real sense, all of these answers are also still with us – all within a system that pits them in competition against one another.

But there's another way to understand what schools today are for, or what they think they're for. And that is to look at what they teach. Here, perhaps, is an even clearer way of understanding what their values and priorities really are.

3. The curriculum

Is there some stuff we just ought to know?

'Yeah.' This is Polly, a sharp, self-confident Year 12 student from the North-East. 'I think probably stuff like what you learn in Maths – percentages, decimals – that's really important for daily life. You learn quite a lot in English: how to speak, how you present yourself. But I think there's also stuff we should be taught in school, but we're not – like tax; all the things you've got to do – debit and credit – I don't actually know the difference! Stuff like that, which you will actually use pretty much every day, we're not taught that, but we're taught really ridiculous things.'

Use seems key here. So I ask, are there some things that are no use, but which you should simply know? Like Henry VIII and his wives?

'I think you don't *need* to know it, it's not gonna help you get through life.'

This is a phrase Polly often uses. She goes on.

'Stuff like that can get you involved in certain social groups. It's a topic you might want to know about because you just want to talk about it, or see a show about it. It gives you a kind of *entrance* into socialising with people you might not have much in common with.'

So what's the point of school in general?

'I think the point of school is to be able to come in, socialise, meet people, work on yourself, but also learn the skills and abilities you need for life.'

Learn the skills and abilities you need for life. It's a pretty uncontentious idea, really. But what exactly are those skills and abilities? Are they the same for everyone? Who decides what they are, and is there a difference between learning knowledge and learning skill? And what about the difference between the knowledge that Polly identifies as specifically and actively 'useful' – such as understanding taxes – and the stuff that is a somewhat arbitrary social tool to get her talking to 'certain social groups'? What about things we *ought* to know, morally?

In fact rather than being uncontentious, the question of what *stuff* we should learn in school is the big one. In England, since 1989, part of the answer is the National Curriculum – a standardised core set of 'things we need to learn'.

Not all countries have one. That doesn't mean a free-for-all – simply that the content that needs to be covered is only tightly defined when it is part of an exam syllabus at the business end of school, rather than specifying content from Year 1, as we do in England. Our National Curriculum was controversial at first, but is now pretty much part of the landscape. It is divided up into 'Key Stages', each lasting two or three years. There are different sets of content that need to be covered in each Key Stage – a particular period of history, a set of mathematical techniques, a degree of complexity in writing – but the organisation of this is fairly loose. We also have a typically nonsensical clash of messages: that academies have the freedom not to cover the National Curriculum, but they do have to cover a 'broad and balanced curriculum'. And, in the view of Ofsted, that means covering the National Curriculum.

'You don't have to get us a wedding present,' says the invite. 'But if you want to, here's the list.'

Mind you, it's a decent list. The National Curriculum really isn't a particular problem. Sometimes you get scare stories about teaching sex ed to five-year-olds, but at each stage it's carefully calibrated. In this instance, the compulsory thing at primary is actually 'Relationships Education', not the full SRE (Sex and Relationships Education) – and the advice is both vague and sensible:

> *Establishing personal space and boundaries, showing respect and understanding the differences between appropriate and inappropriate or unsafe physical, and other, contact – these are the forerunners of teaching about consent, which takes place at secondary.*

When it comes to History, at Key Stages 1 and 2 (primary school) the list is:

Changes in Britain from the Stone Age to the Iron Age; the Roman Empire and its impact on Britain; Britain's settlement by Anglo-Saxons and Scots; the Viking and Anglo-Saxon struggle for the Kingdom of England to the time of Edward the Confessor; a local history study; a study of an aspect or theme in British history that extends pupils' chronological knowledge beyond 1066; the achievements of the earliest civilizations; Ancient Greece – a study of Greek life and achievements and their influence on the western world; a non-European society that provides contrasts with British history.

Again there is both latitude within this, with a wide range of approaches possible, and a decent attempt at covering some big topics. I'm not sure anyone reads the National Curriculum and thinks, 'This is bullshit – we need to be teaching something totally different.'

To be honest, though, primary content is much easier to set out, precisely because it is the first, most general stuff that kids encounter and needs to provide a foundation for later on. By the time we get to secondary, the National Curriculum is only the skeleton outline of what stuff we learn. The detail is defined far more by the GCSE and A-level syllabuses – both during the years those courses cover and because schools tend to work backwards from the endpoint to discover what to cover in earlier years, in order to get there.[1] These syllabuses are necessarily highly prescriptive, with comprehensive lists of what will be assessed in each part of the exam, although even here one can make decisions about which exam board and which topic to choose that can shape the individual school's curriculum in different ways.

But calling these things 'content' and 'lists' is a bit misleading. A curriculum or syllabus isn't merely a list of factual knowledge. There are, in Polly's phrase, 'skills and abilities', too. But we should be cautious of putting too hard a barrier between 'knowledge' and 'skills'.

This is such an important point, and is worth emphasising. In my own specialism, English, you can know what a metaphor is, but be unable to describe with subtlety the effect of a particular one. The first is a factual unit of knowledge – the second is often called skill. But the word 'skill' can be problematic. After all, the 'skill' of describing that metaphor is in reality a whole series of pieces of knowledge, from knowing the vocabulary to use, to understanding sentence structure, to an awareness of the precise ways in which the sounds of words impact on the reader. And yet even if one were to have all of these separately, there is the further 'procedural' aspect to be learned – the ability to utilise them all together in a coherent way, on demand. Something like long multiplication might seem a purer example of a skill – but when you break that down, too, you see that the *skill* is actually composed of quick, highly drilled *recall* of the individual multiplication tables and a learned procedural routine to string that knowledge together. Even everyday physical skills – driving, for example – are inextricably linked with both knowing specific things (what the clutch does and when to use it) and practising specific methods of applying them (how far and how slowly to lift your foot to get to the biting point when you use the clutch).

What this means practically is that we don't simply need to answer the question 'What should we learn?' After all, that would mean it was enough just to pass your driving-theory test. No, we also need to answer the question 'How should we learn it?' – because the process defines how well and in what ways you learn to use the knowledge that you acquire.

The late Sir Ken Robinson (one of the key educational voices of this century) made the case powerfully, in a series of hugely popular online talks,[2] that we often get that question of 'How we should learn?' pretty radically wrong. His thesis rests on the idea that our system of education was designed in a different age, and with different assumptions.

Ironically, this is actually a very old idea – throughout the history of education, people have argued the same thing. There's even a (satirical) book from 1939 entitled *The Saber-Tooth Curriculum*[3] that dramatises an imagined argument in Neolithic cultures between those who want to teach 'traditional' subjects like 'tiger-scaring' and those who make the point that, in the absence of sabre-toothed tigers, maybe we should change the curriculum.

Robinson's version of this is to argue that today's schools are being run according to nineteenth-century priorities (which, as we saw in the previous chapter, prioritised compliance and social cohesion). He calls it a 'factory model' that educates kids in 'batches' and destroys individuality. He tells us that kids in kindergarten are creative, divergent thinkers and that, by sixteen, education in this authoritarian, fact-based model of 'right' and 'wrong' answers has knocked this out of them.

Robinson is very persuasive, even if his talks are littered with the emptinesses that are characteristic of so many TED Talks: 'The problem is, they're trying to meet the future by doing what they did in the past.' As a teacher, you come away thinking, 'Yes, things *could* be different', albeit with a nagging sense that there might be budgetary constraints on doing all this lovely stuff. In fact his claims here are deeply contested, but as they sit right at the very centre of the debate they are worth examining.

Robinson presents a twenty-first-century version of what many call 'progressive' education. This theory of 'how we should learn' has its roots in Jean-Jacques Rousseau's *Emile*, a vastly influential text that crystallised enlightenment views of children as 'little scientists',[4] eagerly exploring the world and learning through practical activities, testing the truth of mini-hypotheses, possessed of an innate developmental motor that facilitates education. In the modern context, this is often described as a 'child-centred' approach and involves things like 'discovery learning', where children are allowed to 'discover' the content of a lesson rather than being told it. More than anything, progressive teaching is associated with the prioritisation of 'thinking skills' such as creativity and problem-solving.

So what's the alternative? Let's call it 'traditional'. This essentially means teaching a defined set of knowledge and doing it in a direct way – the key technique is literally called 'direct instruction'. In many ways this sounds like a denial of the importance of *how* we learn, with a simple focus instead on *what* we learn. But it isn't. Traditional as it may be, its advocates back their arguments with the latest insights of cognitive science and argue for the role of core knowledge in enabling the process of learning. E. D. Hirsch, an American educational theorist, is their current high priest. His name is going to come up a lot. For the last four decades he's been making the case that kids need to have a consistent, fact-based 'core knowledge curriculum', because without a solid vocabulary and general knowledge, none of the wonderful thinking skills, creativity and empirical thought that Rousseau and Robinson wanted to see nurtured are possible. You need the building blocks of culture in order to decode culture, he argues, and the way to acquire those blocks is simply to put the damn things together, one by one, even if it's boring. Most importantly, these building blocks – rather than being individualised to each child's circumstances – must be blocks of communal knowledge, the stuff that *everyone* needs to know, otherwise some people are left out.

I was trained at a time when this was far from fashionable. I did all sorts of progressive shit in my early days. And when I say 'shit', I mean it. I once carefully washed out a tin of dog food and refilled it with chunks of Mars Bar set in lime jelly. Then I ate it in front of the class, for a reason I cannot remember (although I do remember the food poisoning).

To be fair, that wasn't the fault of progressive education. As I tell my students, you have to take responsibility for your own mistakes. But in terms of what you might actually see in the classroom, 'progressive' tends to mean students doing self-directed projects, defining their own area of interest; or being given a problem to solve before being given the rules with which to solve it. It might mean group work, where students are each asked to think in different ways, sometimes literally with different 'thinking hats' on; or it might mean an activity where students are required to move around the room to different 'stations', where they look at different topics.

All of which, certainly in secondary schools, you are less and less likely to see. Michael Gove's colleague Nick Gibb, a keen reader of Hirsch and Minister of State for Schools both under Gove and (remarkably) on two further occasions spanning twelve years, describes explicitly the transition and the rationale. 'Michael and I discovered in opposition . . . that the degree to which a school was progressive . . . was the degree to which its results would be underperforming.'[5] From then on, once they came to power in 2010 and throughout the next decade, there has been a steady push away from progressivism. In practice, this means quizzes to embed core facts, an emphasis on teacher-led activities and a much more defined set of 'stuff' to learn.

And if you imagine a spectrum of educational approaches that has 'skills-based' progressive at one end and 'knowledge-rich' traditional at the other, there is one school in particular that has planted its flag firmly at the latter extreme – and which can tell us a lot about the complexity of both what we teach and how we teach it.

Michaela Community School in Wembley is known as the 'strictest school in Britain'. Its motto is 'Knowledge is power'. The two things are not inevitably linked, just as permissiveness and progressive education are not automatic bedfellows; we'll look more closely at how different schools manage pupil behaviour later on. Even so, there is a philosophical kinship between strictness and knowledge-based teaching: both recognise the authority of the teacher, and prioritising efficiency in the delivery of knowledge often relies on rules and structure. At Michaela, a 'traditional' focus on knowledge is combined with – in the words of the self-styled headmistress and founder, Katharine Birbalsingh – traditional 'small-c conservative' social values.

As you come up to the school, it is pretty forbidding: a grey block, right on the main road. The yard is small, the stairs down to the reception narrow. In the playground are six massive signs, simple block letters against bright backgrounds that bring to mind an odd collision between Orwellian sloganeering and primary-school chirpiness:

I AM THE MASTER OF MY FATE
I AM THE CAPTAIN OF MY SOUL
DO YOUR DUTY

On the other side:

WORK HARD, BE KIND
ESPECIALLY WHEN IT IS DIFFICULT
TOP OF THE PYRAMID

Notices aside, it's striking how ordinary it is – how lacking in flash. As a school, it presents as a scrappy upstart. In the reception are the

normal things you'd expect – kids' artworks, articles about the
school. There is also a series of six framed portraits. Two are of
Queen Elizabeth II – young and old. Then there is Nelson Mandela,
David Cameron, Boris Johnson (prime minister at the time) and
Katharine Birbalsingh. One can see how this could be fuel for her
critics, but I see something more straightforward and perhaps naïve.
The Queen, Mandela, Cameron and Johnson are (or were) figures of
literal and, in one case at least, moral authority. For her students, so
is Katharine Birbalsingh.

Also in the reception is a picture of the school's namesake, Michaela
Emanus. She smiles, a middle-aged Caribbean woman in bright Afri-
can fabrics, somewhere sunny. The story goes that Birbalsingh was
inspired by the no-nonsense, 'warm/strict' traditional style of her
one-time colleague Michaela's teaching and, after her death in 2011,
named the school in her honour. So while it is held up as an example
of traditional British educational values, Michaela Community
School is also suffused with the culture of immigrants from the Com-
monwealth, and specifically the version of it that teaches its children
to be better, harder-working, more loyally British than anyone else.
It reminds me of Andrea Levy's novel *Small Island*, set in England in
the aftermath of the Second World War, in which the Caribbean
characters know far more about England than the English do.

But for all the old-fashioned, 'conservative' quality of the school's
presentation, with elaborate formality in how the kids talk to adults,
and routines of chanting and precisely defined table manners, the
actual feel of the place is pretty far from the classic tradition of British
schooling, for one simple reason. The jockeying, boisterous culture of
bullying and victimisation in the schoolyard, which might have been
tolerated and even condoned in a previous era as character-building, is
totally absent. At Michaela I'm escorted round by two scrupulously
polite pupil guides, who tell me explicitly that there is none of this –
and, having seen the total trust they exhibit in the adults, and the ways
the students interact with each other, I believe them.

In the yard at break I ask my question: What's the point of school?

The answers are prompt and well rehearsed, like this is something
that is talked about explicitly. There's no smirk or eye-roll, or

anything other than a serious wholehearted engagement – a performance of attentiveness that is desperately sincere.

'Later on in life, if you were to look back, you know your education would have set you up for where you are.'

'Very important – you need to know things.' ('Knowledge is power,' says the motto.)

'Have a good education to help you succeed in life.'

'You need to know things, so in social situations you can talk about things.'

What about if you were a plumber? I ask. Would you need to know poetry then?

'Yes, then you could have something to fall back on.'

So a plumber might have a second career as a poet?

They look sheepish, but nod defiantly. Nothing will shake their confidence in the curriculum.

So what *is* that curriculum? The *how* is undoubtedly traditional – but does *what* is taught at Michaela match?

The answer is yes. You can see this traditionalism most clearly in the study of literature. To generalise wildly, 'progressive' education emphasises the idea that one should individualise the curriculum – that students should see themselves in what they encounter, and that they should have an element of choice in how they approach it. A progressive curriculum might emphasise works by writers of colour, to reflect the experience of a student body that contains – as Michaela's does – a majority of non-white children. But in one of the books the school has published, *The Power of Culture*, the teachers explain why they reject this idea of a 'diverse', individualised curriculum: first, so that the students are studying 'the best that has been thought or said',[6] which would be diluted by the imposing of a filter for colour or gender. Second, the 'canon' of recognised writers is a form of cultural currency, and so the teaching of it gives kids – especially those who come from poor or immigrant backgrounds – something that enables them to hold their own in the cultural sphere.

This is clearly in line with Hirsch's notion of the importance of communal cultural knowledge as the building blocks of deeper understanding. But the arguments made are not quite Hirsch's – and are not as persuasive.

Speaking as an English teacher, the first reason given – that you need to teach the canon because it is 'the best that has been thought or said' – is bullshit. I can definitively state that no group of the five or ten best things that have been thought or said would include J. B. Priestley's play *An Inspector Calls*. It is absolutely possible to create an alternative, diverse curriculum where every text is a superb and luminous example of literature. But I know that when I choose texts for my students, I often have the second argument in mind – that it can provide a baseline of cultural literacy to have studied Milton, for example, even though the experience of reading him can at times be a bit forbidding. And to lose this canonical knowledge for the sake of an atomised landscape of subjectively chosen texts would be a loss indeed. Birbalsingh herself says she sees it as the duty of schools to teach 'Mozart, not Stormzy', because it is 'our duty as teachers to expose children to ideas they would not otherwise encounter'.

Polly, our Year 12 student from the North-East, recognises the value of the 'traditional' approach that provides general, common cultural background when she describes the historical knowledge of Henry VIII acquired at school as, in her words, an 'entrance'. But is this 'entrance' the straightforward idea that Hirsch presents of general knowledge providing a foundation to then build further knowledge on – or is it more about signalling your membership of a particular group?

The sociologist Pierre Bourdieu was the originator of the term 'cultural capital', now used in a thousand school-improvement documents as shorthand for building that Hirschian foundational cultural literacy and knowledge. But the original use actually denoted the ways in which privilege is hoarded and transmitted via education. And for all the egalitarian intent behind the democratising of knowledge that Hirsch promotes, there are ways in which cultural capital – even if in the possession of the underprivileged – can still be an arbitrary key that unlocks a wider world, not because you *need* it for understanding, but because *having* it marks you as part of the elite. Unfortunately, if we as teachers embrace this idea of knowledge as social currency, we run the risk of perpetuating its value and bolster-ing the ways in which it can be used to exclude.

Consider the reintroduction of Latin, championed by Gove towards the end of his tenure in Education. This wasn't a surprise – Latin acts as a symbol for all the wonders of 'how things used to be' before progressivism. In fact, as we saw in the previous chapter, it was the foundation stone of those very first Augustinian grammar schools, and continued to be central in their modern descendants right up until the last few decades. It involves specific knowledge, learned in a traditional, direct way. And yet it is also the epitome of the 'sabre-tooth curriculum'. Like the sabre-toothed tiger, it is quite literally dead, and we certainly don't 'need' to learn how to wrestle with it. That is what makes it, to followers of Bourdieu, a perfect example of the gatekeeping quality of cultural capital. You don't need to know it – but dropping a Latin tag into conversation acts as a marker for a kind of exclusionary intellectualism (as certain ex-prime ministers have ruthlessly exploited).

That isn't the argument commonly made for its reintroduction, though.[7] Instead we're told that, as a language predicated on a uniquely logical grammar, the process of learning Latin trains the mind in ways of rigorous critical analysis, and allows a far clearer understanding of the more ambiguous and diffuse rules of grammar in other, living languages.

But of all the educational research that has fed into the 'traditional', knowledge-rich approach, the most clear-cut and persuasive is the idea of domain specificity. This tells us that knowledge or skill in one domain does not necessarily help in another – totally contradicting the notion that learning one subject (in this case Latin) might build general skills elsewhere. To my mind, the easiest way of explaining domain specificity comes from Hirsch himself. Quite simply he says, 'You can be good at reading about dinosaurs but bad at reading about mushrooms.'[8]

Take a moment to think, and you instinctively know what he's get-ting at. Imagine you and your partner are reading the Sunday papers. Your partner loves football and you love the stock market, so you each pick out the relevant section and read happily. But if you swap, your pleasure will quickly fade, faced with an incomprehensible roll call of managers, players, positions and tactics, while your partner will frown in concentration and then cast aside as 'boring' the article on bond dividends that you so recently devoured. Hirsch's point is that your skill at reading is not a general one, but rather is predicated on your knowledge of, and familiarity with, a particular subject.

A famous experiment with chess players demonstrates the fallacy of transferable skills. Chess is often touted as making such demands of the logical, analytical side of the brain that it cannot fail to increase general tactical skills. But when chess players and non-chess players were actually tested, it was clear that the skill that playing chess developed was . . . in playing chess. Everything else remained unchanged.[9] While *The Karate Kid*'s guru Mr Miyagi claimed that cleaning his floor, painting his fence and waxing his Chevy were all perfect training exercises for self-defence, Hirsch tells us that Daniel probably ended up as the Carwash Kid.

Domain specificity is absolutely key in making the case for the importance of focusing on 'knowledge' in a traditional sense, rather than on transferable skills. But somehow this aspect of the argument gets lost when it comes to Latin, and we get stuck on reasoning that is surprisingly progressive. It's almost as if the elevator pitch for a 'knowledge-rich' approach chimes so perfectly with a 'small-c conservative' mindset that the two become elided into one, without critically analysing the more detailed ways in which they don't actually correspond. In a way, Hirsch's notion of the need for foundational knowledge to unlock education is so close to Bourdieu's ideas about cultural capital passing on privilege that we can slip from one to the other without noticing.

This is a persistent issue with the proponents of knowledge-rich education. The argument for a focus on knowledge is not the same as the argument for which specific knowledge should be included. Surely we can accept the importance of cultural literacy, of knowledge and of the canon, without accepting that we have to stick to the traditional (and traditionally exclusionary) content of the canon? Interestingly at Michaela, despite the vigorous promotion of dead white males, they *do* teach a diverse English curriculum. In the same interview that Birbalsingh issues her panicked war-cry in defence of the bard, she also refers to the fact that they teach Andrea Levy.[10]

Admirable as I find the school, this aspect of the way Birbalsingh presents their 'mission' is worrying. If you follow her on social media, she often talks about the things 'they' say (she can be a bit reductive on Twitter/X, and overly fond of grouping all the people she disagrees with into one amorphous 'they'), as a straw man to set against Michaela or her own views. This is a tendency of both traditionalists and progressives in education: they each define the other as their opposite, but in practical terms most education takes place in the space in the middle.

The arguments sometimes meet in the middle, too. If the traditionalist aims to 'expose children to ideas they would not otherwise encounter', that is not necessarily an argument for including Shakespeare at all: one has to admit that he gets a fair amount of exposure already. In fact if that was the rationale, you might end up pitching a highly individualised, progressive curriculum based around each child's prior deficits.

The broader point remains, though: the teaching of a simplified, standardised canon is a reassuring way of thinking about what knowledge students need to navigate our culture. It's just that the criteria for entry into that canon are still somewhat arbitrary. To take refuge in 'the canon' as immovable shirks the question of what culture we might actually want, as opposed to the one we happen to have. We can agree with wanting to give our children cultural literacy while not wishing to maintain one specific (often racially exclusive) version of it.

But what about subjects where the content is less subjective? I don't mean Maths and Science, where certainly at secondary level the content demanded by the exam system is highly prescriptive and there is little room for manoeuvre. I mean subjects like History and Geography, or Religious Studies, where there is a vast array of potential material to cover, and choices have to be made. One clearly can't say a given historical period is the 'best', in the way one can for a writer or artist. So is there a canon of historical and social knowledge that traditionalists advocate and progressives reject?

When I ask Safiya, in Year 8 at a school in Merseyside, if she is clever, she smiles. She smiles a lot in our conversation – sometimes genuinely amused by something, sometimes reflexively. She comes across as both shy and super-confident. This smile is an embarrassed one and comes with a series of uncharacteristic pauses. Throughout the rest of our conversation she talks in a delicate torrent of precisely spoken Bengali-inflected Scouse – she was born here, but her parents speak no English at home.

'I . . . I don't think I'm the most intelligent, but I'm glad to say that I've gotten . . . extra knowledge.'

It's a politician's answer. She smiles.

'I'm happy where I am now – I'm in set one.'

I laugh. I tell her that I think she does feel quite clever, but that she's also quite humble and doesn't like to brag.

Safiya smiles helplessly and happily and gives the faintest of nods.

We have talked so far about her desire to be a doctor, and the importance of science for this. But now I ask her about the 'other stuff' the things that are not so directly relevant.

'In Year Six I really only thought about Science and Maths, but when I started Years Seven and Eight I realised how interesting and how much knowledge you can gain from the other subjects. It might not benefit me *all* the time, but the subjects like History – I really do *love* History, and I really do *love* Geography. The point is just to gain more knowledge of the outside world and what's happening, because if you only focus on one subject then you won't have a passion for anything else.'

It's both exhilarating and exhausting listening to Safiya. Her hands make quick, sharp movements as her words tumble out.

So there's stuff that you learn that is good, even though you don't need it directly?

'Yes.'

I ask now about History specifically. The topics you study, I say, are presumably all about the history of Britain, and Europe. Do you think you should be studying the history of Bangladesh?

'Yes.' She is definite at first, then she hesitates. 'I guess so. We do topics that are other countries, but we only highlight the countries that are really poor or are really rich. We had this one lesson – I think it was Geography – about Asia, and this one lesson was "Why is Bangladesh so poor?" and I actually understood, from outside things that my parents would not have told me. But unfortunately in History there are only subjects about Britain.'

Safiya leans forward intently. When she speaks she has a habit of looking past me and down, as if trying to figure out a difficult problem – all the time with her hands moving in those quick, light, private gestures.

'I remember asking my mum if she could help me with one of my History homeworks and she said she never learned about Europe, only about Asia. I understood, and I knew it was out of her control, but I remember that *vivid moment*.'

The phrase 'vivid moment' is dropped with a fierce intensity.

'In History, there's only Europe. We always go through the same thing – the troubles in Europe, and then how Europe became so successful.'

I have the sense that Safiya is saying something she hasn't articulated before. She looks puzzled as she speaks.

'I guess it's like a repeating pattern. We never see the real, major points of other countries and what's affecting them. When I would go to other countries, people would probably think that Britain's such a *high-class* community.' She smiles. 'Which is true – Britain is very successful – but it doesn't help other countries. It doesn't put the work in that it needs.'

I have to remind myself she's only in Year 8.

'When we think of the world,' says Safiya, 'we don't think of the whole world, we think of little countries being independent – and that doesn't always work out. Countries can fail, and countries can be successful, so I feel that we should all learn different things about what can help, so we can change it one day.'

She looks up at me.

'Which is why History should be pinpointing all the other stuff. Maybe not Bangladesh, but other countries we could learn about and could benefit us.' Her face is serious for a moment. Then she beams.

A twelve-year-old can't give us the answers as to what we should teach. But it's clear that Safiya is sensitive to something both subtle and profound in the nature of our curriculum. As with literature, or indeed any subject, choosing what to teach is an expression of values and priorities and perspective. Safiya agrees that for most people, Bangladesh is not high on the list of their priorities in the curriculum, but she also shows me that there is a fine line between celebrating 'our' history – meaning, British or European history – and creating a subtextual narrative that says Europe is special and that progress runs in one direction, and that failure is something that only happens to the 'little countries'.

The progressive response to this dilemma is the individualisation of the curriculum, along with the ideas of decolonisation and diversification. The traditionalist response is to say that collectively owned knowledge – an agreed canon – is necessary for the sake of public discourse and individual access to knowledge. The English system's compromise between the two is a self-consciously traditional curriculum with space at the edges for a more individualised approach – as in the National Curriculum's requirement for the study of 'a non-European society that provides contrasts with British history'. But whatever option is chosen, a shadow is cast. Because there is no magical non-political curriculum – any choice expresses a set of values.

This bias, to term it bluntly, is inescapable. And it goes further than this. We've already seen that the question of *what* we learn is also the question of *how* we learn it – and just as the curriculum choices that we make express values, so do the broader ways in which schools work. Every aspect of school culture teaches us *stuff*. One of the concepts much discussed in education circles is 'the hidden curriculum'.[11] The term was coined by Philip Jackson in 1968 and describes the idea that while there is an explicit bunch of knowledge that is transmitted directly, there is also a separate but no less important set of skills, norms and assumptions that are implicitly taught by the wider environment the child is in.

Polly puts it well: 'Everything that you learn in school – from it being academic work, to being able to, like, take turns, socialise, talk, stand up in front of a class – I think all of that will be very useful as you get older. Even though they're not put as life skills, I think they are, in a way. From the simple things like having to put your hand up in a lesson to speak, to how to work in groups – I think it's all very important for when you go into working life.' She pauses. 'Obviously as well as your academic subjects – your actual "what you learn".'

Polly's description of basic socialisation is a straightforward and pretty uncontentious version of the hidden curriculum. But there's another side. In any school – like Michaela, or Polly's school, Lingsby – there are phrases that you hear, attitudes and prejudices that the kids learn and hold in common. They learn this from their peers, from social media, but also from the ways in which the school's expectations and method of approaching things can cast a shadow. The order in which you teach something, or the way you frame it, can teach as much as the explicit knowledge within it. That's what Safiya is getting at. It's one of the arguments against concepts like Black History Month – while it may foreground an important topic that has been overlooked, it also segregates it into a particular subject and month, reinforcing a mindset in which the topic is less main-stream and therefore less important. It becomes a one-off lesson rather than a central element of the curriculum.

Philip Jackson was a sociologist. In fact many of the theories that underpin the 'progressive' view of education are heavily influenced by the sociology of the sixties and seventies, infusing them with an attitude that sees the proper use of education as a means to challenge authority and social control. As such, the hidden curriculum of hier-archy and order and conservative social values reflected in a 'traditional' approach is something to be torn down.

But the 'traditional' approach as it is presented now, in the twenty-first century, is something far more technocratic – the focus on, in Polly's words, 'what you learn' has a very functional mindset, self-consciously divorced from the politics of class and society and underwritten by the cognitive science explained so well in books by Dan Willingham[12] and Daisy Christodoulou.[13] They tease out the relationships between long- and short-term memory, between vocabu-lary and reading fluency, between factual knowledge and creative thinking, and ultimately present a knowledge-rich 'traditional' peda-gogy as a practical solution to learning – not as a hidden curriculum of control. At the same time an exclusionary concept such as 'cultural capital' is reformulated as a functional tool for building more complex knowledge and understanding.

It's an impressive transformation. But does this practicality override any concerns about the hidden curriculum? Does traditional education's rebrand as a cognitive tool for a fairer system erase the need to question the subtle ways in which the school environment teaches us our place in society? In my view, clearly not. Once again, the accommodation is obvious. We need *both* sociology *and* cognitive science to make sense of what we should learn, and to interrogate whether we have got it right, because the curriculum is many things. It can simultaneously be a practical list of the building blocks needed to construct higher-order thinking and a normative structure that socially conditions children into compliant adulthood. Kids like Safiya may well be served best by a knowledge-rich approach – but that doesn't mean there is no cost to it.

Up till now we've discussed what kids learn at school as if it was monolithic. But at a certain point, kids choose – and they don't all make the same choices.

At KS3 (aged eleven to fourteen roughly) the subjects in the National Curriculum are: English, Maths, Science, History, Geography, modern foreign languages, Design and Technology, Art and Design, Music, Physical Education, Citizenship and Computing. SRE and Religious Education (RE) are also included, but there are caveats stating that parents can opt out of parts of each.

What is fascinating about that list is the order. Now nowhere does it specify this, but any teacher knows that, give or take the odd position, this is the pecking order. Kids know it, too. And when you get to KS4, where students do their first public exams (mostly GCSEs), this isn't just inference from a list – this is encoded into the accountability measures, as we saw in Chapter 1. The subjects at the top of this list are literally worth more than the ones at the bottom.

There are good reasons for this, not least the centrality of English, Maths and Science to many careers and paths of further study. But again (as we saw in Chapter 1) if a school wants to get a good Progress

8 score and climb the league tables, then it has to be fairly dictatorial and restrictive when it comes to which students are taught which subjects: it must insist, for example, that the most able students take the most EBacc subjects, while the least able are guided to take more vocational and practical subjects. In practice, this means streaming the students, and that of the nine or ten GCSEs they take, they only get to 'choose' perhaps two of them.

Polly, who is now approaching her A levels, has some thoughts on this. She wasn't a high-flyer when she was younger. Neither of her parents went to university, but Polly says that she always wanted to go down the academic route. 'My mam's on universal credit. So she does struggle a bit.'

She aims to go to university, locally (in Newcastle), and stay at home to save money. She's very focused on this – on the idea of teaching as a career – and has chosen three A levels (Health and Social Care,[14] English Language and Psychology) to fit with this. But when I ask about her subjects at GCSE she says, 'I wouldn't have chosen those, if they weren't the only options I had. I think that was very unfair actually. We were put in different blocks, so depending on your academic level, you were put in a certain block. The highest level was like Triple Science, where you do individual grades for each science. The one I was in was Combined Science, and I still had to do a language – which I didn't mind. But the only two options I had left were Cooking and Media Studies.'

The point about the National Curriculum as a whole is that it also has embedded within it a set of values and priorities, and when this is combined with a competitive ranking system, it results in kids being assigned a relative value in the system, according to their academic stream. With this system, we say very clearly that clever kids won't be made to do Cooking because they're better than that – so the ones in the next stream down, like Polly, have to.

There is a phrase for this, which the likes of Hirsch and Gove and Birbalsingh are fond of using: 'the soft bigotry of low expectations'. By expecting less of those who are considered less academic, or by making allowances for them, we are actually engaged in a kind of discrimination. And when you consider that to be 'clever' in Britain also means to be, on average, less poor, less disadvantaged, then the notion of 'weaker' students doing more 'vocational' courses starts to sound like the well-oiled process of inequality replicating itself.[15]

But there's another way of looking at it, too. If you take kids who have little cultural background in education and are perhaps already predisposed to disengagement, and you force them to do subjects that they can visibly see other 'posher' kids are more at home in, you are asserting to them in the strongest possible terms that who they are is not good enough. Even more: if you make the overwhelming moral imperative of education the need to 'get' good grades so you can 'get' a good job, and at the same time constantly reinforce the need to excel in *every* subject (even the ones you don't feel you really chose, and can't see the transactional need for), then you run the risk of some kids – the ones whose engagement with school is the most fragile, and whose understanding of the purpose of what they are doing is the most rudimentary – starting to feel that all this isn't really for their benefit anyway.

There isn't an answer to this. But every time January comes around, when in my school we ask kids to choose their GCSE options, something gets under my skin. I think the reason this all bothers me so much is the hypocrisy. We say to students that they can choose their GCSEs, when really they can't. And we say to them that we value all outcomes – that you're not worth more if you're clever in a particularly defined academic way. But you are.

In many ways Michaela Community School, for better and for worse, is the most honest school I've ever been to. Here, the values of the education system that elsewhere are hidden and elided under layers of obfuscation around 'fulfilling your potential' and 'individualised pathways' are nakedly on the surface.

At lunch – 'Family lunch', as they call it – we discuss what you would do if you won the lottery. This isn't a random topic; it is the prescribed topic that everyone is discussing. The kids dutifully engage. 'Dutifully' might imply reluctance or disengagement. But not here, not with the Michaela conception of 'duty'. I hijack the conversation and turn it towards school.

What's the point? What is school for?

'To allow you success in your career.'

'To help you learn the things you need for your career – for a serious career, like lawyer or doctor.'

But what if you didn't do that? What if you were in a different career – like a bricklayer? I ask.

'If you didn't get a good job, then maybe you did something wrong.'

What is not a good job?

'Maybe picking up litter or something.'

But if we didn't have people picking up litter, we'd be in trouble, I say.

The boy shrugs.

Michaela is hyper-competitive, hyper-regimented. The routines are carefully planned, centrally, with slick effectiveness. Kids move seamlessly from one part of the school to the other. They speak with a clipped, practised formality.

Here's the structure for lunch. You sit in tables of five or six kids, with someone at the head of the table. Today this is me – it might be a student or a teacher on another day. You stand behind your chair and a teacher comes in. They raise their hand. Everyone raises their hands and there is silence. They announce the first poem – in this case 'Ozymandias' – then dive into the first line.

'I MET . . .'

'A traveller from an antique land . . .' The kids half-chant, half-shout. With some lines they do gestures.

'MY NAME . . .'

'Is Ozymandias, King of Kings . . .' Some make a crown with their hands above their heads.

'LOOK ON MY WORKS, YE MIGHTY, AND DESPAIR.'

The noise is deafening. Behind me a girl is practically screaming.

Then, with a gesture from the teacher, it drops. 'The lone and level sands stretch far away.'

We sit.

Kids respond to the environment they are presented with, and the genius of this school is to micromanage the social environment to make it serve the learning environment. There is no conflict here – it is all about learning, discipline and success. The hidden curriculum has been brought to the surface.

When I ask one of my guides why she chose the school, she says, 'My parents chose.' She smiles. 'That's how it always is.'

The other guide agrees. 'At first I was scared, like I didn't want to go. You prepare for the worst. But then I started to want to go.'

'And then you turn up in Year Seven and in the first assembly everyone shakes your hand,' adds the first girl. 'All the teachers know your name. I've seen them with flashcards and pictures, learning the names.'

And there's the rub. This is a stunning place. I don't believe anyone who says the kids are unhappy here – at any rate, they are no unhappier than in any other school and, frankly, the absence of bullying is probably the single most impressive and important achievement here. If my conversations with kids from other schools have proved anything, it is that feeling unsafe, feeling threatened, is kryptonite for learning. If you can eradicate that with some rather cringy chanting, then fair play. And yet the whole essence of the school is built around the need to win – to gain power and control at the top of a hierarchical system. TOP OF THE PYRAMID, as it says in the playground. It is the logical outcome of a system that is designed to create winners and losers: a school with a hard-nosed, ultra-realistic focus not on creating a better world for all, but on ensuring the success of its students within the education system and society as a whole, as they are. It may not be fair, but life is unfair. Michaela accepts that. In fact, it embraces that.

And that, in turn, is the logical consequence of one very simple and fundamental assumption: that we even need to know who's best in the first place.

4. Rank order

When I was a kid I was effortlessly good at school. I read voraciously – stupidly – and I had strange little obsessions, like tropical fish, or insects, or Russian literature. Apart from PE and meeting girls, I cannot remember anything being a struggle. I had my challenges, as any kid does, but they were emphatically not academic. When I got a place at Oxford, I was thrilled. I felt like a powerful drug the sense of myself as gifted. I had conversations with people in which they were impressed with me and I was impressed with myself. I think I genuinely believed that I could do just about anything. On my good days, I still believe it. Yes, as I might have mentioned, my desk is messy and my inbox is the stuff of nightmares. Yes, I have a tendency to think I know the answer before I've properly checked whether I do in fact know it. Yes, I still struggle to tell my left from my right. But, I tell myself, I am *definitely* clever.

The thing is, though, that as I have gone through my working life I've worked alongside people whose qualities are arranged in different configurations. People who have read less, but have absorbed more of what they have read. People who are slower to make decisions, but better at holding to them. People who struggle more with the act of writing, but are clearer-sighted about what they want their writing to do. And, despite all my cleverness, some of these people have been far more successful than I have. Does that make them *better*?

Comparison is both odious and essential. Our social hierarchy is formed on the notion that people are comparable – and our wider culture thrives on the idea of superlatives, of being the best. John Wayne is the best with a pistol, Sherlock Holmes is the best at solving crime, 'Maverick' is the best of the best, goddammit. But one of the oddest things about the idea of being the best is how it falls apart as you look closer. You see this every time a newspaper tries (yet again) to decide the best footballer of all time, or the greatest film of all time, or the finest restaurant in the world. The ranking of qualities becomes more and more subjective – unless you take refuge in the numerical, at which point context overwhelms you. 'Dixie' Dean scored the most top-flight goals in a season – but that was in the 1920s, and no one pretends he would have scored the same in the modern game. *Avatar* is the highest-grossing movie of all time, but does that make it a bigger success than *Star Wars*, which changed the movie business? It all depends on what you mean by 'best': what you're measuring and how.

Even 'Maverick', dare I say it, was only the best of the young men in the US at the time who felt that becoming a naval pilot was a viable career and was not held back by being Black, gay, disabled or ethically opposed to the military–industrial complex.

We can't all be the best. But we are all ranked by our schooling. And when we look at each new cohort of school leavers, blinking in the glare of the August sun, jumping in carefully coordinated leaps of rehearsed joy with their exam results in their hands, do we really think that the A grades or D grades tell us something about 'them'? Or do they instead tell us everything about where they live and how they live, and where they came from?

That's the question of this chapter. To answer it, we need to explore the notion of meritocracy that underpins our conception of school, as well as digging into the way market forces operate in education. But first, let's begin with a close look at how exams actually work – how they are structured, and how grading is assigned – before we try and get a clearer view of the ways in which they don't.

Famously, our modern understanding of what constitutes an exam – the application of the same standardised test to a number of different people, so that you can compare their responses and rank them – has its origins in imperial China. It first appeared around 1,600 years ago as a method of selecting scholars for the civil service. There were sporadic appearances in the West during the Middle Ages and early modern period, but the real start of their consistent use in Britain begins, unsurprisingly, with the start of universal state education.

When it comes to exams as they are used today, there are certain basic points that it is worth stating baldly:

- When we say 'exam', we mean a test sat under controlled conditions that is 'summative' – summing up the knowledge learned over a given period and checking how well it has been retained.
- While there are many qualifications that do not depend on actual exams – using combinations of coursework and practicals instead – the ones based on a single summative assessment in an exam hall are seen as the 'gold standard'. This may or may not be bullshit, but it is a fact.
- Our current education system in England has those 'gold standard' exam grades as its primary output. If you ask someone how well they did at school, it means what grades did they get; and if you ask if a school is good, it means what grades do the kids get in general. Again you may like this or not, but it is the general rule, and the language is very simple – 'performance', 'results', 'achievement', 'scores'.
- The attributes that exams (and other qualifications) *explicitly* measure are twofold. They measure how good Kid X is at Y. They also measure how much better Kid X is at Y than Kid Z. These two things are awkwardly entwined. But they are also taken as an *implicit* measurement of intelligence, organisation, hard work, moral stature, social worth and suitability for a variety of totally unrelated jobs.
- Exams and other qualifications have a second function, besides measurement. They also exist to serve as a goal for students to work towards – a teaching tool to force them to internalise knowledge. This is far from insignificant.

We will come back to these last two points, but for now the easiest way of thinking about exams is as a test of knowledge. 'Here are some questions – do you know the answer?' For some subjects, in some contexts, that is exactly how exams are put together. Science is a good example of a content-heavy subject that often plays out in this direct way: *Label the muscles in the diagram; name three cell types in plants.*

It gets more complicated when 'problem-solving' questions come in – important for both Maths and Science assessment at GCSE and Maths KS2 SATs – where a scenario is presented and inside that scenario there is, effectively, a 'hidden' question. Classic examples often involve trains travelling in different directions, or a variety of multi-ethnic characters with bags of apples. These questions are designed to relate abstract concepts to 'the real world'. There are two motivations for doing this: to make the abstract more accessible and therefore easier to grasp; and, more importantly, by using an unexpected context, to ensure that students actually understand the problem and the concepts involved rather than simply regurgitating a piece of information acquired by rote-learning.[1] Even so, both direct factual questions and problem-solving have straightforward binary answers.

Things get much more challenging when we have to judge diffuse and complex processes of learning. As a teacher of literature, I have to mark essays that answer questions like '*Hamlet* is more about death than revenge: how far and in what ways do you agree with this statement?' and that run over four or five pages. To do so for my A-level class I have to assign a numerical value between 0 and 30, organised into six different 'levels', based on how well the essay fits a series of descriptive sentences corresponding to five different assessment objectives (AOs). For example, for AO2 (*Analyse ways in which meanings are shaped in literary texts*), I might have to distinguish between an answer that has an 'excellent and consistently effective use of analytical methods' and one that has a 'good use of analytical methods' or, God forbid, merely 'some attempt at using analytical methods'. On one level, this is nightmarishly vague and subjective. On another, there is a sense to the vagueness – it allows the professional judgement of an expert to have a role. It certainly makes standardisation a challenge, though.

How assessment works is a potentially limitless subject, and much has been written about it. The point I'm making is simply that the term 'exam' encompasses a very wide variety of possible structures, none of which works with flawless precision, and many of which can be decidedly subjective.

They can have deeper methodological flaws as well. In the previous chapter we encountered E. D. Hirsch's argument that you cannot teach reading comprehension as a generalised *skill*: being good at reading about dinosaurs does not make you good at reading about mushrooms, because your ability is informed by your level of prior knowledge. He's very clear about the implications of this – that teaching reading comprehension skills, with unseen, context-free extracts where you have to 'pick out the main idea' and infer the meaning of words from their contexts, is educationally empty.[2] Instead, he says, reading needs to be developed by constantly broadening the frame of reference, by learning vocabulary and by developing a base of general knowledge that provides the key information needed to interpret unfamiliar texts.

Interestingly, despite the clear influence of Hirsch on the current iteration of the curriculum in England, reading comprehension is a key element at both SATs in Year 6 and GCSE English Language and is tested with unseen, context-free extracts, where you have to 'pick out the main idea' and infer the meaning of words from their contexts (amongst other things). I'm not saying that I agree with everything Hirsch says, but it does seem astonishing to me that we spend so much time establishing the idea of evidence-based teaching, and knowledge-rich curriculums, and overlook this glaring anomaly. If we taught reading comprehension using texts that contain the actual content we want to teach, and if we got kids to answer questions on texts covering ideas and knowledge they had actually studied, we'd not only be assessing their actual abilities, but we'd also avoid the basic unfairness of the 'unseen' test passage. Because it's not *really* unseen, is it? There's always going to be a difference in the levels of prior knowledge that the kids have. Like the time my students in Sunderland had an unseen passage in their GCSE English Language that referenced Piccadilly Circus, and some of the less worldly amongst them inferred the presence of lions and acrobats.

But the question of what goes in exams isn't the only problem. The wider organisation of exams – the ways they are graded and sat – impacts on the way we learn from them, and on how students are ranked. The two key reforms of the 2010s were the change from modular exams (where each unit of work could be sat at a different time throughout the course, and then re-sat individually to improve the grade) to linear exams (where everything came down to one set of final examinations that could not be separated out) and the removal of coursework. Instead of spreading assessment through the year, the entirety of a student's grade was derived from their performance in two or three two-hour exams – and schools were told that only the first time an exam was sat would count for the performance tables.[3]

This intentional narrowing of the field for success is matched by the way our grading is structured. Some exams are 'norm-referenced', meaning that you get a grade according to your performance compared to the other people taking the test – so the top 10 per cent of students would get a Grade A, for example. Others are 'criterion-referenced': you get a grade according to how well you match a given set of criteria – everyone who gets a certain mark gets an A. BTECs and other 'vocational' courses are often criterion-referenced, with specific skills thresholds that candidates need to clear – as are many familiar checks of competency, such as the driving test – while something like the entrance exams used by Oxbridge, or the UCAT test that many medical schools use, are norm-referenced, slicing off the top percentage of the cohort for consideration and discarding the rest.

GCSEs in England are, strictly speaking, a mixture of both, with something called the National Reference Test acting as an extra pool of evidence to adjust the boundaries.[4] In practice, though, what this means is that, with the notable exception of the Covid years, they behave roughly like norm-referenced tests, where there will always be a similar proportion of different grades, with roughly one-third of students failing English and Maths.

Essentially, this means that education becomes a zero-sum game – there have to be winners and losers, and we establish this in one single, country-wide window of time. We don't do this with other key skills. Imagine if we made everyone do their driving tests on the same day, no matter whether or not they were ready. Obviously it would be stupid on a practical level – picture the queues and the beeped horns, as thousands of seventeen-year-olds simultaneously stalled on roundabouts around the country – but it would also not be conducive to getting the majority of them to pass, which is surely what we want, right? And then imagine we simply accepted that those who fail their driving tests first time are just not meant to drive. That they are second-tier; that they don't have 'the qualifications'.[5]

We seem somehow to have got stuck on the logically absurd proposition that everyone develops at the same speed, reaching their potential at the same time. We forget that exams and other qualifications are developmental snapshots, *evidence* of ability (and the lack of ability) rather than *proof* of it.

But even if exams *were* perfect, there are still limits as to what they can tell us – and what we are morally justified in doing with the information they provide.

Nowadays a 'meritocracy' is considered a good thing. In a meritocracy, everyone has more or less the same sorts of opportunity, the same chance to gain qualifications through education and then the same chance to progress, so those who achieve more and go further are deserving of their success. If innate talent has helped them on their way, all the better: a system that recognises and rewards talent is one that elicits the best from society. It has to be a great improvement on wealth and decision-making power being handed down by class and birth, with all the incompetence in public office and wasted ability that implies.

In fact the person who came up with the term, Michael Young, a sociologist writing in the fifties, thought meritocracy was a bad idea. Profoundly unfair as the class system was in Britain, those at the bottom of it were not seen as being to blame for their poverty. Wealth and education were divorced from moral worth by the unfairness of the system. Move to a meritocratic society, however, where instead of accident of birth we have accident of talent, and suddenly you have a narrative where poverty is exactly that – failure.

In an imaginary 'perfect' meritocracy, this is bad enough. But any real society is far from perfect. There are two key processes that can go wrong: how we reward the best roles in society (those we want to encourage people with the highest merit to occupy); and how we define the best candidates for those roles (how we identify merit in the first place). It's a commonplace to say how the first process has become corrupted. The rewards in our society are far more often a product of market forces than of intrinsic good. Success is measured in monetary terms – getting a salary rise for good performance – and then, by a process of semantic slippage, worth becomes about money as well, until one ends up trying to defend the differential between the wages of bankers and those of nurses.

As for the second process, though, at the heart of identifying 'merit' is the school system. The equation seems simple: good grades = high-merit candidates = high-status role in society. It's so simple that we implicitly accept it, even when it is blindingly obvious there is something amiss. For years, for example, it has been an accepted fact that the levels of privately educated students at Oxford and Cambridge are disproportionately high. As a result, recently there has been a concerted (and successful) effort to increase the representation of students from lower-income backgrounds – and a concerted backlash. Newspaper headlines have phrased this as 'privately educated pupils to lose out' and 'parents say children are edged out'.[6] They describe attempts to bypass privilege as 'social engineering'. There has even been a suggestion that this will lead to a brain-drain, whereby our brightest Etonians may well go to America instead.[7]

Leaving aside unintended benefits like that, the response reveals the way in which we persistently think *what* a child achieves is all that matters, and *how they achieve it* is irrelevant. In this way of thinking, the privilege of a private education (or indeed a supportive home, money for books, absence of stress) may be unfair, but in the end it will produce a person with greater capacity – greater merit – and, as in any efficiently run market, resources should be allocated according to who can make best use of them. But the opposite might also be true: in the same way that running uphill makes you fitter than running on the flat, someone with fewer resources might end up being mentally more agile and resilient – and when finally placed on a level playing field, the state educated might then outpace the privileged private-school candidate. To arrive at a true measure of the privileged candidate's abilities maybe we need instead to *discount* their schooling.[8]

This logic doesn't apply to everything. If you are recruiting someone on the basis of how much French they know, it doesn't mean much to you if the reason they know less is because they weren't taught it properly. But if, on the other hand, you are choosing candidates for their potential to excel at Oxbridge, or to succeed at a competitive career, then you have to bear in mind not only what they have achieved, but what they will *go on* to achieve – and judging that absolutely *should* be informed by the circumstances of their education.[9]

Privilege distorts the workings of meritocracy. But privilege isn't simply about the rarefied competition for places at elite universities, or the difference between private and state education. It runs through *all* schools from top to bottom. We talk about education as a vehicle for 'aspiration', 'social mobility' and 'achievement', and yet, as the political philosopher Michael Sandel has pointed out, 'the hard truth is that education overwhelmingly reproduces advantage rather than restructuring it.'[10] The statistics to support this statement are stark.[11] No matter where you are, what school you're at, what ethnicity or what gender you are, what happens at home fundamentally frames what happens in school. A school like Michaela does exceptionally well for disadvantaged students, with progress scores for those eligible for Pupil Premium funding far in excess of what most non-disadvantaged students get in the rest of the country. But within the school? Those who have the advantages still do better than those who don't. This is known as 'the disadvantage gap'.

So what counts as 'disadvantage'? Pupil Premium, the statistical marker for disadvantage in UK schools, is the bluntest of blunt tools. It encompasses all children who have received free school meals at any point in the last six years, plus those who have been in care at any point in their lives. This means that it includes the following children and treats their circumstances as identical:

- Janice, who lives in a loving home with her mother and father and two brothers in a small terrace. Her mother is a carer to her grandmother, who lives next door, and her father works for a low wage as a teaching assistant.
- Arthur, who was abused at three and has had five different foster placements, including a traumatic return to his birth mother, where he witnessed her being assaulted.

- Aljaz, whose father is a doctor, but whose certification is not valid in Britain and so he currently works as a porter while moonlighting as a cabbie to earn enough for extra tuition.
- Viola, whose mother died when she was six and whose father is clinically depressed, and who comes to school so dirty that her head of year has contacted social services on four occasions.
- Bobby, whose parents split up three years ago. During the acrimonious divorce, his mother (with whom he lived) ended up without income for six months and claimed free school meals for him. Now he divides his time between his father (a barrister) and his mother (retrained and now working for the BBC).

For obvious reasons, these are not real kids. But their circumstances are. One of the terrible aspects of teaching is that you know all the awful things that happen – those grotesque stories in the news or that crop up as plot points in prestige drama – they *really* happen. Every school has abuse going on behind the scenes in some of its families. Every school has bereavement, has trauma, has poverty. And the sad fact is that every school I've been in has also witnessed deep neglect, hunger and malnutrition.

It does not take a great leap of imagination to accept that a student who lives in a two-bed flat with eight siblings and a mum who passes out with the needle in her arm cannot really be expected to compete with a classmate who has three square meals a day, three foreign holidays a year and a quiet desk to work at, with the aid of a tutor once a week. True, some who fall into the Pupil Premium category will not be as disadvantaged as others. But even allowing for such an unsatisfactory marker, the point about disadvantage remains, and it is worth looking specifically at how these various forms of disadvantage affect pupils' ability to do well at school and, in particular, at exams.

One example of how this happens is illustrated by an offshoot of the Marshmallow Test. This was a classic bit of psychological research done by Walter Mischel in the seventies. In it, five-year-olds were given a marshmallow and told that if they refrained from eating it for fifteen minutes, they would be given a second and could eat them both. They were then left alone with the marshmallow and their actions were filmed. The children were tracked in a longitudinal study over the ensuing decades, with the results finally published in the nineties. Those who demonstrated impulse control at the age of five, and didn't eat the marshmallow, were found to have greater 'success' in the adult world – income, education and absence of addictions.

A few years back, I did an assembly on the Marshmallow Test. This is excellent material for an assembly, for two reasons. First, there is a wholesome message, which is so seductive for teachers. It fits perfectly with a worldview that says small acts of self-denial now – following the rules, doing your homework, waiting patiently in a queue – will pay off later. Second, there are some *really* cute videos of kids trying not to eat marshmallows.

But then a friend of mine pointed me in the direction of another study.[12] Tyler Watts, Greg Duncan and Haonan Quan had noticed that the ninety children in Mischel's original test were all recruited from a pre-school on the campus of Stanford University, and this came from a restricted and relatively affluent social group. So they re-ran the experiment. This time they picked 900 subjects, from a cross-section of society, and they controlled for background. The end result was that the kids' background had a major influence on whether or not they ate the marshmallow.

Put crudely, if you grow up with less food, a marshmallow in the hand is worth two in the bush. And if you don't trust adults, then you don't believe that second one is coming anyway. It threw into question what lies behind 'impulse control' – and, indeed, whether that was actually what was being measured. This is perhaps the single most important point about disadvantage. People who are struggling with poverty or abuse or trauma do not necessarily make bad decisions – they make decisions that look bad from an outside perspective. We all, at all times, juggle priorities. And sometimes there genuinely *are* more important things than getting that homework done.

Another way in which disadvantage hampers children's engagement with school is acutely diagnosed by the sociologist Diane Reay in her hugely insightful book, *Miseducation*. She puts it like this: 'It's primarily working-class children who turn out to be losers in the educational system.'[13] She anatomises the ways in which schools are a middle-class world, encoding middle-class values, and subtly (and not so subtly) skewing achievement towards those who already embody those values. This effect encompasses everything. It ranges from language and vocabulary to course content, to frame of reference, to basic rules.

Imagine a child whose parents work shifts. They get their own dinner, maybe with a cousin or an aunt, and sit with it in front of the telly, and get themselves up for school in the morning. They speak in local dialect with everyone in their family, never being 'corrected'. On any questions about any subject at school, their parents defer to the school, saying, 'I never did well at that.' They go on holiday to a caravan park an hour away or on a week's package holiday to Mallorca once every two years. They have an encyclopaedic knowledge of Sunderland AFC, dogs and fishing, but have only ever been to museums with the school. This is a loving, warm home. The child is happier and healthier than many, from any social background. But when they come into school, from the first moment they are identified as not quite fitting.

The teacher on the gate says, 'Do your tie up properly' and 'Those aren't school shoes'. The child goes into the classroom and says 'aye' when their name is called, but is corrected. In Geography they are talking about cities, and the teacher asks, 'Has anyone been to London?' They haven't. In History the teacher asks, 'Who here's been to Hadrian's Wall?' They haven't. In English they are corrected when they say 'us've' instead of 'we have', when they say 'I got wrong' and when they say 'borrow me a rubber'. When they write a story, they're asked to describe a really spooky location, like an old haunted house, but they've never been in or seen a really old house, haunted or not.

At lunch, they get told off for not sitting properly at the table. In French they have no idea why they are learning the subject, because every time they go abroad, people speak English. At the end of the day they have a detention because Mr Wright thought they were being really rude when they pointed out his shoelaces were untied, even though they were genuinely just pointing out his shoelaces were untied. And that night they don't do any homework, because no one tells them to.

These are individually small things. But the unfortunate point about our system is that it is designed to work with the support of a wider cultural awareness and with the support of educated parents. And kids without this slowly, incrementally begin to feel that school is not the place for them.

There is a vicious circle at work here – and it's in places like Sunderland, where I work, that you see the ways in which literal disadvantage and cultural disconnect converge to create whole communities where education is so meaningless, and hope so distant, that further underachievement becomes inevitable. If you break Progress 8 scores down by region, London comes first, with a positive score of 0.23, and the North-East is last, half a grade down on the capital at -0.27.[14]

Where does all this leave us? We live in a meritocratic society that demands we measure our young people in public examinations. Meritocracy is problematic, but flawed meritocracy is worse – and ours is flawed in part by its very reliance on exams. Exams don't measure as well as we think they do, and the way they are designed and implemented can compound this. Even if they did measure flawlessly, educational achievement is inextricably linked to home circumstance in a variety of ways, both practical and cultural. While we know that, on the individual level, this link can be broken by young people who succeed despite multiple challenges, on the aggregate it means that even when they do comparatively well, disadvantaged young people are still outstripped in the rankings by their more privileged peers and are denied the most competitive places in society. And for a young person from a disadvantaged background growing up in Britain today, this inequality is visible and pervasive and deeply disheartening.

So are we at the point where we need to put the exam system out of its misery? Unusually for the complexity of education, the answer is clear: no. Because what are the alternatives? Coursework is one – but it's arguably undermined by the level of (cough) 'support' that students get (although clearly it can be made to work, as its presence in creative subjects testifies to). Continuous assessment (where grades are based on judgements and tests throughout a course) takes away the incentive to fix learning into long-term memory via revision. And teacher-assessed grades, as we had during Covid, where teachers made a summative judgement at the end of a course, have the potential to play into the preconceptions that teachers have about their pupils.[15] All have their benefits too, of course, but there is no doubt that none of them offers a meaningful alternative on its own, without the anchor of standardised exams. Even the persistence of the disadvantage gap isn't really an argument against exams per se: it is the disadvantage that causes the gap, not the exam itself.

The simplest answer – of just not assessing – is the worst. Because, for all the issues that come with it, teaching is at its most fundamental level bound up with assessment, not only in terms of the way we do it culturally, but in terms of the way our brains learn. We process knowledge using assessment as we go – as anyone who has tried to learn the spelling of a word using the classic 'look, cover, repeat' technique knows. Cognitive science tells us that the revisiting and revising of knowledge, the cumulative learning that takes place, the checking and recalling of ideas with or without prompts are part of fixing it in the long-term memory. And, on a really practical level, anyone who has ever actually met a child (or an adult, for that matter) understands the basic moral point that our behaviour is socially determined, and that if something is not checked, then it often starts to atrophy.

There is one qualification, introduced around fifteen years ago, that does offer a profoundly different way of thinking – although, as we will see, it is also far from straightforward. The Extended Project Qualification (EPQ) is offered mostly at post-sixteen and is described as 'equivalent to half an A level'. It's an odd beast – students choose their own 'project', which could be literally anything (I've seen the construction of a bicycle, the performance of a musical, an essay on the legalities of the Palestinian Authority, and a novel, amongst others). They have no teaching, but simply a 'supervisor' who offers coaching and helps them decide where to focus their efforts. What they produce is then assessed, not on the basis of how good it is, but on how good their process has been: how independent they were, how much they researched, and so on. The key point is that the assessment should not be of the absolute standard of anything – but of the distance travelled.

I'm a big fan of this and have seen some truly outstanding examples. But there is, again, a major caveat. The EPQ is probably the qualification that I've seen having the most profound impact on individual students. But it can only work if there is no pressure on it. Schools have to be able to let students fail – and the course has been designed to allow this, by not being part of the main suite of qualifications that schools are judged on, or that students use to get into university. If there was more weight on the EPQ, the freedom to experiment and fail would be curtailed – and the inevitable inconsistencies in marking and grading would become problematic. Which takes us right back to the need for exams.

Perhaps the most important point I think we can learn from the EPQ is the way in which lowering the stakes, and letting go of the need for a hard-and-fast answer to that question 'Who is the best?', can actively *improve* the core educational impact of it, even as the validity of the data produced is undermined.

This is not the only paradox of our examination system. In many ways, paradox is the best way to understand it. To my mind, there are three core contradictions that cannot be ignored. First, to teach without testing whether something has actually been learned is a dangerous game. But to teach to the test can undermine the usefulness of what you teach in the first place.

Second, no qualifications system can *actually* indicate someone's fitness or ability in the messy complexity of adult life, or rank them relative to their peers. But to pick one example, we need doctors and we have to be sure they know where your liver is.

Third, exams are not fair. There is a wealth of evidence to show that how you do in exams is dictated by many other factors, not least whether your grandma died the day before the test. But here is the crux of the problem: every other option for assessment is also not fair, although in different and sometimes worse ways. If you are going to try to assess how much students have learned, exams really are the best of a bad lot.

(The last of these paradoxes is the rather ugly and inconvenient elephant in the room because, as we've seen, the need for education to be fair is the great struggle of the modern system. As teachers, we know that we're losing that struggle. And yet we still claim that, even if imperfectly, we reward merit. The hypocrisy is corrosive, and in my view lies behind much of the weird combination of apathy and stress that we sometimes see in our schools – apathy because of a lack of hope that one can achieve, and simultaneously stress because so much seems to depend on it.)

Does that mean we're just stuck with exams? Maybe – but if, instead of valorising exams, we acknowledge that making these judgements is a lot harder than it seems, and that there are significant errors in many of them (even aside from the furore over teacher-assessed grades used during Covid, management consultant Dennis Sherwood has estimated that in normal years around one in four exam grades is 'wrong'[16]), then we might be able to move away from the ridiculous over-specificity of how we use this information.

To go back to that earlier question of entry into elite universities, the most absurd part of the outcry over the effort to increase the numbers of state-school entrants (apart from the inherent absurdity of worrying that private-school pupils who are over-represented by a factor of five might lose out) is that *all* the candidates will have top grades. Oxford and Cambridge are not picking between one student with three Cs and one with three A*s. All of them will have combinations of As and A*s. Really the process of selection is one of trying to make the most fine-grained of judgements, when that simply isn't possible. It's like choosing the best fish at the fishmonger's when they all weigh the same. I mean, one *might* be better – but you won't know until you eat it.[17]

So one suggestion is that we simply stop pretending we can make these decisions. Rather than employing or selecting on the basis of being 'the best', why not choose on the basis of being above a thresh-old: being 'in the group of people who would be capable of making the most of this opportunity'. I can't imagine anyone saying it to Tom Cruise, mind. 'You're in the top group of people within the wider group of people capable of flying this goddamn plane, Maverick.' But on second thoughts, maybe that might actually work. We'd save ourselves two hours of macho ultra-competitiveness, and Goose might still be alive, goddammit.

I know – there are obvious challenges with this route. Once we've established who sits within the relevant group, how do we then allocate scarce resources and university places? The simplest way would be by lottery, but that is a significant challenge to the way our most prestigious institutions have organised matters up to now.

Whether or not we pursue that line of thinking, though, the underlying point remains: we don't need to ban exams, but we do need to flip the way we see them. They are important tools for teaching, but we must not mistake them for the teaching itself. Other ways of motivating, reinforcing and assessing achievement are valid, even when they do not produce 'robust data'. In many ways, the problems that dog things like coursework are problems not of pedagogy but of the way grades are used and their artificially heightened importance. Because the fundamental problem with exams is this: they support a system of ranking that is based on a narrow definition of what constitutes academic achievement, a definition that favours children with relative privilege. It is a system that mistakes specific achievement for general potential and then allocates resources and opportunities and privileges accordingly.

This whole approach derives from a way of thinking in which the only fair and reliable way to assign value is to let the invisible hand of the market decide, via competition. Applied to education, it results in exams that are not a way of fostering achievement, but a means of engineering competition between pupils as the mechanism by which we assign them with value: who deserves what.

This has a further effect on the education itself. In a market where grades are the currency and ranking is the goal, the engine that drives the whole system is the competitive maximisation of outcomes – the need not to get every student past a threshold, but to extract the highest possible grades from every pupil, regardless of their inherent utility or whether the effect on the pupil is actually desirable or worthwhile. We end up with a system that prioritises good grades at the expense of a good education.

And one reason we have ended up with this way of thinking about education is because it's also how we think about the institutions that deliver that education. The ranking of pupils doesn't happen in a vacuum. It is itself an outcome of how we rank schools, both through performance tables and through Ofsted (whose four single-word judgements are also referred to as blunt numerical grades, with 1 being 'outstanding', 4 being 'inadequate', and the 'good' grade of 2 being the pass mark). All three processes feed into each other, magnifying and reinforcing the way we think of education as: (a) a transaction with measurable outcomes; and (b) a market where parents can exercise choice and schools must compete with one another.

What success or failure in this marketplace actually means, though, is where we need to look next.

On a bright Monday morning in September I receive a one-word text halfway through period two. The text says: *NOW*. I know instantly what it means. We have received 'the call'. At 8.30 the following morning Ofsted will be here.

. . .

I left a dramatic pause there, for all the teachers reading. The rest of you might not know exactly what is happening in that pause, but teachers know. There's a quaking, a jelly-like feeling in the gut, a cold sweat and a sudden instability that makes one want to sit down. I imagine it's not dissimilar to how people reacted to 'The Vikings are coming!' or, more recently, 'There's a hen party at the next table!'

Just as kids have exams, so schools undergo their own ritualised process of comparative ranking. And there are no two ways about it, Ofsted – the Office for Standards in Education, Children's Services and Skills, which conducts the school inspections – is genuinely terrifying. I don't mean personally. Lots of inspectors are very nice people; I know and work with some. But no matter how much one rationalises it, there is a fear that comes with the process of inspection that few other experiences can quite match.

This is my fifth Ofsted. In the course of the twenty-year span of my experiences with inspection, I've been through it five times and have seen a few different iterations and perspectives. But I've never been in truly car-crash territory – the kind of inspection that sits at the back of my mind as I walk, wobbly-kneed, across the yard to the Head's office on the morning of 'the call'. Here are the things I think about:

- Have I got any clean shirts?
- How long can I live off my savings if I am sacked?
- Am I going to puke in the middle of the playground?
- When our intake collapses and we have to make mass redundancies, will I be able to look my colleagues in the eye ever again?

Because no matter how sanguine you are and how well prepared, what gives an inspection its peculiar psychological intensity is that a negative judgement, as well as being a massive blow to the school's morale and self-image, can have huge practical implications. The intake of new pupils can drop as parents send their children elsewhere, which means a fall in budget: schools are funded per pupil – so each one who doesn't come represents a drop in income of around £5,000. That money is paid on a lagged timetable: so if you are down one year, you have no prospect of making the money up the following year and can be forced into hiring freezes or even redundancies. There are no other savings a school can make; 80–90 per cent of budgets comprise staffing, and the rest is mostly utilities and essential services. The students who don't come are invariably those whose parents pay attention to Ofsted and who have the resources and know-how to make a change. If the student body alters in the wake of a negative judgement, it is likely to become more deprived and less motivated.

You are also likely to see a higher turnover of staff. The staff who leave are likely to be the ones who can – the ones with ambition and good references. Sometimes the perversity of the process means that you lose the young, cheap, enthusiastic staff and keep the old, cynical, demoralised ones who are at the top of the pay-scale and are serving out their time to retirement. Given the length of time between inspections – two years, if the judgement is 'Requires Improvement'; four years, if it's 'Good' – these impacts can become a spiral of long-term decline; or, in the modern climate of academisation, the prompt for an aggressive takeover, with the attendant decapitation of leadership.

There are legitimate arguments that these effects might be an important part of the process of improving school quality. But there's no denying the fact that they're bloody unpleasant for the people involved, and all of them can rapidly make a child's experience in the classroom worse.

This is the fear that haunts you – the worst-case scenario – and it comes with an agonising twist. Because the worst bit about Ofsted (the very worst bit) is that they are not really judging *you*. They are judging how the kids are: how they learn, and how they behave. And while kids are lovely and I have boundless hope for the future because they *are* the future, I also invite you to a very particular form of the common exam-room nightmare.

Most people describe this as a dream where you are back sitting an exam, your mind a blank, terror congealing around your ankles. But imagine instead sitting an exam that consists of testing not what you know, but what 1,500 hormonal teenagers (at least forty-three of whom properly hate you) can remember about their Geography lesson from last week.

I'm being flippant, but there is something deadly serious about this. In the wake of the tragic death of Ruth Perry, a headteacher who committed suicide in the aftermath of her experience of inspection, the discourse has opened up about the impact of Ofsted on teachers, and in particular on headteachers. The combination of judgements that feel both highly personal and arbitrary, that are of you but not really within your control, that come without warning and yet can be life-changing, both personally and for your local community, can be psychologically devastating.

As for our own inspection, everything turned out okay. By which I mean we were awarded a 'Good' judgement and everyone could breathe again and focus on the actual business of teaching. But I describe all this because the Ofsted inspection process and its results tell us several very important things about the way schools are ranked, and why some schools 'succeed' and some 'fail'. First, although the grade a school receives is intended as a reflection of the state it is in, the quality of the education it provides, it is not simply that. It is also a sentence: it has a direct bearing on the school's trajectory towards success or failure thereafter. Second, it is Ofsted's job to take the holistic view, to look beyond the performance tables derived from the student's exam grades, and to dig into the daily *experience* of the school, in order to tell us definitively and objectively what a 'Good' school is – and how that differs from an 'Outstanding' school or an 'Inadequate' one.

The problem with this is simple. The Education Endowment Foundation, the body created to collate, compare and disseminate educational research, has averaged the data on the disadvantage gap across schools that have received different Ofsted judgements. The pattern is clear. For each category, the gap is essentially the same, hovering at around 11 per cent: whether a school is outstanding or inadequate, poor kids still underachieve.[18] And research by the Social Mobility Commission (SMC) shows a clear correlation between the number of poor children in a school and the likelihood of it being judged 'Outstanding' or 'Inadequate'.[19] This tells us, in the starkest possible terms, that what we call 'Outstanding' schools have two key characteristics: they are still hobbled by the same inequalities, and it is much easier to be outstanding with richer kids in your school. To put it even more bluntly: for many schools, the Ofsted judgement is a measure of their privilege, not their educational excellence. And while it's true that the new inspection framework introduced in 2019 places less reliance on exam results and has shown itself willing to knock previously outstanding schools off their perch, the same pattern of inequality seems to persist.[20]

This is not to say, by the way, that kids don't get a good education at 'Outstanding' schools, or that 'Inadequate' schools are totally fine. It's not a criticism of the schools, or their leaders, either. It's merely that our expectations of good schools are so geared towards the needs and experiences of the more affluent students that it is easier to succeed when that is your student body. And behavioural issues in schools often stem from disengagement with education – something far more likely when your students, for often very legitimate reasons, believe that school does not address their needs.

The specific issue with Ofsted is that we are forced to translate this complex set of social circumstances into a blunt grade. During every inspection I have been through, I've always come away with the sense that the inspectors are principled, perceptive human beings who probably can see the qualities and flaws of a school with significantly more nuance than they are allowed to describe in their reports. In fact they often say as much – in the feedback they give to senior leaders they explain the detail and context that they explicitly cannot express in the report. You can see the conflict in them as you speak to them. They actually understand that a school is too complex to capture in a grade – and yet the mechanisms of inspection require them to do exactly that. They understand that the process of the two days they are with you is intensely artificial; that kids are on their best behaviour and that staff are terrified; that no one slept last night; and that, when they leave, normal business will resume. They understand that just as exams have little relationship to real life, so an inspection day has little relationship to a normal day at school.

In fact one of the oddest points about inspection is that, because it is so high-stakes for the school, and so rule-bound on the side of the inspectors, you can find yourself (as I did in a previous school) arguing that the difference between 'Good' and 'Outstanding' depends on the significance of one specific piece of evidence – in this instance, a crisp packet dropped by a student. The need to grade makes an absurdity of the whole process.

That's not to say we don't need to judge and inspect, in order to maintain and improve school quality. But badging schools with cliff-edge descriptors is not really about school improvement. I had a conversation with Amanda Spielman, head of Ofsted at the time, while on the SMC, trying to persuade her to change the grading system, but it was made explicitly clear that a numerical grade was seen as essential to help parents choose between schools. Parental choice sounds great, but of course it means a choice only for those parents who have the wherewithal to *make* a choice – a smokescreen of a supposed free market in education that is anything but. Even if we had a system of grading that didn't act as a proxy for identifying the most middle-class schools, ask yourself whether it is morally acceptable for a kid to attend a substandard school because their parents are unwilling, or unable, to put in the application on time – and that will tell you whether we should build a system of inspection that acts primarily as a tool for the crude marketisation of education.

This first part of this book began with the question 'What is school for?' That question has taken us on a tour through the systems and structures of education in England. I've looked at the ways in which we have tried to describe the function and success of schools through performance tables, at the history of schools and their differing purposes, at the nature of what we teach and how we teach it, and at the methods and impact of how we rank students – and how we rank schools. Before we embark on Part Two, let us return for a moment to that question, and specifically to the very simple answer that is most often repeated by the pupils themselves: 'So you can get a good job.'

What this tells us is that we have entered into a compact with our students that is fundamentally transactional: do well at school, get good grades and you will get a good life. The problem is that the students can see perfectly well that a large chunk of their curriculum has no direct bearing on what they want to do at A level or in later life, and it's equally clear to everyone that how well you do in life is not *really* going to be decided by how well you do in Geography GCSE.

When we teach GCSEs we tell our pupils, 'This is the stuff we need to know in general', but the truth – as they can see – is that the specific content is organised in a way that fits with the highly specialised nature of study at A level and beyond. In other words, we say that we are offering a rounded education that imparts general skills and equips someone to navigate the world, but *what* we teach and *how* we teach it are actually reverse-engineered to fit the demands of the next stage of the exam system. Something is taught in the way it is taught, not because that is the only way, or even the best way, but because it fits with the needs of the students who go on to follow the most academic paths. In many ways, 'general' is exactly what it is not. That doesn't mean that all the content covered is 'wrong', or that everything pupils do has to be 'relevant' to them. But we can't tell them something is important to learn because it is generally enriching and will get them a good life, then expect them to believe us when their experience says that it's exam-focused, designed for academic specialisation and will do nothing of the sort.

As I have argued in this chapter, the heart of the problem is that the idealised 'meritocratic' logic of our system results in schools whose purpose is not the general education of all pupils according to their natural aptitudes, but rather the sorting of kids into the positions in society that they 'merit', according to an academic scale. The most pernicious result of this is that the pupils themselves can see the lie for what it is.

They can see perfectly well that this system works fine for those at the top, but not for the rest, and that the ranking system has an inbuilt bias against those from poorer backgrounds. That we reward the winners in this system, and pretend to the rest of them that the education we are offering them is something it is not. That all our attention becomes focused on a certain narrow definition of success. That school becomes a place where disadvantage is entrenched, not challenged. And when fairness is exactly what we promise kids, the absence of it is toxic. The by-product of the drive to succeed in a rigged game is stress and apathy.

To turn this all around we need to rethink the idea that school is a place whose sole purpose is to produce results that can be quantified. We need to recognise that what goes on in a school is about so much more than what can be measured in an exam, and that the idea of education simply being an investment for the future leads to an endless deferral of the *now*. It's the difference between thinking of a house as a 'property' and thinking of it as a 'home'.

If we want to build a more equal education sector, we have to start by telling the truth, both to the pupils and to ourselves. Because what's in the textbooks and the exam hall and the Ofsted report doesn't even begin to describe the ways that children actually *experience* the process of education – or the deeper lessons they learn from it. So what is school actually *like*? And what do schools *really* teach us? These are the questions that we will address now, in the second part of this book.

PART TWO

What is school really like?

5.   A world of contradiction

Like any teacher, I have certain things I do again and again. Certain lessons, certain questions, certain spiels that I trot out. This can be good – practice makes perfect – and it can be bad. I used to have a routine with kids who struggled to follow rules, where I talked about all the rules in the world, all the things that made society work, and I said that a life without rules would just be sitting in a damp forest, killing animals for food: You wouldn't want just to sit in a damp forest, killing animals for food, would you?

I hadn't read the file properly. If I had, I would have known that this specific child *did* want to sit in a damp forest, killing animals. He said 'Yes' with a particularly disturbing glint in his eye.

Some spiels work more reliably. Like when I ask kids, Why do we study literature?

They look bemused at first. They might mention GCSEs. They might frown and say they don't know.

So now comes my answer: All your other subjects ask you to close down knowledge – to box it up into answers that you can put a tick or a cross next to. The study of literature asks the opposite. It asks you to blow things open – to allow uncertainty, and ambiguity, and contradiction, and paradox.

I like saying this. It makes me feel heroic – which, after all, is a key motivation for being a teacher.

And that is what life is, I carry on. Whatever you go on to do, you will find out that the answers in life are far more like the answers in literature than in all the other subjects.

I might be wrong, of course. But when I look at what schools in England are really like, it seems to me that uncertainty, ambiguity, contradiction and paradox lie at their heart.

★

Let me try to explain.

In 2002, during my training year, in an impressively haphazard piece of decision-making, I accepted a post teaching English at William Ellis School in Camden. I had never lived in London. In fact I'd been looking all over the country at other possibilities – Doncaster, Carlisle, Brighton – but it ended up being London, and it ended up being William Ellis, because the sun was shining on the day of the interview, there was a nice pub opposite where I had a decent Guinness and, most importantly, they offered me a job.

If I'd thought about it, I might have said that I didn't really believe in single-sex education. But I didn't think about it. And so I ended up teaching in a school which, for all of its many charms, was eternally marked by the smell of teenage boys in nylon blazers who'd played football energetically all lunch and then sprayed Lynx Africa liberally over the *outside* of their clothes. I did try to tell them why this was wrong. I didn't get anywhere.

It's hard to identify why it is that schools develop a particular culture. And in many ways that culture can turn out to be an illusion, or wishful thinking. Every teacher will talk about 'our pupils' as if 'our pupils' are a different category, forged in different fires from the ordinary run-of-the-mill kid, even if this has little basis in objective fact. But I remain convinced that the one exception is that there really was such a thing as 'Ellis boys'. I could spot them a mile off. It was a place where the most astonishing mix of kids had been thrust together – deep deprivation mixed with affluence and cultural capital of a level that only North London can provide. Kids of actors and singers and New Labour grandees sitting cheek-by-jowl with chippy cockneys and traumatised refugees. But they all had a particular quality: a hectic warmth, a bullish, swaggering sensitivity. They'd behave in ways that were halfway between the impish mischief of a *Beano* comic and the charismatic menace of Tony Soprano – but always with an implicit acknowledgement of the school as a tight community, and of teachers as people you trusted, even as you mocked them.

'Fuck off, sir' was a classic Ellis phrase.

And 'tight' was the word. The pupils really were cheek-by-jowl – no teacher had anything so outlandish as their 'own' classroom, and later on in my time there, in an effort to engineer more space, the school actually had to take the roof off to build an extra floor while we continued teaching below. Combine that with a workforce predominantly filled with cheap, inexperienced teachers like me, Australians on extended gap years and a core of grizzled old hands, many of whom religiously got tanked in the pub over the road every Friday, and you had a pressure cooker of intensity and camaraderie.

So when I arrange to speak to Conrad Landin, an ex-student from those times, I feel an unexpected flush of emotion. He had been a bookish kid who used to come and sit on the raggedy sofa in the English office – next to the single computer that all nine teachers shared – as a bit of a refuge. I'd left the school when he was in Year 10, but after seeing his name on a byline for a couple of articles online, I got in touch to find out how his memories tallied with my own.

It turns out he's had a stellar academic career, including studying at Cambridge. Now, at close to thirty, he's a long way from the kid he was, but it's amazing how quickly the past comes back – and how natural the conversation is. After we've got through the reminiscences about this teacher and that kid, Conrad tells me how he found school quite isolating.

'If you don't really fit in,' he says, 'and I don't really think I did, you end up with a barrage of stuff coming at you, which seems to encourage you to capitulate and to do your best to fit in.' He looks thoughtful. 'I think I was probably less happy than I could have been. If I'd tried to conform a bit more, I would have been happier at the time – but less happy now. In a way it was a pretty formative experience. But having said that, I felt pretty alone.'

I feel surprisingly upset, hearing him say this. It's different knowing that a kid is struggling and hearing them, as an adult, describing their unhappiness. And there is an odd disjunct between my memory of Conrad – thinking of him as the epitome of a 'good' student, a kid who wanted to catch me at break to talk about books, and who seemed to warm to teachers – and the more mature knowledge that the ways in which he pleased us also caused him pain.

As he speaks, there is another doubleness – a confident, articulate, successful adult still carrying the baggage of his childhood. The

vulnerability peeks through. I wonder if it does in all Conrad's conversations, or if there is something so specifically unguarded about
talking in this way – teacher and pupil, fifteen years on.

I say to him that there were other kids who were struggling just as
much – but that there was something very open about him. You
wore your heart on your sleeve, I say. You arrived at secondary school
fully formed – you came to us as a nerdy, academic, left-field kid, and
you left us like that too. Where did that come from?

'Yes,' Conrad agrees. 'But I also think that when I arrived I was shy,
I was lacking in confidence, I think I was quite insecure. And probably
that didn't change that much in the time I was at Ellis – but I think the
time I was at Ellis, in the long run, the time I had to . . . to defend that
relationship against the wider society of the school, that really helped.'

So in a way, I say, there was one kind of learning – the lesson-
based stuff – but there was also another – an antagonistic kind of
trial-by-playground. I think of my romanticised memories of the
rough and tumble of the 'Ellis boys' and wince.

He nods. 'But that was also the way in which some teachers interacted with you. If you're dealing with a class of twenty-six quite
unruly kids, there'll be a bit of a lowest-common-denominator factor
in there, in terms of getting the attention. Teachers can become quite
antagonistic themselves towards students who are actually interested
in learning.'

That's pretty strong, I say.

Conrad qualifies. 'Maybe it's more like it's a bit of an inconveni-
ence.'

I tell him that I think one of the reasons we, in the English department, were quite warm towards him was the sense we had that he was
vulnerable, and that he was quite misunderstood by adults as well as
by his peers. As I speak, I feel disorientated by the complexity of this
conversation – the odd intimacy of it. I've not seen this person for a
decade and a half, and even then I don't know how well I actually
knew Conrad. But for all that, when I saw him, I saw him every day.
There is a vertiginous strangeness to this. It makes tangible the thing
we teachers know, but rarely dwell on: our afterlives in the minds of
all the students we taught, for good and for bad.

Most of the time we overlapped at Ellis, I didn't actually teach Conrad – I just spoke to him in and around the corridors or in the office. I couldn't remember whether I had ever formally taught him, to be honest, but he reminded me that I did, for a six-week period. I had left the school to go travelling with my girlfriend (now my wife) and I returned in May to find that there was a job at Ellis, after my replacement had peremptorily quit. Conrad's class was in Year 9, and I picked them up after they had finished SATs (these were the days when Year 9 did a SATs test, too). We talk a bit about how weird SATs were – how you were told that they were about measuring the school and not the pupil, but that the pupils nevertheless had all the pressure, despite not giving a shit.

'But then we had you,' Conrad tells me, 'and we didn't write a single word in our exercise books for the whole six weeks. And I think they were the best six weeks – the most educated six weeks I remember doing. It was the fact that we had finished the SATs. There was nothing really that pressing. And we read *Flowers for Algernon*, and we watched *Blade Runner*, and we just talked a lot about ethics and sort of values – big things. And that taught me that if you're not up against the clock for something (like SATs), with such a conflicting message about what you're actually measuring from it, lessons can be different. Literature can actually be the best way to understand the world.'

This is the jackpot of teaching, I think. What a great comment to hear. I smile stupidly while Conrad says this, and then I'm embarrassed at myself. It's easy to get sucked into a conversation like this, laden with the freight of nostalgia. But I remember that time more clearly now. I remember how little of a shit I gave. How I was actually only on a supply contract, and was spending most of my mental energy finding a flat. And how some kids in that class were simply baffled, and will have learned literally nothing in those six weeks. Somehow my best teaching moment and my worst were one and the same.

That tension between the contradictory impulses of teaching – between the pressure to learn content and the opening of space for thought; between the knowledge imparted and the experience felt;

between the need to drive for success and the need to scaffold happiness; and between the impulse to control and the impulse to free – seems to me the very heart of the matter. I want to demand rigour *and* freedom, to say that life is messy and teaching doubly so, to say that challenge and discipline matter, as do cheeky moments when the mask cracks and the teacher swears and the kids giggle. I want to insist that real life sits in real, human, empathic interactions – and that sometimes we need both to draw a line in the sand and to remember that the line is arbitrary.

Because these contradictory impulses are the reality of school. On the one hand, there is the simplistic narrative of 'get good grades, get a good job'. On the other, there is how we *actually* move from the world of school into the world of work – and what makes us successful. On the one hand, there are lessons, curriculums, teaching methods. On the other, there are the infinite ways in which your social world shapes your time at school, the impact of friends, parents and the wider communities that schools inhabit. There are the teaching plans and the academic lessons, but there are also the tacit and implicit ways in which school teaches moral and social codes. There is the way that school should work in theory, and then there is how it feels when things are tough, and when nothing connects. We should think about how best to fit our education to the needs of our pupils, but that should also mean looking at the kids who don't fit – those who behave badly, or who can't cope with the mainstream.

It is this messy, complicated relationship with school that I want to look at in the next few chapters, and I'll begin where that contradiction and complexity really take hold: at the transition from primary school to secondary school, which for many kids marks the start of their disengagement from school.

6.   Growing up

I remember vividly the day my eldest son went to school for the first time. I have a photo of it. He stands in my drive, beaming shyly in a red sweatshirt that will never again look that clean. At the time, he felt so old. The baby I had held was being handed over to someone else and there was both a relief and a heart-stopping strangeness to it. You walk to the school door and then . . . what, you just leave? You walk away with an untethered lightness, a sense of uneasy freedom like being drunk or very high up, and yet all the time you're thinking, 'Really? I just leave him?' Now, at eleven, he grabs his stuff and walks out of the front door without a backward glance.

The most disorientating aspect of parenting, and of teaching, is that kids change. What they are at one stage is not what they are a few years later. And yet one of the infuriating things about the conversations on education that we have in the public forum is that they are often about 'school', full stop, as if school as an experience remains unchanged between early years and sixth form. Teachers argue fiercely about points that turn out to be entirely specific to their stages – and solutions are proposed for one kind of school that turn out to have been formulated for another kind entirely. The traditional-versus-progressive debate that we discussed in the first part of this book is a good example. For many, this is either about teaching like a fifties grammar school – rows of desks, content, taking notes – or letting kids 'discover' the laws of physics in an anarchic, lefty sixties-inflected science lab. But this entire characterisation is founded on an assumption that we're talking about secondary education. Both models, as well as the conflict between them, look very different when you're talking about four-year-olds.

Frank, Head of Paul Hendry Primary in Chiswick, puts it bluntly: 'Four-year-olds are not ready to sit round a table in a group of thirty and write sentences. They can't do it. And so setting children up to fail at that age leads to many of the issues that many schools experience about school refusal, about feeling a failure by the time you get to Year Two.'

Frank's school is in a stunning location by the Thames. On my way there, walking through the leafy streets of West London, I feel like I'm in a different world from the bland suburbia of most schools I have visited. 'Jazz brunch' is offered at the local pub. Then in between white stucco terraces beside a thin slice of scraggy grass is wedged a huge chunk of thirties municipal architecture – a handsome, slightly shabby block, with gated tangles of scooters at the front and a tiny yard to one side filled with sandpits, slides and buckets of toys.

It's a classic London school, in that it is poised at the intersection of three demographics: the owners of those beautiful stucco houses (probably worth a few million pounds each), who send their kids here before they do the entrance exams for private school; the steadily squeezed locals who have lived here for generations; and the children of the endless churn of temporary Londoners – immigrants, refugees and those who came for work, but who will leave for housing before their kids get much older.

That hugely polarised intake is a factor in the way Frank has structured the teaching at the school. Early-years teaching takes place in an environment that feels more like a playschool than a classroom. But that doesn't mean no teaching takes place. 'The adults facilitate more than they dictate what the children do at any time.' In Frank's school he's bucked the general trend and has elected to continue this approach into Key Stage 1. 'There are long periods of the day that are protected for child-initiated activity, where children are in a very familiar environment, they have access to all the resources there are, and they lead their own activity. The role of the adults is to look for teachable moments – to be able to spot and observe what children are doing, and what the thing will be that they need to learn in order to move on, in whatever activity they are doing,' says Frank. He points outside. 'So, for example, at the moment it's very hot outside, so they have set up a spa.'

Later I watch the spa from the window of a classroom. The narrow strip of playground is below me, and beyond that is the curve of the river, with the clustering glass towers of the City in the distance, and the clunky new blocks at Vauxhall in front of them. There's no uniform here, and the kids are a riot of colour in the sunshine. There is a slide, and a makeshift pool lined around the edge with decking planks. One child sits on their own in the shade underneath the slide, and the others crowd around the pool. A teacher points to a chair, then moves it. The kids shift around, regroup. A little girl drops down to pull off her socks laboriously. The teacher gets another chair and brings it round.

'The guidance given by the adults might include things like sign-writing, handling money and change, depending on the needs of the child,' explains Frank. 'Perhaps it's about management of the child and leadership, and how do we make it fair? Or perhaps it's about how do we make a paddling pool.'

He is at pains to say how skilled the interventions from his staff are, and how the students still do all the elements of the KS1 curriculum. The trajectory they follow is not straightforward, though – there are leaps and shifts in learning. But this is something widely recognised, certainly in early childhood. And what is fascinating is that, while Frank and his team seem to be flying in the face of current 'traditionalist' orthodoxy, E. D. Hirsch, that great sage of knowledge-rich schooling, talks at some length about how significant a high-quality pre-school is for subsequent learning. In many ways, Paul Hendry Primary is simply extending pre-school and delaying the onset of formal schooling – something that has been done with great success in Finland for years.

But what does the start of more formal schooling look like, from the perspective of the very youngest students?

Logan, Alice and George are all six years old – which means they are in Year 2. Here is some important information about them:

- Logan and George would rather go in a cave, while Alice would like to climb a mountain.
- Alice prefers socks to shoes, as does Logan.

- George would love to meet a badger the size of a bear.
- All three would drink snot rather than eat a spider.

They go to Brushmount. It's a tiny school in an ex-mining town on the Cumbrian coast. The road winds past a vast expanse of bare, wide sand, split by the shifting meander of a river. You drive over a bleak, heather-purple fell and then down through a few scattered houses and along the single pebble-dashed street of the village. The school is tucked down a little lane, and you can see the isolated grey cube of a prison across the field from the schoolyard.

The Head, Liam, tells me that the building is so old and knackered the insulation is made of compacted horsehair, and every time it rains they put buckets out. But it is a warm and wonderful place, with little knots of kids in mixed-year groups dotted around a bright and cheerful building – with adults who talk with that special primary combination of kindness and performative mock-strictness.

When you woke up, I ask the kids, and you realised today was a school day, what did you think?

Logan, a tiny dot of a thing with big eyes that swivel as he speaks and little baby teeth that bite over his lower lip, begins to speak. He carries on beginning for a while. 'Aah.' He looks up. 'Uh.'

Did you think, 'Excellent, I've got school today!' I prompt.

He shakes his head, smiling shyly. 'No, cos I don't like school.'

'I love school!' weighs in George. He is perky where Logan is vacant.

'Well, I kind of like school,' qualifies Logan. Then he sticks the boot in. 'But I have to spend boring time doing stuff – boring stuff instead of fun stuff. But then sometimes I just don't like stuff.'

I turn to George, which reminds me quite how small the chair is. Being in a Year 2 classroom is like being Hagrid. In the background the lesson is still going on. Eight small children sit in that special primary way, cross-legged, necks craning back to stare up at the teacher.

You say you love school, I ask him, but is there any bit you don't like?

'Probably – I like English a lot, but maybe English.'

I love how keen George is still to like the bits he doesn't like. He has big specs and spiky blond hair.

Alice chips in with, 'Maths.' But then she says, 'I'm really good at Maths!'

I'm spotting a theme here.

Logan is adamant, though. I try to get him to say more. 'The bits what I find boring are Science.'

'I go to the Science club loads!' says Alice, beaming.

When I talk to Liam, he says Logan hasn't had an easy time of it. In fact a lot of the children have really struggled with coming out of lockdown. He says the kids came to them this year very significantly behind in physical development. It's a reminder that the physical elements of play are hugely significant at this age – with muscle tone, fine motor skills, physical confidence and dexterity all having massive consequences, both for later learning and for a successful and healthy life. As a curriculum, and as knowledge, this is stuff that might seem peripheral if you apply a secondary-school perspective, but that is actually fundamental to the quality of educational provision for very young children.

'I don't like when, at the start of the day, you know how we do that stuff with Miss Hall,' says Logan. 'I don't like that stuff – that stuff is a little bit hard, so I don't like that stuff.'

Is hard stuff bad? I ask Alice.

She thinks carefully. 'When I put my hand up and I'm waiting for Miss Andrews,' she says, with a puzzled, slightly forlorn look on her face, 'my hand just gets tired, so I need to switch hands.'

They are adorable, these kids. At one point we talk about the bluebottle busily trying to get out of the window. The kids tell me his name is Dave. I wouldn't say they are hugely reflective about school, but nevertheless there is a lot one can tell about their relationship with it. To me, it is as clear as day that while the other two are brimming with enthusiasm for anything and everything, Logan is already disassociating himself from school. Later Liam will tell me exactly how much there is going on at home for Logan. As ever, being a teacher involves witnessing the most heart-rending sadness.

Tell me the things you like, I say to Logan.

'I like lunchtimes and breaktimes. Because lunchtime is nice, and breaktime I can just play stuff without anyone bothering us.'

Who would bother you?

'If I'm playing with people and they spoil the game, I'll just play on my own.'

Alice chimes in breathlessly, 'We're going on a school trip, and I'm dead excited.'

Beside her, Logan's big eyes stare absently up.

Primary schools have certain qualities that we all recognise. The shrill delight of the playground. The slow, off-key chanting. The Comic Sans notices, and the teachers standing with hands clasped, modelling an elaborate formality. The language is distinct, too. Lots of 'we' and 'let's', a conscious attempt to forge a sense of group identity: 'At this school we do it this way.' Assemblies and projects have clear moral messages – with a deep sense of cohesion and community. If early years sets up the basics of social interaction, Key Stage 2 could be characterised as a more specialised version of this: an extended lesson in how to *be* in school.

Then, at the end of Key Stage 2 (Year 6) we come to the crucial moment when students make the transition from primary to secondary. By now they are ten or eleven years old and the focus has moved firmly onto SATs (the standardised tests in Maths and English) – and, with it, a growing awareness of where they sit in the academic hierarchy.

Back in London, Jared, Kacey, Miles and Oni are in Year 6. Both Jared and Kacey say they are 'average'. They tell me there are some people in their class who work at Year 9 level and, when I later meet Oni, I can well believe them.

As I often do, I ask if she's clever. It's an interesting question for kids, because they unfailingly know what they think the answer is, but find it disconcerting to be asked directly. At first Oni says, 'Depends.' Which is a good answer. It's probably what one would say about the notion of 'cleverness' if one was an academic researcher. In fact it's said with such an air of astute emotional maturity that I smile. Everyone always makes a face when I ask that, I say. They don't want to admit they are clever. But I think you are.

'Yes,' Oni says.

Miles tells me, 'Not really' when I ask the same of him.

Interestingly, of the four of them, he's the one going on from this state primary to a hyper-academic private school. He must have passed a test to get in and, when I talk to his teachers, they say he's been having intensive tuition for a couple of years. It hasn't given him much confidence, though.

At this stage, everyone is focused on where they go next. They sometimes look back with regret on their younger years – a kind of precocious nostalgia. Kacey says she looks at her sister in early years and wishes she had the chance to play around like that still. Unlike the younger years, they have some subjects they think are boring – but they haven't reached the general, dull-eyed ennui of the thirteen- and fourteen-year-olds of Year 9. Their lessons have now become relatively similar to those they might have in secondary school: written work, information from the teacher, maybe group work. But when I talk to secondary-school pupils about their memories of primary school, they are remarkably consistent.

'It was more fun.'

'I wasn't naughty in primary.'

'Everyone just got on.'

It's roughly how I feel as well, to be honest. Even at the end, when things had begun to take a more formalised educational shape, I remember the primary classroom as one of emotional safety. I remember the way the teacher felt like another parent, the way the other kids were known to you, the way there were class jokes and routines.

And when you went up to secondary, everything changed.

What's difficult about school? I ask Angela. She's in secondary, but only just – Year 7, tiny, blonde hair, big grin.

'People that are older than me,' she says. 'Because I used to be Year Six, and I used to be the oldest, biggest, toughest.' She smirks to her friends, who giggle. 'And I was very cool, but now there are people older than me and I'm very worried.'

The way she talks hovers carefully between a self-aware jokiness – playing at being young and worried – and actual worry. At that age, childhood becomes oddly self-referential. My eldest son does it, too.

He puts on a baby voice and plays at being younger than himself. When I see this, I think it's a way of protecting yourself, of facing up to your own sense of vulnerability.

Angela carries on speaking, and I can hear that hint of babyishness lingering at the edge of her voice. 'My dad actually said, "Enjoy your time being the oldest in the school, because next year you're going to be the youngest."' She hesitates. 'We didn't bully people of course, but the other years are very tall.' 'Very tall' is said in an exaggerated, mocking tone of childish wonder. She giggles again, half-giddy, half-uneasy. 'I'm very tall of course,' she jokes.

Ask a secondary teacher and they will talk about year groups as character descriptions. Year 7 are all like this – eager, bright, needy, childlike. Year 8 are scatty, naughty, silly. Year 9 are raging balls of hormone. Year 10 are edgy, half-grown, awkward. Year 11 are somehow both world-weary and puppyish as they tear desperately towards adulthood. Every child is unique, of course, but there is a truth to the generalisation. School is not just the sum of what you do to children while they're there   it is a process they are going through. Lessons are not merely standardised packages of learning, to be received unmediated and stacked up neatly. Rather, they are absorbed in the midst of the fierce heat of puberty, distorted and changed, and heightened by a self that transforms as it listens. And that process takes on a variety of shapes, which in time become familiar.

If you teach for long enough, you get a feel for these different trajectories. There are the kids who bounce brightly through, fresh-faced till the end. There are the ones who start with impossible wonder etched in their wide eyes, but slip into sullen fury and never emerge again. And there are the ones who struggle through the tempests of adolescence, but suddenly reappear – human, smiling shyly when you mention to them quite how much of a misery they used to make period five on Friday. Most of the time this journey seems like something that you observe, something that just happens, like death and taxes. But there is a classic primary-teacher comment that we secondary teachers get grimly used to: 'What do you *do* to them?'

It makes my hackles rise, but I do get it. It isn't simply the monstrosities of being a teenager. There is something else at work in the interplay between biological, social and educational development. Something that makes kids who seem to like primary school – who understand it and do well – slowly switch off as they settle into secondary. It's not a universal experience, but for my own pupils, in Sunderland, there is an uncomfortable truth. Where they are from, in the North-East of England, achievement at the end of Year 6 (the end of primary school) ranks second out of the nine regions of the country. But as we've already seen, by the time of GCSEs it is ninth.

The transition to secondary is, I think, the key fault line in our system. I'm not sure I can overstate how radical a change there is in the emotional organisation of a school between primary and secondary. At a really basic level, there is the shift from having the same teacher in the same classroom each and every day, to a system in which the kids move from one class and one teacher to another. This change alone – from a continuous culture, shaped by the same teacher, to one in which they slip between worlds several times a day – is transformative.

Let's look at a day in the world of Year 6. At the school that my own children go to, it begins at 8.45. They troop in through their own entry door – all sixty of them in the year. Uniform is a sweatshirt and school trousers/skirt. The kids divide into two groups and each group goes into its own classroom. On the walls are pictures they have drawn, stories they have written. The teacher takes the register: the same teacher they have seen every day all through Year 5 as well. They sit in their seats – the same seats they sit in every day.

Today they have several lessons: English, Maths, Humanities and Music. All, apart from Music, will be taught by their class teacher in their classroom. The English and Maths lessons are as normal: they start with some class reading, then pick up on a discussion of how to write a newspaper article. A few students contribute eagerly. The teacher asks someone to distribute exercise books. They work at clusters of tables, in small groups. Some kids are focused, some less so. A teaching assistant is in the room – the same one they always have. There is a rhythm of explanation, task, feedback. The teacher circulates.

At break they go out into a yard, where they are the biggest. Where everyone *plays*. There are conflicts, but playtime is for fun, and everyone understands what fun is – it involves running and chasing and pretending.

After break comes the Music lesson – where they go to another room and a teacher they also know well, who used to teach them in Year 4, leads them in making sounds with a variety of percussion instruments. And after lunch come Maths and Humanities, and then an assembly, where parents are invited to watch the pupils perform their demonstration of the Great Fire of London (with no actual fire, sadly). Everyone performs, everyone is clapped.

A year later, when I watch the Year 7s start at my own school, there is a recognisable pattern. They begin like primary kids, saying, 'Good morning, Mr Wright!' every day, asking eagerly about which pen to use, and running around the yard playing intricate games of tag. They expect you to know them instantly, because you waved at them once. They talk familiarly to you, like you're a friend. They seem oblivious to the fact that they are one of 260 pupils in their year now, and that I really don't know who they are. But over the next few weeks this starts to sink in.

They have perhaps thirteen subjects, sometimes with lessons only once every two weeks. Each lesson might follow a roughly similar plan – or it might not. The teacher might be at the door, greeting them, sending them to the place on the seating plan they occupy. They might get their own book or find it on the desk in front of them. Sometimes they might have a supply teacher, and then all bets are off.

They move independently, without a teacher chaperoning them all the time. They are self-organised – or try to be. In lessons they come slowly to the realisation that each teacher is a monarch in their own classroom, but that these classrooms are also quite different places. What goes in one will get you a detention in another. And you have so many teachers that no single teacher is the person who knows everything about you. The people you see far more regularly are your peers.

Then some of them have a rush of blood to the head. They see the older kids and gaze adoringly at some species or other of bad behaviour. They copy it and get shouted at. Maybe detentions. Maybe even suspension. They gain a reputation. Others double-down on their positive attitude. They gain a different reputation. Some slip into the background and the standards of their work slip a little, then a little more. And after a year you have a cohort of Year 8 kids. For these pupils, bouncing wide-eyed in the first rush of hormones, school is increasingly a place defined by your social, peer-to-peer relationships. Some of this is just growing up. But some of it is about the strange abruptness of that shift from primary to secondary.

Not all kids experience it this way – in some areas of the country there are middle schools, which cater for Years 5–8, smoothing the transition. And increasing attention is being given to the idea of all-through schools, where the same institution caters for kids from the age of three to the age of eighteen. Reach Academy in Feltham, on the western edge of London, has this structure. Like Michaela, Reach was set up as a Free School, and like Michaela it has attracted a lot of attention for a tight behaviour policy and a knowledge-rich curriculum. But it feels very different. For one, while in Michaela the rule is that one should use the 'Michaela full stop' – a disconcerting 'Miss' or 'sir' at the end of every sentence – here the children call the staff by their first names. Within the shared ethos of 'warm/strict', Reach is at the warm end. But if you ask the teachers, being an all-through school – avoiding that cliff-edge transition to secondary – is far more central to their ethos and success than their behaviour policy is.

Every year group is limited to sixty children – both in the primary and secondary phases – and has a section of the purpose-built site to itself, with a dining area in the centre and classrooms around. They eat in a similarly formalised way to Michaela, with routines and structures like set conversation topics, clearing up for each other and standing at the appropriate times, but at Reach Academy these vary over time, moving from the tightness needed to establish norms in the early years, to a structure that allows more personal responsibility as they grow older.

The curriculum is carefully designed to match: planned and

sequenced with the whole of the school career in mind, and not just the Key Stage or phase. And perhaps most significant of all, in their impressively realised ethos, is the idea that, in the words of Ed Vainker (the co-founder of the school, alongside Rebecca Cramer and Jon McGoh), 'School is necessary but not sufficient' for the success of their students.

'An all-through trust – which quite a lot are – can easily have three kids in a family going through, which means a twenty-year relationship with that family.' Vainker says they didn't articulate this at the start, but 'It's definitely why we wanted to be small, and it's definitely why we wanted to be all-through.'

What this enables them to do is maintain an impressive level of focus on their community: on working with parents and kids outside school as well as in it, through their charity the Reach Foundation – a body that not only provides youth and family services, but also convenes a wider group of schools and local-government bodies to coordinate their response to the needs of the young people in their area.

They have maintained this community focus in the face of powerful market forces. Not only have they resisted the urge to increase the numbers in each year group, keeping a tight control over that coherent all-through student experience, but they have also worked to keep the student body representative of the area as a whole. For its first few years Reach was on a temporary site, while the school building was built. During this time it was inspected and received an 'Outstanding' judgement. Developers noticed, and started buying up the land around the site that Reach was now preparing to move into; they marketed the houses they would build as being next to an 'Outstanding' school. Before the building was even occupied or the houses built, the plan to found a school that provided for the least advantaged was being subverted. Having chosen to locate itself in an under-served area of Feltham, Reach was now going to be surrounded by an increasingly affluent population.

But the school had other ideas. When Reach finally moved in, it used the freedoms that academies have over entrance criteria to mandate that the number of deprived students in its intake could never drop below the average for all schools in the borough. It was, by design, gentrification-proof. What's more, it used the incentive of a place at the school to draw in the most deprived children, specifically targeting its perinatal services at certain at-risk parents, and then giving priority to children entering at early years who had engaged with those perinatal services. As a result, Reach still has 38 per cent of its students eligible for free school meals – and it has ensured that it has worked with those families with as much continuity and intensity as possible, not only through the primary and secondary phases but, in their own words, 'from cradle to career'.

There are lots of great schools, many of which are not all-through. But at Reach we can see a model that takes a neat shortcut to bypass many of the destructive effects of the transition from primary to secondary – and that begs the question why we change schools when we do, and in the way that we do. Yes, kids change and have different needs at different times – and sometimes that includes needing a new start. But the consistency of approach that the three-to-eighteen structure allows, the careful building of routine and independence hand-in-hand, and the controlled expansion of children's worlds from age five up to eighteen surely takes some beating.

It also represents a deeper ethos – one alluded to by Vainker in the phrase 'School is necessary but not sufficient'. It is a view of school in which, as Vainker puts it, 'destination' is more important than 'achievement' (in the narrow sense of grades). At Reach, they describe a 'life of choice and opportunity' as the goal. Crucially this is not just about grades in the collective sense leading to more university places, and so on – instead, he says that 'Schools can and should seek to tell a story about a good and a productive life for all of their students.' This is in no way at odds with preparing students for the world of work – as one can see with that 'cradle to career' catchphrase. But it's a completely different way of thinking about what equipping someone for a working life involves. Indeed, Vainker makes the point that the hierarchy we have set up in schools, with academic achievement at the top, doesn't necessarily fit with that ideal of the 'good and productive life'. 'Plenty of people who go to university have staggeringly boring jobs,' he says bluntly.

His students do well at school – Reach as a whole is highly

successful in the terms that the system sets up, the Ofsted judgement, the performance tables – but it seeks to do more than that. Reach wants 'a life of choice and opportunity' for its students, which means grades, and knowledge, but something else, too. Its answer to that 'something else' is in the services it offers around the school – in the vocational offer at its sixth form, but also in the mentoring and support that its Foundation offers young people, even after they've left school. It runs programmes up to the age of twenty-one and partners with local universities, too. It is, in a word, a holistic model, in which an abrupt transition from primary to secondary education has no place.

The school, and the support around it, is inspiring. But it's also unusual. It speaks to the strange uncertainty of the world we live in now – where the old routes into lifelong careers no longer exist; where opportunities are hoarded and jobs are contingent and temporary; where teachers struggle to articulate to their students what the possibilities actually are. In many ways the anxiety about exams has increased precisely because they no longer seem like a guarantee, so we flee to the upper heights of the achievement range and pray that we get A*s all round. Alternatively, we shrug and say, 'What's the point?' If school is there to get you that life of choice and opportunity, it has its work cut out. What Reach recognises is that the actual process of school – the mechanics of what it really does – is so much more complicated than simply getting the grades and dancing off into the sunset.

7. The social world of school

A girl doesn't want to go to her lesson. She comes to me and says so. 'I'm not going,' she tells me.

Why? I ask.

'I don't know anyone in that class.'

I pause. She's been truanting, this girl. She's known to me. I know what she means by this. I know it is a precursor to half an hour of fruitless arguing and/or chasing her around the school, after she wanders off.

Doesn't that make it easier? I try. It's like a fresh start.

'No,' she says. 'I'm not going.'

You know you can't just say that.

'What?'

You can't just tell me you're not going to lessons.

'Well, I'm not.'

We look at each other.

Saying something doesn't make it so, I tell her gently. Even as I say it, I know that I might be wrong on this one. I know that if she really digs in her heels, the only thing I can do is exclude her, internally or externally – both of which will, needless to say, involve her not going to her lesson.

'I don't care,' she says. 'I don't even *like* any of the people in it.'

Outcomes – whether it's the grades you get or the career you find – rarely describe the way we feel about school, and what we hold on to from it after we leave. In fact in all the ways we can answer the question *What is school for?*, there's a simple truth. It's the same if we answer the question *What is life for?* Life – and, for many kids, school – is about love. Not romantic love necessarily, not all-guns-blazing Romeo and Juliet stuff, but the fierce love of teenage friendship – and the ways in which that can blaze and warm a whole life.

I remember those moments. We all do – and if you don't, then I bet you feel the lack of it. I remember the art field-trip in the Trossachs, running away from a goat, drinking a pint in a pub and crying in a field in a melodramatic way that I was certain was pretty impressive to certain girls. I remember – because it was 1994 – singing the theme tune to *Friends* in an un-ironic passion, arms around each other, convinced that no one had ever been friends like this before.

My best friend at school later introduced me to the woman I'd marry. I call him most weeks. We've lived together, holidayed together and camped together with our kids. He has enriched my life significantly more than my study of French verbs ever did.

There are certain tropes that, as teachers – and as parents – we return to again and again. 'If you carry on like that, you'll end up in a dead-end job' is not a nice thing to say to young people, but in different forms it is something most teachers will say. We also have 'I treat you with respect, and I demand the same in return.' And there is that old favourite 'School is about learning, not hanging around with your mates.' But is it?

In 2019, a few months after I had been appointed to the Social Mobility Commission, I took my colleagues in the Commission north and brought them to visit a school in Teeside. I arranged a tour, and a meeting with pupils. We do this a lot in schools. There are often pupils – probably on the school council, top sets, maybe sports stars – who are so regularly involved in things like this they begin to have an air of professionalism in the way they describe the school.

I still remember the students I met on my first trip to my current school, back in 2013. I'd been searching for a head-of-sixth-form job for a while, at the same time idly contemplating a move out of London to the North-East, where my mother was from. But it was all half-hearted until a close friend's father died unexpectedly, only six weeks after his son's wedding. It jolted all of us – and so, after travelling to Leeds for the funeral, I went on up to Sunderland for an interview. Teaching interviews being the strange, intense, gun-to-your-head affairs that they are, I had to ready myself to decide whether I wanted the job over the course of the day, so that I could accept it there and then, if it was offered.[1]

I vividly remember walking round the school on that morning, chatting to three excited Year 11s. Two of the three would go on to be in the first year group through the new sixth form. That morning the three of them – all girls – were brilliant guides, talking with just the right mix of candid truths about the school, polished enthusiasm for the whole sixth-form project and giggly exchanges behind my back as I tried to look serious and professional. They carried themselves with a sense of total ease around the adults, an implicit assumption that we were all on the same page. It was a sense of ease that is characteristic of the ones in the top sets, the ones for whom school is a place that reaffirms the things they have been taught in their homes about success and status.

When I organised that visit for the Commission in 2019 I asked to select student guides in a slightly different way. Instead of my criteria being 'to present a positive impression of the school to important visitors', I used 'persistently in trouble and likely to say something challenging'. With the help of a willing Headteacher, I picked from a spectrum of ages and outlooks, but all united by the fact that they came from backgrounds that ranged from unsupportive to highly disrupted.

We gathered in a classroom, sitting round tables. The kids had that look of faint distrust, combined with the excitement of being legitimately out of lessons. A couple of the girls kept turning to look at each other and giggling. Rob, at seventeen the oldest boy, sat in polite attention, but wore huge white trainers that spoke the universal language of rebellion.

The conversation was fascinating. A couple of the students stayed sullenly silent, but most began to open up as it became clearer and clearer that they were genuinely allowed to say what they wanted. We heard some interesting nuggets of information – about the prevalence of pyjamas on the streets of Hartlepool, the sense that their neighbourhood was 'different' and that they were 'different' as a result.

And, from Mia, a really clear sense of where her priorities lay.

'I'm not being funny, but my mates are everything. I don't really care about what I'm doing in lessons.' Mia spoke with a kind of performative defiance. Eloquent and bright, and willing to escalate any minor disagreement into a blazing row, she was a 'name' in the school, someone whom teachers spoke of with the assumption that 'of course you know *her*'.

And if you had to choose, between your mates and success in school, I asked, which would you go for?

She smiled. 'My mates.'

Back in 2013, my tour around the school in Sunderland ended in me getting the job. The process of starting a new sixth form is pretty intense. You have to appeal directly to kids to join you, with no track record, no evidence of being any good at what you do. Sixth formers have choice – and you need to tread a careful line between enforcing strict working habits to get them to succeed (which they want) and fostering a relaxed and communal atmosphere that treats them as almost-adults (which they also want). Without past precedent, you find yourself open to challenge on every decision you make – both from students and from teachers. You can't take refuge in 'This is the way we've always done it.'

At the same time you have another tightrope to walk. Your funding is linked to pupil numbers. Your staffing is linked to funding. Your pupil numbers are linked to the subjects available, which is dependent on your staffing. And both your staffing and your pupil numbers will, in the long term, be impacted by your results and your Ofsted grade.

So you need kids to join. But if they don't do well, they bring you down. So you need to be strict. But they then don't want to join if they perceive it as too strict. However, maybe the ones who don't want it to be too strict aren't the kind of kids you want in the first place. Maybe they are the ones who will bring your results down.

The way I tried to square this circle was by selling the students on the idea of the sixth form as a community – as a place of friendship, and engagement, that was also focused on academic success. We had events every term: a Christmas party, a summer barbecue, an Easter activity day. And at the start of their time with us we went away on a weekend to the Lakes, the whole year group of around eighty students together, and did activities specifically designed to push them out of their comfort zone. I wanted them to mentally invest in us, to forge a bond with the school that would allow me leverage to push them when it felt less comfortable for them to be pushed. I wanted their identification with the sixth form to be such that adversity brought them in, rather than pushed them away.

This is not a new idea. Many schools employ these strategies. In its classic form, this is the same thing England's great public schools have been doing for centuries, with their obscure rituals and complex rivalries. It's what the US Marines do when they strip down the identity of their recruits during basic training and then build them back up again. It's also what the Mafia does (at least, based on my working knowledge of *Goodfellas*).

Nor was my execution of it particularly innovative. I did the basics. Far more intensive are XP School in Doncaster and its various iterations across the world, which use a much more refined and focused system of experiential learning and team-building, with students organised into 'crews' rather than classes. Fascinatingly, the school that many people take as the polar opposite of XP – Michaela – seems to do something very similar in its championing of 'the power of culture' and 'the Michaela way'. In both instances the schools are reacting, as I had done, to a recognition that the social world of school is not a sideshow to the main event. It is, in many ways, intrinsic to the pupils' engagement. It defines the way they react to the messages that school gives. And it needs either to merge seamlessly with the social world at home, complementing and supporting it, or it must dominate and overpower that home environment with a more compelling alternative.

Think about it like this: if we say to a young person that they need to get their GCSEs in order to become worth anything, and then they go home to their parents, who have not got GCSEs, and hang out with their friends, who don't care about their GCSEs, and visit their nan and their uncle and their cousin, none of whom got any GCSEs, then we are asking them to make a choice. We are presenting them with two dissonant ideas – that GCSEs are important for your worth, set against the worth they find in all of these people who don't have GCSEs. We're asking them to choose: school or their social world. Setting aside the ethics of such a choice, the practicalities are simple. For a fifteen-year-old kid, the teacher is often the last person to trust – and the easiest belief to jettison.

One option is to ramp up the necessity of grades, increase the stakes, but if we do that, we should not be surprised if a good portion of our students (those for whom the world we describe increasingly isn't the world they see) choose to disengage. And the more black and white we paint this world, the more absolute becomes their rejection of it.

The two girls from my tour in 2013 who joined the sixth form became students whom I knew well – I taught one, and supported the university application of the other. They were lively, intelligent, charming. School, for them, was a place of no dissonance. Doing well in their classes, getting on with teachers and aspiring to university were all things that, far from causing mental anguish or conflict with other deeply held beliefs, simply reinforced their sense of self. School was, for them, a place of social success as much as academic success. The two were in sync.

That wasn't the case for Mia, the student who spoke so eloquently to the Social Mobility Commission. After our visit, I stayed in touch with the school, and checked in on her every now and then. She's now in her first year of sixth form and has developed into a reflective and intelligent young woman, still with a highly developed sense of drama.

When I ask her my standard opener – What is school for? – her answer is pretty typical.

'To improve on learning, to socialise, to help with social skills and, obviously, to take you on to further education or apprenticeships.'

She gives me a serious look, like she's delivering a speech onstage. It occurs to me how her 'goodness' is just as performative as her 'naughtiness' once was. So I dig at the social part of her reply. What are those social skills?

She thinks. 'Like, social cues – how far to push someone.'

I smile. Pushing against the rules is good for you then?

'To a certain extent, yes.' She qualifies it. 'Obviously, if it goes too far, you're purposely putting yourself in a position where you can't learn any more.'

Again I smile. We both know the subtext. We're being frank here, I say. You tell me about the times where you felt you were really pushing.

'Year Nine and Ten – definitely in Year Eight it started. But Year Nine and Ten it was like, right, I can't be bothered. This is just ridiculous. I just don't want to do this any more.'

What was the prompt? I ask.

'To be honest, the start of it was probably mainly my social group.

But then, obviously, you kind of learn these certain behaviours. Then it doesn't matter who you are around – you just purposely portray these behaviours that you have learned.'

As I listen to Mia, I notice how her speech is a slightly awkward combination of high-register words, phrases taken from her sociology and psychology classes, and the local syntax of 'us' and 'me'.

I remind her of the visit of the Commission – of her comment that mates were more important than anything else in school. Was that how it felt at the time?

'Definitely. Because when you're in that type of mindset, you kind of feel like the whole school system betrays you. You kind of feel like – because obviously you're doing this to yourself – you're doing all these behaviours that the school system's gonna give you consequences for, and they're gonna make you feel like that – but in the same sense, it's kind of like a cycle where you're only here for your friends, you're not here for anything else, cos if you go into lesson, you're just going to be told to go to the BASS.'

The BASS was the Behaviour and Support Service. In Mia's school, it was a room with a series of booths in it. You had to sit in silence, getting on with work. Grim as it might sound to call it a trend, that's exactly what it was – schools all over the country started setting up these 'isolation booths'. Since then there has been a reaction against them, leading to a great tearing down of MDF up and down the country.

Her teachers tell me that Mia is pretty accurate about what life was like for her in Year 9. She was in and out of the BASS, sometimes given exclusions, always in conflict with the school. And it certainly felt to her as if it was the school that was trapping her in this behaviour.

'The more the school pressured me to be "good", the more I didn't want to be. I mean, this is just me personally, but it's like the feeling of doing good after being encouraged to, I just had like this thing in the pit of me stomach – I just didn't want to do it, it seemed pointless if I wasn't doing it for me, I was doing it for someone else, I was being forced to do something.'

She pauses.

'But for some reason, now that I look back, why did I feel like the school system was pressuring us to do something, but the peer group wasn't?' She's really thinking, now. 'The peer group felt natural, but school didn't.' She smiles. 'I don't have the answer for that, but it's quite strange, when you think about it.'

One of the key themes of our conversation back in 2019 was how much the social environment outside school impacted upon her. I ask Mia about this. Do you think it makes a difference where you live?

'I think where you live does matter a lot. Because like here, the people I was around lived close to me, so it was not just in school we were socialising, and we were doing the wrong thing, whatever we wanted. On me dad's side, not one of them has ever went to uni, not one of them has ever been to college. And no one ever says, you know, "Stick in." It's always, "Ye kna ye've gorra get those grades because ah never did."'

I can't help laughing. Mia does the voice brilliantly – a harsh, mocking, nasal slice of the North-East. But there is a bitterness to her impression that sits uncomfortably.

'It's like that type of mindset – they want better for you, but they're not showing you a good role model. It's just like they try to stop you smoking by saying, "Y'kna ah started smoking at the age of eleven." It's just hypocritical.'

I'm nodding. What she says reminds me of parents' evenings where mothers sit next to their kids, saying, 'Ah never telt him to use that kind of fucken language.'

Mia's still talking. 'You know that – what they're saying – there's no value in it. In my case, my mam and my dad didn't make it to Year Eleven. So me just going on to sixth form, I'm doing more than they ever will.'

I listen to the pride in her voice, and I feel proud of her, too – but also sad. I don't know her mum and dad, but the thought of their lives being dismissed like that is uncomfortable, in the same way her mockery was. I can't help seeing the place she's in – the positivity of her success at sixth form, and her new-found ambition – as one that has involved loss, too.

So what changed? I ask.

'End of Year Ten, beginning of Year Eleven, me and my friend got in this big argument. Big. At the time I was just drifting out of this social group, and she was like the anchor that kept us there. Then obviously we had this big argument and she was giving us a hard time in school, and I just kind of thought, "I don't need this any more. I don't need all these moralities that they've put on us, when I know how I feel. I don't want to be this person, I want to be this 'good' person I've been hiding for so long." And it was like hiding, because you never want to show emotion round them.'

Her eyes are gleaming. This is a rare moment of proper vulnerability from Mia.

'They're kind of like vultures, you know,' she adds.

She shifts in her seat, flickering between composure and teenage awkwardness. 'The turning point was then, when I thought, "I've got nothing else tying me to this person." I just kind of, like, buckled down.'

Mia did. I remember it. I stopped having conflict with her and, instead, we had conversations about work and exams. She turned up for revision classes.

'You look at people now in the lower years,' she says thoughtfully, 'and you see the exact same thing. They talk to me about sixth form and about what it's like, and I say it's the best thing that ever happened to me, but then they say, "I couldn't" and "I wouldn't dare." But I can see that they want to. But they just can't.'

I think of all the times I hear this. It's a kind of fear, isn't it? I say.

'Definitely. In some cases it's fear of other people, fear of rejection, fear of disgrace from your peers. But there's another kind of fear. Like fear of this other person. You don't know how to be good. You don't know who this person is that you're becoming.'

I watch Mia. The person she's becoming is pretty impressive. But I'm not sure how much of a hand in it the school had.

The famous account of William Golding's writing of *Lord of the Flies* says that he was inspired by his experience of teaching. It led him to reject Rousseau's notion of the natural goodness of children and to posit a latent savagery, waiting to burst through, once the civilising hand of society's rules and conventions was lifted.

I've taught *Lord of the Flies* for a number of years. For one of those classes, when I was going through a period of more experimental teaching, I made use of the observation classroom that my school had set up. This was a room with CCTV and a one-way mirror at the back, designed to provide teachers with the space to demonstrate or record lessons without the distraction of other people in the room. I told my class that we were going to use this room for a one-off IT lesson. They didn't know it was rigged, although anyone sharp enough would probably have spotted it. When we arrived, I made a point of fiddling with the computer, then told them to wait in silence while I fetched some IT support. Given my normal capabilities, this was entirely believable. But instead of heading off down the corridor, I doubled back and snuck into the observation booth. There, I watched the class and recorded their behaviour.

It started gradually. Turning round to chat. Then talking more loudly. Shouting across the room. Throwing paper balls. The point at which I hastily popped out of the booth door and back into the classroom was when a small boy hopped up on a table and started to cross the room by jumping from table to table, shouting, 'I'm Spiderman.'

They calmed down quickly. And then, when we watched the video back, we discussed why they had done what they did. Why was it that, in the absence of the teacher, the rules stopped applying?

'I just wanted to have fun,' said one.

'I don't know,' said many of them.

'You follow the rules because the teacher's there. That's why there are rules.'

What was interesting, though, was that in their brief window of freedom they didn't fundamentally change their natures. Spiderman was like that in lessons, too – a show-off, a bit immature. They simply responded to the circumstances.

I think of this when I hear Mia describing how rules were there to be pushed against. And I think of all the other things people do that push against rules – things that we don't object to, in quite the same way. I think about my tour guides from 2013 and how they also 'pushed'; but they did it in emotionally astute middle-class ways.

One of them – Becky – is still at my school. She completed her A levels, did her degree, then returned as a trainee teacher. We then employed her; she's a member of the same department as me. After I speak to Mia, I catch up with Becky. I remind her of that day she gave me a tour, all those years ago.

'I probably spoke too much,' she says, laughing.

I took the job, I reply. You must have sold it pretty well.

We talk about how she felt about school at that age.

'I probably have a skewed perspective,' she says. 'I loved school. I wanted to learn. I felt very accepted – the school was a very warm place for me.'

I ask Becky about her friendship group – about what gave her status in the group.

She's surprised. 'Within my group?'

Yes.

'That's a really difficult question.'

It seems like the idea of status doesn't fit with her sense of how her friendship group worked.

'We weren't the popular ones,' she says.

But did they have expectations of you that you felt you needed to meet?

Becky thinks. 'I suppose I was very lucky, from a young age, with the people I was in education with. Those people you saw me with on the interview day, I was friends with them from a young age. And they were conscientious and hard-working people – so, in that sense, there was a pressure on me to be conscientious and hard-working. In Year Eleven we went to a revision group in the morning, so we all walked in early together. I might have gone anyway, I suppose, but because there was that pressure – that everyone I was friends with was going – I would go, too. If I'd been in a different social group, those pressures could have been more negative.'

I move the discussion on to sixth form. How did that transition feel, for you? I ask.

She smiles. 'I think, because we were the first year group to go through, we felt – I think everyone would agree – we felt special. It was a very warm environment, like a family. You were cared about, your individual goals and desires were cared about, and everyone who worked there wanted the best for you.'

It's lovely to hear this – lovely to hear that we succeeded in creating this environment. But I point out to Becky that even if she had not been 'popular' in lower school, by the time she got to sixth form she certainly was. It's like the parameters of what high-status behaviour was had changed, I say.

She agrees. 'If you talked to any of us, I think they'd agree that we started to mix more – that the boundaries kind of broke down.'

It seems to me, as I listen, that there are two very different social environments at play here. The antagonistic one that Mia describes in the lower school, which Becky simply opted out of, creating her own little bubble, and then the more inclusive environment in sixth form. Both Mia and Becky see that threshold, after GCSE, as a real change – and I agree. The act of choosing what you're doing, the sense of agency and control, completely alters the nature of the contract between student and school.

I return to the idea of 'pushing against' authority. I describe Mia's comment to Becky, and she says she can't really think of herself doing something like that – testing the boundaries of what she could get away with. 'The most rebellious thing I did was write my name inside my locker,' she says.

But in lessons, I go on, my memory of you was that you were quite willing to push me, and to interrogate me. It wasn't pushing in an aggressive or an unpleasant way, but it was assertive.

She nods. 'I absolutely loved that in lessons. I always felt I was the most vocal person in my lessons, but that didn't intimidate me or scare me. You know when no one wants to answer and everyone's looking at you? I was always the person to answer – like I was the nominated sacrifice. But I was always willing to do it.'

And there's a status that goes with that, isn't there?

She nods.

I point out to her that it isn't only the social world this affects. When I taught Becky literature, what marked her out wasn't just her work ethic. It was the way she listened and responded to feedback. She wasn't an automatic high-flyer. At AS, she worked hard and got a B – but she then refined the way she wrote, in essay after essay, until she got an A* at A level. There was learning there – but there were social skills, too. There was teaching from me, but it was in combination with the rest of her personal context.

'Definitely,' she says. 'I absolutely learned through the way I socially interacted in lessons.'

It strikes me, as we talk, that Becky has much in common with Mia – but their experience of school was poles apart. Mia was at home in a world fundamentally at odds with the values of British education; it was not that she hated school, or that her family or her community hated it, but that the ways in which she understood getting respect, and attention, and even love, conflicted with the ways school tells us we should get them. It took a jolt for her to release that world, and even though she says she is happier now, there is still a severance in it somewhere. Mia's success at school has, quite simply, cost more than Becky's.

But is it worth more, too? Has the social struggle Mia experienced given her something that no grades could? Does she have a breadth, and a strength, that comes only from adversity? Or does she remain brittle, ill-at-ease in a world that she navigates at one remove?

All school is social, really. Maybe the difference lies in whether your social world and the world of school operate in tandem, or in opposition. And maybe we could do better by acknowledging the force of this. Sometimes teachers – and schools – can see friendship as an add-on. But if we value it and bring it into the centre of the curriculum, nurturing it with extracurricular activities and trips, allowing bonds to form and re-form, giving space in the safe environment of after-school clubs, maybe the experience of friendship will start to become less dictated by where you grew up and will be a source of confidence, of power, of support. And if we think this is important, we cannot leave it to the chance pattern of council investment or charity interest. We need all schools to have this provision, and to provide it for all students.

Maybe then we can do two vital things. Guide those peer relationships, in the way that good parents always do – but also recognise the skill and strength it takes to navigate them, and value these in our pupils when we see them.

As important as peer groups are, though, they are always second on the scene. They colonise a space established by the home environment. And if we want to understand the ways in which the context that a child comes from impacts on their schooling, then we have to look not only at friends – but at family.

8. Parents

When I watch my own children, the thing that astonishes me is the way their love for me is such an implicit assumption. They don't say it – they show it, and not in grand gestures, but in the casual way they drape themselves across me on the sofa, the way they speak without filter or affect, their total lack of self-consciousness around me. And, much as I hate it, they even show it in the way they are so rude, argumentative and utterly shit at tidying up after themselves.

Kids can be fractious with parents *because* they are at home – because home is the place, when it works as it should, where you have no anxiety about rejection or not belonging. There's a pattern that you learn to recognise, as a teacher, when parents of kids who are meek, mild and obedient in school say they've been struggling at home. I always reassure these families: their children are expressing their frustration at home because they are comfortable, because they have a secure attachment. The ones I worry about are those where home is a place of stress and school is the release.

We've seen already the impact of the home environment on grades. But there's far more going on here than just 'less money equals less education'. For a child in complex circumstances, school can be a completely different experience, in a whole host of unseen or overlooked ways.

Take Benny – Benny is eleven. He lives in Carlisle. He has a smile and a swagger, a way of walking with both hands in his pockets and his blazer swept back behind them. His eyes are bright, but he often looks to the side and down, when you're speaking to him. He's inattentive, but clever. His books are neat, and he takes pride in them. Sometimes he gets in fights – and sometimes he loses control so much that teachers can do nothing with him.

'What it is,' says Benny's dad, Nathan, 'is I'm a single parent of four kids. Their mam walked out on them a year ago, left them with social services. We weren't together – I was in a hostel at the time. I got a phone call: come and collect me children.'

The children range from two to eleven. Before their current home, they had spent several years moving around. They left Manchester because 'There's just no respect at all. It's absolutely diabolical. All the gun crime and everything else. All the druggies – people stabbing each other on street corners.'

There were, and are, other factors at play in the family's circumstances that Nathan skates around, and which I won't go into. But the world they left was one that contained trauma and disruption, and significant risk to all of their lives.

Nathan is a small man, sharp, eager to talk. He looks worn, but alert. He's relentlessly positive. He describes the moment he had to take charge of his children as 'The best thing that ever happened to me. Turned me life around.' Now Nathan has a new girlfriend – and she has two children of her own, one of them autistic. They live together in the council flat that Benny's mother abandoned. 'I do everything for them,' he says.

He does. Social services have been so impressed with his turnaround that they invited Nathan in to speak about his experience. He's engaged with them at every step of the way. And Benny has settled down in the year since all this happened.

What is school for? I ask Nathan.

'Routines,' he says. 'That's what gets you through life. Your "please" and "thank you"s.' He says he hopes Benny gets a good job.

What do you mean by that? I ask.

'Army. Or engineer.'

At school, though, Benny's success is fragile. He is easily provoked. On those occasions when he does lose control, he moves restlessly, pacing, a half-smile on his face, his brow furrowed. He won't listen. He seems possessed by something stronger than he is – an energy from somewhere that is hurt deep inside him.

I watch Nathan as we speak. He smiles. His feet move. His body moves, too, as we talk. His voice is fast, perky, oddly disassociated from what he's talking about. I think about his small flat. About his income: Universal Credit only, benefits capped at two children.

About the six children who are actually living there – his four and his girlfriend's two. I think about days when my own two children are too much for me. I think about the neighbourhood Nathan lives in, and the things Benny saw when he was younger. When I hear the details of why the family left Manchester, I feel sick.

Benny's path to adulthood seems desperately narrow. School is both the least of his worries and his only hope.

Two hundred and fifty miles away, in Bristol, Elena speaks in tumbling, excitable bursts. I ask how she felt about school when she got up that morning, and she tells me, 'So not bothered. I was so mad, because I had such a good dream – do you know who Alex Turner is? – I had a dream I met him and then I woke up and I was so sad!'

Talking to Elena is a bewildering experience. She is filled with energy, in a strange mix of nerves and confidence. She has even prepared notes for me, although we soon discard them and just talk. At one point she tells me about her family's education. They are from Albania.

'I think my dad dropped out of school – he went into the army. My mum, she had to drop out of college because she didn't have enough money. It makes me really sad, because even today she says, "Elena, I want to do this and that, because I want to become a nurse" and I'm like, "Of course, I'll take my brother to school – I'll do anything, because I want you to be happy, I just want you to do your thing" and she's like, "I need my English GCSE", and my teachers were like, "You can pay about sixty pounds to do your GCSE . . ."'

The words pour out of her: a torrent of vivid excitement, leaning forward, all intent on how much she wants to help her parents and how much she does at home. There's something performative about it – as there is with many fifteen-year-olds – but, with Elena, there is a peculiar intensity.

I suggest to her that maybe she feels a little bit of pressure from home?

'I do feel my parents pressure me to do well. I'm not gonna lie. They have changed now – my dad goes to therapy, but before they were very strict.' She laughs. 'Honestly, it wasn't my fault, because I didn't even know English properly. They would be like, "Oh, you did really bad." They wouldn't even allow me on my tablet if I didn't read that day.'

Listening, I feel my sympathies turn. That's the kind of thing I tell my children. I begin to wonder how much of this pressure is simply reasonable parenting. I remember the difference between the histrionic way I would talk about my parents at fifteen and the way I think of their parenting now.

When Elena gets on to her brother, she sounds furious. 'He has so many things, and I'm jealous of him because I never got those things. He's always on the TV all day, and he's so stuck up.' She takes a breath and launches dramatically again. 'I know what makes him like that – my parents being lenient with him, because they were so strict with me.'

To be totally honest, by now I'm feeling for Elena's parents. They can't seem to get anything right, in the eyes of their daughter – veering wildly between too strict and too lenient. It seems striking to me that much of what I've discussed, both with Elena and with Nathan, is about this idea of parenting as discipline, as the establishment of routines. And again, as a parent myself, I recognise this, even as I hope that's not all it is. But what has this got to do with school?

Everything, I think. As teachers, we are quite literally *'in loco parentis'*. We stand in for parents – and kids know this. Hell, they pretty frequently mistake us for their parents. That's not to say that teaching and parenting are the same, but there is a shared DNA – and a reliance on a commonality of values between home and school. The difference is that school needs to provide something that home often, and perhaps by definition, cannot: space. Space to be a different person, to test boundaries, to experiment. To be free from the pressures and guilt that home can bring.

Elena calms down a little. 'I think it is because they changed,' she says about her parents' attitudes towards her brother. 'Of course I'm not gonna be horrible to my brother, I'm not gonna be like, "What's wrong with you?"'

I love the construction she keeps using – 'I'm not gonna'. She distances herself from herself, stands back and watches her own actions with approval. It's a phrase that conveys the absolutism of being a teenager, the raw self-construction.

I tell Elena that she seems very self-possessed, very confident. I ask where that comes from.

'That does come from my parents,' she says slowly. She takes a deep breath. 'I have this thing where I'm really scared they're gonna leave me, if I don't do well.' Her voice catches. 'Sorry if I cry a little bit.' She composes herself. 'When I was two months old, my parents left me with my dad's aunt because they couldn't take care of me. So they decided, "We're going to go to Germany, gonna make money for her, get her money." They came back for me when I was five years old.'

It's shocking to hear her say this. Elena gives an overwhelming impression of fragility. There is still that sense of something performative – a telling of a story about herself – but that doesn't negate the genuine unease in what she says.

'Now I really want to do well for them. I don't want to disappoint them, because of this fear that they don't need me, they want to get rid of me.'

I say nothing.

'My parents have reassured me multiple times, they say, "Elena, you are our daughter – we would never do that."'

I can picture those moments. I imagine being those parents, or being Elena. I have the familiar sense of watching a kid struggle and knowing that the best thing to do is simply to wait and let them talk.

The way children are parented affects their experience of school. And whether you believe that the parents' job is to put in place boundaries, so that their children behave respectfully at school, or that the parents' job is to provide an endlessly tolerant and loving home, so that their children are secure and confident, the bottom line is that home and school are a double act – and that double act has to evolve organically. For some kids, like Benny, the solidity of school in a world that is so scary and changes so frequently is essential. His daily life is one where, as his dad recognises, the routines and structures are lifesaving. The ways in which school reached out to Nathan and supported him, the positioning of school as a mediator between social services and the family, the structure that school provides – all of this, despite the worries about what the future might hold, has steadied the situation, has kept Benny and his siblings safer than they might have been.

For Elena, on the other hand, school has been a place that has allowed her the chance to breathe, outside a demanding home. It has balanced a very different set of pressures: letting her access therapy in school, and supporting her in mitigating the intensity of the academic pressure that she places on herself. Her needs are very different from Benny's – and her teachers have reacted to those particular circumstances.

But these kids are not outliers. That home–school double-act is in place for everyone. All of the inequalities in income that have so much of an impact on outcomes are better described as inequalities in home environment. School – barring institutional failures – is a place where the kids in any one school get pretty much the same deal, from when they arrive to when they leave. The differences between children and the way they interact with school come overwhelmingly from the context outside.

This is not the same as saying that poverty equals bad parenting. But it does equal different priorities, different stresses and different ways of thinking about yourself. And poverty is only one of the many aspects at home that influence schooling. Your whole social context – friends, family, the jobs they have, the telly they watch – provide the backdrop to what you do in school, and vice versa.

Sometimes it's more than simply the backdrop. In primary school, and particularly in early years, homework is designed largely as an exercise in structured interaction with parents. But that's also true later on. GCSEs, with their final exam structure whereby all the knowledge gained over two years is tested in a three-week period, are dependent on revision at home. You cannot do well simply by doing your best in class. Home study is not something I'd argue against – learning to revise in your own time is a valuable skill, and is a core part of fixing learning in long-term memory – but we rarely acknowledge quite how important this aspect of the system is, in terms of the simple maths of the time you need in order to absorb the volume of content that you need to cover. The necessity of working at home means, in practice, that home and school cannot be meaningfully separated even in the seemingly hard-edged academic sphere. It means that a school needs to take into account what is going on – and what is lacking – in a child's home life, if it is to have a clear view of how school might be affecting them.

In Essex, one school is working closely with a local charity, Thepwell Family services, to change the way they support the parents who struggle the most.

On the day I visit, it is holding its weekly parents' group drop-in. It takes place in a few simple rooms off a car park near the high street. There's a kitchen, plus a room set up for stay-and-play. It's busy: packed with parents, babies and young people studying with the local college on their foundation-degree programme. I'm fed – not just once, but again and again – chickpea curry, deep-fried bread, pakora. It's hard to tell who is who. Some people are referred here by the school, some have come with friends, and others have been coming so long they've started to volunteer.

I sit down in one room and begin to talk to a few parents. Sophie sits opposite her friend, Keira. Sophie is older – maybe mid-thirties – while Keira could be one of my students. They tell me they come every week. Both of them have young babies and they do stay-and-play, but they also come to spend time with other adults.

Sophie struggles socially. She thinks she's bipolar, but hasn't been diagnosed. Whether she is or not is immaterial – she was struggling to get out of the house before this. Her baby is stimulated here, and her toddler too, in ways that they wouldn't be with her in her tiny flat; and she is kinder here, more able to interact positively. She has begun to volunteer and has taken Keira under her wing. Sophie tells me she has no friends outside this group, but here she is trusted, and given responsibility.

On the other side of me is Amal and her friend, Mariam. Mariam has only just started coming. I turn to her and ask her whether she likes it.

'My son died,' she tells me.

I freeze.

'My son. He was fourteen. He died on the seventh of July.' Her eyes are big and blank. Amal carries on talking to someone else on the other side of her. Mariam tells me more. It seems like a compulsion for her. She tells me about her other children, but returns to her son. She tells me that her son was so wonderful – everyone thought so, everyone at school and at home. She tells me how, one long summer evening, he climbed up on the roof of a block near their house with some friends and slipped. She tells me everything: the way she heard the news, the funeral. Everything.

Afterwards, as I walk back towards the train station with Jennie, who runs the Foundation, she tells me that Mariam has been talking to everyone like this. Perhaps she has no other outlet.

Sometimes it's hard not to feel that all the things we do in schools are vain attempts to push back at the sheer volume of misery in the world. Some children are so hurt by life before they even step through the doors of school that it's easy to give up on them, there and then. And some families have such a weight of pain that it's hard to see how they can keep standing.

There is a world that I imagine sometimes, where we get everything right. Where there is a system for this: a network of support, a friendly face who guides parents through the difficulties of raising a child and holds their hand in moments of grief. Places to go, people to see, courses that teach you what every child needs; outreach centres that are warm and kind and welcoming.

But even in the real world, where so much is inadequate and ill constructed, there is one vital way in which school is the partner to home and acts *in loco parentis* in a simple and profound way. It was something we all became starkly aware of during the Covid pandemic: the simple fact that, for most of the working day, schools serve a fundamental, and perhaps primary, function as childcare. With the schools shut, parents (and the employers of parents, the clients of the employers of parents, the employees of the clients of the employers of parents, and so on, *ad infinitum*) suddenly realised how essential this aspect of school was: it provides a safe and reasonably stimulating environment for their children, freeing them to do their jobs.

Because what we have to remember is that the very concept of childhood – the idea that there is a period of time when a person should not be expected to fend for themselves, to work, to be subjected to the pressures of adult life – depends on there being an environment in which childhood can take place. And as soon as you start to think of school in these terms (as a place for kids to be kids, to grow up in), then the inadequacy of the transactional approach becomes starker. And so does its inaccuracy.

People often say nostalgically, 'It takes a village to raise a child', probably thinking of some imagined collection of cheery cottages, and bemoaning the atomised nature of modern life. In truth, though, even the bleakest high street contains networks of community – the most isolated estate has bonds of love, which just need to be activated and enabled. And in the meantime a school, with its stable routines, its neighbouring classrooms and its warm and relentless nosiness, is perhaps the closest thing to a village that we have.

If we recognised that, maybe we could start to see how the links between school and home are worth nourishing – and not simply because schools might 'get' something out of them.

9.   Community

I moved out of London almost a decade ago, but in many ways I still miss it. Not in any considered way − not with any serious sense of wanting to live there still. But when I visit, when I walk through the streets on a summer night and the pavements are crowded and hot, and people sit late in the park and shout from wide-open windows, there is a dusty magic, a ramshackle brassy glamour that still makes my blood run.

In the middle of a trip to see some schools in London and the South-East I stayed for one of those glorious July nights in Finsbury Park. Everything was full and exuberant, from the tiers of stacked fruit spilling out of the front of the shops, to the crowds in the cafés and bars. It was the hottest day of the summer so far, and as I walked past the bus station I saw a familiar face − Horace Parry, a teacher I knew from William Ellis School.

As we caught up, he introduced me to his sister, sitting next to him. Then a young man walked past and Horace said, 'This one was an Ellis boy.'

I smiled at the boy, but didn't recognise him.

'This one, too,' said Horace, holding out a hand to another.

And while we talked, a third boy walked past, held out a hand and, yes, he too was an Ellis boy.

Schools are rooted in their communities in ways that few other institutions are. You belong to them for years − and they are linked to you for a lifetime. A school's name is an identifying tag on Facebook or Snapchat, a name on an exam certificate or a CV, and it becomes an address to locate you socially and culturally. But it goes deeper than that. Your school is the climate you grew up in − an emotion, a colour, a mood that sits with you when you remember the most formative moments of your life. When you meet someone from your old school, that in itself is a connection: a shared pool of faces and names, and places and quirks, for you to pick over.

And all those people who went to that school (at least for a short while) share a tight geographical location. At the end of the school day, they spread out in a web of meandering routes home, through estates and down high streets, via back alleys and parks where fags are smoked and battles fought. They go to houses where brothers and sisters will make the same walk in years to come and, after them, children and grandchildren. They share a frame of reference, even as they are also fractured into different constituencies, different races, religions and classes.

In the morning they are drawn back in again and sit, side-by-side, in the same classroom.

These communities have long memories. Each generation that attends a school has its own version of it – a story that's told with relish or fear, with love or anger. In my school there is a wooden bench in the corridor outside the Head's office. It's where you sit while you wait to go in. When I bring parents past, they often glance at it and sometimes smile at me, a sheepish, half-proud smile as they say, 'I remember that.'

On open evenings, you catch a look in the eyes of a visitor. It says, *Does that person remember me?* Sometimes it leads to an awkward exchange, until the floodgates open and memories pour out. Sometimes, no matter how much you squint, you simply can't place the other person through the haze of time and change.

But these webs of emotion and connection are not merely retro-spective. They exist within a school at any one time. Teachers send their kids to the schools they work in. Parents often get jobs in their kid's school – in the office, in the restaurant, as an invigilator. And when you live in a tight community, with your nan on the next street and your aunt three doors down, you will by default be at school with your cousins, or sometimes your nephew, niece or uncle.

School in these circumstances can become a hybrid place – a place where your relationships are an extension of your home life. I remember breaking up a fight between two girls, only to discover they were sisters. My authority as a teacher felt suddenly wobbly; I had to defer to the family structure instead. Equally, I've lost count of the times where the opposite happens: where internal family dynamics are brought into the school, on parents' evenings or in phone calls or exclusion meetings, and suddenly I'm called on to arbitrate on how a kid talks to his nan, or how much time he should spend on Xbox.

Horace Parry started teaching at William Ellis the year before me, but he was older, with some time in other jobs beforehand, ranging from the family hair salon to tour manager for Soul II Soul. It was the hair salon that he was sitting outside when I ran into him. He's a classic Black Londoner of his generation: Caribbean heritage, with strong links to Jamaica and regular trips there, but deeply embedded in North London. I remember him as calm, gentle in his manner, but qualitatively different in the way he interacted with the kids, from the way I did. Partly it was age and being a father, but it was also about race and community.

'He never taught me,' explains one ex-student I spoke to a few days later, 'but he became a kind of unofficial mentor and has since become a close family friend. He took on much more of a father role. He looked out for me, in the context of knowing where I came from.'

This kind of connection is something Jeffrey Boakye, teacher and author of *I Heard What You Said*, also comments on – how it comes from the sharing of a social experience, like that of race or culture, between a teacher and a student. In particular, in the context of a system that marginalises Black voices, he describes the recognition that he, 'as a black teacher, [has] important knowledge about how to exist in a white education system'.[1]

Horace says this was not something he went into teaching for, but it did become apparent to him very quickly. 'I hadn't consciously thought about that. It was only when I went in to school that I realised, "Oh my God, there's such a need."'

When I ask if there was a particular moment that made him see this need, Horace tells me that those moments are never *not* present. 'It happens every day, right up until today.' But that's not to say that being Black and a teacher is inevitably made up of this experience, he qualifies. 'It's how you position yourself. Are you available – are you prepared to talk to pupils as human beings, and recognise the fact that you and I are the same: I am Black and you are Black.' But what he describes is not something exclusive. 'I've come to recognise that the other ethnicities – including white working class – have such a need too.'

As we talk, some fascinating parallels begin to emerge between the world of North London and my current school environment in Sunderland. At one point we discuss a point that Boakye raises: the ways that relatively innocuous behaviour in Black students can become a flashpoint for sanctions and exclusions. Horace describes talking to a group of Black boys outside a lesson. They've all been sent out for talking, and it dawns on them that they're also all Black. They begin to protest, saying it's racist, but he takes them through the incident, only for them to point out that yes, they might have been chatting, but so were X and Y. And it suddenly seems that yes, there may be some unconscious bias here.

'Then I have to say that old line: "You know what – you're going to have to get used to this." I can't change all the teachers' mindsets, but I can change the boys' mindset. I try to get them to understand and not react in a way that makes it worse.'

There is something deeply depressing in Horace's acknowledgement that he might not change the teachers' mindsets – and perhaps troubling. But it's what he says next that is really interesting. He describes an incident, also in the corridor, but this time between him and another teacher. After a minor issue around moving tables in a classroom, she is disproportionately angry, shouting at Horace down the corridor, to an extent that really disturbs him. He doesn't react at first, but then returns later to talk to her and finds himself furious, reacting in turn to her overreaction.

'I absolutely lost it, Sammy,' he says to me. 'I don't remember, because I was so enraged. But I surmised that she was shouting at me in that disrespectful way because I was Black, and I told her so, to her face. And now I've done exactly what I told those boys not to do. Now I had no proof of that – but it's something that sits in you, and then it comes out.'

In that moment the kinship, the shared community experience, is intense. What Horace is able to do – imperfectly, as ever in teaching – is use his own experience, and the more reflective intelligence that only comes with age, to shine a light on the world those boys live in. As a Black man, he is able to position himself in such a way that he talks about the emotional experience of racism, not just the morality of it. A white teacher simply could not do this for them.

This is where I see the connection with Sunderland. In fact if I'm honest, it's where I see my own deficiency as a teacher. I am not of the communities in which I have taught. It means that in Sunderland I often find myself watching from the outside, seeing my own failure to communicate with kids whose world is so different from my own, and recognising the importance of figures like Jakey and Dean, the local lads who run a community outreach programme from a couple of rooms on our site. Like Horace, they speak to the lived experience of the community. They are from here, they know the families, they understand the circumstances. They *sound* like people the kids have grown up with, and they're trusted in a different way from teachers.

'When they come to the youth club, they get to speak to someone who's not . . .' Jakey hesitates. He speaks with the broad, deep, precise seriousness of a particular kind of North-Eastern masculinity. He tries again. 'I've got a position of power,' he continues, 'but it's not forced on them. I think some kids feel like they have to attend school, but they're attending our youth club by choice, so they're more inclined to listen.'

He tells me about his own childhood, in a stable, loving working-class home in the city – how he was someone who had his own moment in his teenage years when things almost went wrong, but that the support around him from family, and the discipline he learned from boxing and football, kept him from stepping over that invisible line.

'When you start talking to young people about their family life, you find a lot of them are from split relationships, or some of them haven't got a dad. Sometimes dad's away in jail; sometimes they only see him at weekends. Sometimes they just don't like their mam.'

Jakey sees his own role as different from that of a teacher. 'Youth workers will give a lot of time to one person.' And it's often personal – relatable to the kids. They feel engaged with in a way that makes them feel seen. 'I feel like sometimes that's a difficulty some teachers have – they haven't got the time to sit down and talk to kids about *their* experiences.'

It should be no surprise that it's highly validating for a child to receive that kind of attention, especially when it is so rare. And yet in many ways, schools are not designed to attend to these aspects of welfare that Jakey describes, even while increasingly it falls to them to do so. The current model of knowledge-rich learning – where the body of canonical, communal knowledge is seen as the primary thing that a school transmits – leaves less space for the work needed to make kids feel at home in a school community. There's no doubt that when individualised education comes at the expense of providing opportunity, it is damaging. But the collateral damage done to those who feel school does not see them is significant.

This is where Jakey's work is so important. He tells me about Graham, a kid I knew reasonably well. I would have described him as disengaged, badly behaved, someone who underachieved at GCSE and generally seemed a bit of a problem. But to Jakey, who had worked with him for years, Graham was someone who had grown in confidence until he reached the point where he started an apprenticeship with them to become a youth worker himself, and would soon be receiving an award for his work with younger kids. In the conventional school environment, Graham's behaviour was a reaction to the way the teaching staff thought of him and treated him. As with Horace's students, a seed of prejudice had grown into disruption and antagonism. The antidote was a space where Graham felt at home.

Jakey highlights another key difference between the way youth clubs and schools work. 'They're not focused on competition – they're focused on enjoyment.' Schools are so heavily structured around 'achievement', around ability and the climbing of those meritocratic rankings, that children lacking in confidence and self worth can find themselves resenting the place. Not everyone *can* succeed in that environment, and these kids are fully aware of that. Instead they find value in the things they know and can negotiate – the social world around them, the network of relationships that they grow up with. Youth workers are not friends, but their status – a 'bridge', as Jakey describes it – opens up the possibility of success and learning that is on a community's own terms, rather than a capitulation to a middle-class schooling system.

Jo has a similar vision of the way kids can find something at school, besides the academic. She works in the restaurant at a mid-sized North-Eastern comp. 'I was never the brightest. I wasn't in trouble or anything, but I wasn't getting into the learning. I was more . . . knocking about. School was a place you had to come. But, as I say, I was never the brightest.' She's funny, quick-talking, sharp.

Did you like it? I ask.

'I did, actually. I like mixing with people. The camaraderie – the banter, you know what I mean. But I like that about work, too. I like bouncing off people.'

I suggest that what she liked at school is also what she likes about working at school.

'My sons are, like, "Is there something wrong with you?" But I love my job. You bounce off the kids – like I bounced off the staff when I was a kid. I still keep in touch with some of the staff who don't even work here any more, but who taught me.'

I ask about the web of connections that exists in a school like this: the friends, relatives, all bound together. What does it give you, as a child?

'I had it; my sons had it. My eldest was in the same year as my niece, and the next year down was a nephew, and a cousin – and for six years there was always one.'

School is a place of warmth to Jo, but she's not uncritical. She has a clear sense of the difference between school skills and wider life skills. 'One of my nieces left school, really bright, now teaches A-level Maths. But she's like that.' Jo knocks dramatically on the desk, eyebrows raised. 'Hasn't. Got. A. Clue.' She says it with relish. 'Now you can ask my lads anything – one runs his own business, the other two's got full-time jobs – and they're like,' she clicks her fingers, 'switched on. But you ask them stuff what my niece would know, and they wouldn't have a clue.'

Jo herself epitomises this. She described herself at the start as 'never the brightest' – but she's a powerhouse in the school, someone with judgement, nous and real emotional intelligence. 'I've got another niece who struggled,' she says. 'Didn't get the help she needed in school. Now she's a team leader in a nursery – absolutely loving life.' She carries on, talking through the careers of different members of her family after they left school. In all this there is a palpable sense of moral values as the core. Jo describes yet another niece who's a carer, and who gives up her own Christmas to care for the old lady she works for.

What you're describing, I say, is that there are people who, in their lives outside school, are organised, ethical, with good judgement, but those qualities didn't let them succeed at school.

Jo agrees. She tells me about the way in which technology and practical subjects – woodwork, cookery, and so on – have been stripped out. 'Some of these things are what normal kids fall back on.'

I pick up on that word. In fact as I listen to the recording later on, my wife picks up on it, too. 'What does she mean, "normal"?'

What Jo means is very simple – normal *to her*. This is what Diane Reay is referring to when she says that education is middle class. The assumptions of normality are set at a level that seems 'average' to the educated people who have designed it. To me, having a degree is 'normal'. To Jo, not succeeding academically is 'normal'.

Her point is hugely important. Reforms to education in the last decade have been made on the basis that 'lowering' standards or expectations because of a student's background would be to perpetuate the 'soft bigotry of low expectations', as mentioned in Chapter 3. But while it may be right – in fact I think it probably is – to say that we were not serving the interests of the 'disadvantaged' by giving them 'low-value courses', there is a hefty dose of patronising superiority at work here. After all, as I talk to Jo I don't get the sense that this is someone for whom school was a failure, even if it might have been so, from a narrow academic viewpoint.

Looked at this way – seeing a school community as offering and being something more than its academic outcomes – we begin to see the shape of something warmer, more humane, more inclusive. And if that all sounds a bit vague, then it's worth looking at the very real consequences that can follow from its absence.

At around the time I visit Birmingham, the investigative-journalism podcast *Serial* has released a new episode on the so-called 'Trojan Horse Affair' of 2014. This was big news at the time: a group of majority Muslim schools were accused of fostering radicalisation and misogyny, and were then beset by counter-accusations that the original whistle-blowing letter was a forgery.[2] What struck me, on listening to the podcast, was how, prior to the scandals, the schools involved had been utterly transformed. In the nineties the central school in the scandal, Park View, had GCSE pass rates that were staggeringly low, with only 4 per cent gaining A*–C grades in 1997. Teachers and students described a place devoid of hope or expectation. But by 2011 a pervasive belief amongst the staff that their students would never amount to much had been completely turned around, and the pass rate was now 73 per cent. There are many factors that go into a transformation like that – but in this case, bringing the community into the school was key. Religious assemblies, prayer rooms and the active recruitment of Muslim teachers and governors were all part of it. 'They had a really clear ethos and everyone was on board,' one of the (non-Muslim) teachers at the time told *The Guardian*. 'The religion helped to build some of that.' And, it is worth noting, this is no different from the ways in which Catholic schools have been operating for centuries in the UK.

The scandal lay in the linking of a straightforward attempt to engage and represent the community and the alleged promotion of views that were misogynistic and homophobic, and which resulted in a wild maelstrom of accusation and counter-accusation that left the schools, once more, in dire straits. But irrespective of the truth about a highly contested series of events, this much seems uncontroversial: when there is a radical split between the attitudes and cultural values of the teachers and those of the students, it is a recipe for disengagement. It's what Jeffrey Boakye talks about so persuasively. In this instance, if the cultural environment of the students was so strongly defined by Islam, and by parents still steeped in the language and attitudes of their homelands, then a school that failed to try to understand this was surely doomed.

The school that I visit, Michael Cairns Academy, was one of those caught up in the storm, although it was not at the centre of it. It never had the period of wild success beforehand, and instead suffered the worst of both worlds. It has been through two changes of management and an amalgamation since then and is, to all intents and purposes, a new school. But the catchment remains heavily Muslim, with white British students a very small minority. And what's fascinating is that despite those past scandals, the overriding need of leadership is still to reach out to the community, ensuring that school is seen as a place that trusts, values and believes in its children.

The Deputy Head, Alex, is clear that there has been a transformation in the school over the last couple of years, and he is equally clear on why that is: 'It's cultural – in terms of the culture of the building, not the culture of our children.' He describes how, in the aftermath of the years of instability, 'we had a large churn of staff – and of children. A school which maybe was a little bit unloved – standards of behaviour were poor. I think behaviour underpins everything, so teaching suffered, too.'

But the school I visit now is not at all like that. It sits off an unmistakeably multicultural high street, with that recognisably English combination of Victorian brick terraces, headscarves and mangoes piled high outside giant fruit emporiums. The school is a new building, a dullish complexity of high walls, off-centre windows and featureless round pillars in coloured render. But once inside, you're in a calm, spacious world, with polite students, affable staff and a sense of quiet purpose.

'There's been a lot of work with parents, with our community,' Alex carries on. 'We're really trying to push this community hub, community feel.' They have made links with local organisations and charity groups. 'Everything we do now is done in all languages which represent our community. We have an active desire to engage. Often, in previous years, the basic fact of the majority-Muslim school population wasn't recognised.'

The kids I speak to recognise his account. They talk about 'culture days' when they are allowed to wear 'cultural clothing' – or, if they prefer, non-uniform – and overwhelmingly choose to do so.

'Keeping up with the Joneses is hard, with your Nikes and Armani and everything,' says Alex, 'but everyone has one special suit or one special dress.' He adds, 'For Eid, we hand-made little gift bags for every single student – it was a big effort, but these little gestures go a long way.'

This value placed on community is palpable in the school. And when I talk to the students, they universally present their faith as an integral part of how they see themselves. That's not comparable to saying they have the same attitude to it, the same level of observance or the same specific set of beliefs – but being Muslim isn't an add-on, and a school culture that ignored this would be one that failed at some level to see who the students are.

The experience of schools in circumstances like these, where the need to reach out to community is imperative and is done with sensitivity and inclusiveness, is heartening. But there is a tension that accompanies public debate about what should constitute 'belonging' in Britain today, and schools are far from immune. If you want an unfiltered version of public discourse on this subject, spend some time in the classroom: you will hear comments made explicitly that even the *Daily Mail* would only hint at darkly: about how refugees are rapists, and Black people are given priority in the NHS, leaving white people to die on the street (both of which I have heard from children). But you'll also hear a quieter and much more heartening consensus, where teachers listen to and guide the attitudes of the students in their care. At schools like Michael Cairns the multiple identities that their students hold are not in conflict. For this community, celebrating Muslim identity *is* celebrating Britishness.

On another hot and muggy July night, two weeks after my visit to London, I am back in Sunderland and make my way slightly reluctantly up the back stairs of a local sea-front hotel. In the bar I scan for familiar faces and see, with a jolt of unfamiliarity, a group of figures in evening dress. They are colleagues and, not for the first time, I feel underdressed. Round here, people take their nights out seriously – and at Year II Prom, it's not only the kids who want to make an impression. I, on the other hand, have a tendency to think a checked shirt is the height of smart-casual sophistication.

Prom gets a bad press. Creeping Americanisation, apparently. A parade of grim flouncy dresses and spray tans. The commercialisation of childhood carried to a glittery extreme. And there is plenty that night to fuel that narrative. Some children are dropped off by their parents. Some come in specially hired cars. I see a Mustang, a limo and a gleaming black Rolls-Royce. One pair even arrives in a horse-drawn carriage, complete with feathery plumes and a top-hatted driver. As they step out of their vehicles, there is the unmistakeable feeling of an ersatz red-carpet event, with dresses that generally adhere to the maxim 'the bigger, the better' – sequins, tulle, glittering headpieces, corsets – and suits that lean towards the brash, with loud checks and gold chains and white waistcoats much in evidence. Phones are out, selfie follows selfie and an appreciative audience gathers.

I look at that audience. Nans, dads, mams (not mums – this is the North-East) and a host of younger kids all watch the parade, ranging from giddy to teary. Sometimes their elder siblings turn up, too, kids I taught a few years back, now at uni or working, sometimes with children themselves. They come over to say hi, to say thanks again.

The leavers keep on coming. They step out of their vehicles perfectly poised on the cusp of adulthood, made up into what they imagine grown-ups to be. Their eyes dart sideways, their faces both embarrassed and euphoric. The girls teeter on their heels, in the folds of their wedding-cake dresses, and shriek delightedly at themselves and their friends, while the boys slowly warm up, from hands on shoulders into awkward and then heartfelt hugs.

I stand at the back of the throng and talk to two girls, best friends, who for five years have giggled their way around the school in a strange little bubble of innocence. All the things there might be in their lives that are sad and troubling – and there are many – can be forgotten for a moment as they stand, gobsmacked at themselves in matching purple dresses, their make-up applied with the aid of a member of staff in a room booked by the school specially for them at the hotel.

Teacher after teacher approaches and speaks to them. When we catch each other's eyes there is a jolt of pure emotion, a heart-wrenching wonder at the ways childhood can be so hard and so magical. Later in the evening, one of these two girls will be so over-whelmed that she starts hyperventilating. We'll take her out to the front again, empty now, her friend as ever by her side, and practise breathing. Another member of staff will stop and talk to the two of them gently, joking with them in the softest, kindest way.

But right now, up front, more and more students arrive.

For each of these children, stepping out of their shiny cars, I remember the difficulties, the moments of panic and anger. And yet here they are. Prom is just a symbol, but symbols have power, and in this moment they do seem like they have changed, and grown.

Forty-nine teachers are here tonight, most of them voluntarily, paying for their own tickets, wanting to participate in the celebration with the kids. We play bingo together, count down to confetti can-nons, then all dance in a hectic mass, bouncing first to generic hits and then, as the evening progresses, they bring out the big guns. Every prom or school party I've been to in Sunderland has played these: 'Cha Cha Slide', 'Macarena' and a weird happy hardcore song called 'Children of the Night'.

And *everyone* dances. Teachers, students, boys, girls. Boys dressed as girls, and girls dressed as boys – because, every year, the flounces and frills are only part of the story. Girls in suits and a tall, strikingly made-up boy in a backless blue gown mingle, with no comment at all from the other students. A colleague grabs me and makes me spin her, to cheers from the kids and the teachers. Another colleague – the head of Maths – bounces with a glowstick in each hand like he's in a field in 1990, despite having turned up in full tuxedo and shiny shoes.

Throughout the night, kids grab teachers and ask for photos with them. Two students of mine give me an *Avengers* tie. A group of boys dance for the whole time, sweatily holding each other's hands and hugging.

At the end I stand with a couple of other teachers at the door as the kids drift out into the night. They say 'bye' and 'thank you' as they go. We remind every girl in a long dress to lift up her train, so it doesn't get wet on the steps – some of the boys do it for them. Many of them wear the flip-flops we provided for when the unfamiliar heels get too much. From the door I watch a group of boys at the bus stop opposite waiting for the night bus. Every now and then they duck behind the sea wall, presumably to drink from illicit supplies. There will be parties and after-parties. People will be sick.

As the two friends leave, I ask if they had fun.

'It was difficult,' says the one who had been hyperventilating. She has the serious, unquestioning honesty of a five-year-old. 'But it was great.'

In this book I sometimes try to use the proper terminology and call them pupils or students. But most of the time I find myself reverting to 'kids'. Because that is how I see them. They are children, and they live with us in our school for half of their waking lives. It's easy to criticise things like proms from the outside – but when it's your kids, your pupils, you don't see that. You see simply the sheer exhilaration of being sixteen and having your whole life ahead of you.

Ignore the flounces and the frills. Most important of all is that an event like this is safe, and warm. Like a first trip abroad with your class. Like the day at the end of term when the teacher brings in cake. Like all the ways in which schools are not simply factories, they are also homes. And celebrating this in a way that makes strong, positive, hopeful memories – sometimes for kids who don't have many of these – is far from the least that schools do.

10.   Privilege

Schools may well be communities as well as simply places of education. But what changes when the organising principle behind those communities, instead of geography or culture, is money? Because if disadvantage impacts educational outcomes, then so does privilege.

Full disclosure: I went to a private school at the age of twelve. It didn't feel like a big deal at the time. But now, when I refer to it, I always (slightly awkwardly) emphasise that I got a scholarship, that my parents wouldn't have been able to afford it otherwise, that I felt out of place. My discomfort is born out of years of arguing against the unfairness of our education system. I have explicitly criticised the private sector, and the role it has – and so I feel the need to hedge my privilege, to excuse myself. I somehow want to absolve myself of the taint of the private schoolboy.

But of course the irony is that my explanation doesn't lessen my privilege at all. It merely underlines it. My academic aptitude and my childhood in a bookish household, surrounded by love, were far more valuable to me and my prospects than being educated at any particular school. But somehow the idea that education can be bought – that your success is a product of the money spent on you – feels far harder to stomach than the idea that you were just incredibly lucky in your personal circumstances and the natural inclinations of your character.

The difference, I suppose, comes down to the notion of merit – and what education *means*. Somehow parental support and genetics are part of your intrinsic merit, while your bank account is not. And if, as we saw earlier, in modern, meritocratic Britain the idea of fairness is key, then nothing feels quite as unfair as the fact that you can buy success.

And buying success does seem to be what is happening here. There are many statistics I could quote at great length about the proportion of private-school pupils in jobs, from medicine right up to prime minister.[1] These arguments have been explored exhaustively. But to me the most persuasive is pretty simple – that 29 per cent of Russell Group university places go to private-school students, while only 7 per cent of students actually attend private school.[2]

There is a clarity to this statistic. Going to a private school does a really direct thing – it gets you a better 'education' (with the major caveat that we're taking the meaning of 'education' to be that class-inflected odd construction of 'excellent' results and 'excellent' university). There is a clarity to the incentives with the schools as well – they know they are there to get you that better education, to the point where during the suspension of exams in 2020 and 2021 private-school grades soared massively, under pressure from fee-paying parents.

But the problem with private schooling in Britain is more complicated than this straightforward transaction. It isn't simply about the grades. Historically, private education has been, almost by definition, a route to power. Not necessarily power in a straightforward political sense, but economic, social power – the power of networks, of being a professional, of 'polish'. And private schools are very aware that these qualities are not the same as straightforward academic achievement. They come from social cues, from norms of behaviour and expectation, from attitudes and assumptions about who you are and where you belong. And in many ways, this boils down not so much as to where you go to school, but who you go to school with.

Jackson is mid-forties, privately educated and lives in a pretty suburb of York. His kids are now both at private schools and have been 'for ever – since nursery, really'. When I ask why, he laughs. He's affable, intellectual – polished in fact. 'Good question. My wife and I were both privately educated, and there wasn't an enormous amount of thought that went into it. I think it would have felt quite difficult for us to do something different. We had the money to do it, and I think it would have felt quite . . . radical for us to send our children to state school.' He speaks carefully, and honestly. 'I have over the years had second thoughts, and then third thoughts. My views have moved back and forth over time.'

When you think about what your kids get out of education, would you say the knowledge they are getting or the social world they are in is more important? I ask.

'Difficult. I'm not sure of your categories. I think the most important thing is that my kids are not exposed to terrifying other children, who might do horrible things to them. Make of that what you will, but that's probably my prime motivation – it's protective. I mean, I end up exposing them to other things: they are around a bunch of spoilt little arseholes who will grow up to be spoilt big arseholes. But it's not as big a fear as the fear of what might happen to them in a more "normal" environment.'

As I listen to Jackson, I'm very aware of my own position as a parent. I have never considered private school for my children and, despite my own background, would describe myself as opposed to the idea in principle – but I did carefully research the schools in the area that we decided to move to, and in many ways they were the deciding factor. I engineered their environment in a similar way to Jackson; his worries about the social environment for his children are not a million miles from my own. In many ways my 'principled' decision-making has been significantly easier because I know I definitely can't afford private school.

In a sense, both Jackson and I exist on a spectrum of middle-class attitudes to education. We see it as important – we base life-choices around it. We have differing levels of agency, and differing attitudes, but similar concerns. Only there is one vital difference. I've spent twenty-two years in state schools. My wife went to state schools. I know what they are like – they have become the norm for me. Yes, I want my children to attend the best possible version of this norm, but when Jackson describes the 'protective' impulse – the need to avoid being exposed to 'horrible things' – I can't help but think there is one element of this that is a simple fear of the 'other'.

This is the stereotype of private schooling – that it is about exclusivity and separation. But that isn't the only view of it. Melvyn Roffe, Chair of the Heads' Conference (the HMC), makes a persuasive and passionate case for the way private schools can integrate with their communities and offer something more.

'All education is a social good,' he says. 'But further to that, I would argue that the work we do, the education that we provide, is in itself preparing young people to do good, socially aware things.'

His own school, George Watson's College, clearly does do this. Roffe tells me of partnerships, of voluntary work, of a variety of ways in which the school contributes to the wider community. He talks with great pride about the careers of ex-students – about one who is working in the NHS, another for the UN. But it seems to me that the values he is describing – values that have led to these outcomes – are not unusual in the state sector, either. They are the values that many schools and teachers try to inculcate. In itself, this seems to mark out Watson's as a good school, and Roffe as a good head – and having looked round the school and talked to some of the kids, I think I'd agree. But this doesn't really seem to have much to do with why the independent sector should exist in the form it does.

We talk about proposals to change the charitable status of schools. His view is simple: this will increase the social division that private schools represent, not decrease it. By driving up fees and removing incentives for assisted places and so on, private schools will become more socially exclusive or will go bust – either way, not improving the net good of education.

I find myself half-persuaded. But there is something in this argument that doesn't sit right. One of the most fascinating quirks of the private-school demographic is the way in which the percentage of kids who attend them has remained remarkably stable, even as the pattern of wealth distribution and the average income in the UK has shifted dramatically. Around 7 per cent of kids attended private schools in the sixties – and the figure is the same now. One might reasonably have expected increased wealth to have created more demand for private education, but it didn't. In fact, between those two points, the cost of private schools has soared, as has the social exclusivity of the students attending them. It's not too much of a leap to see the stability of that number as a reflection of the fact that the core *job* of the private sector is exclusivity. If *everyone* sends their kids to private school, it loses its USP.

Even those well-meaning attempts to mitigate this exclusivity with assisted places come with their own compromises. Keiran is from a far less privileged background than his peers at private school in the Midlands and receives financial support. I ask if he feels like there is enough money at home.

'I think we're – I wouldn't say wealthy, but we have enough. Never like we can't get crisps or anything.' (I love this as a measure of relative wealth.)

Keiran tells me he lives with his mother, and that she's a teacher. He tells me he came to the school because the children of lots of her friends came here. Listening to him, I have no doubt that he sees the difference between himself and his peers. But I also have no doubt that he is not 'disadvantaged' in the sense that some of the other children I've met have been. And this, I suspect, is the general picture in private schools. While there may be many in financial need, the cultural knowledge required to gain access to private-school schemes, and the confidence and resilience needed to take advantage of them, inevitably mean that they will not help the most disadvantaged in our society. In fact I would probably argue that uprooting someone from their cultural background and placing them in an institution where they are divorced from their previous identity is far from a recipe for happiness in any case.

Of course charging fees is not the only way that desirable schools can become exclusive. Jackson touches on this when I ask what it would have been like if his family had had less money – if private education had been more of a stretch.

'It certainly would have made a difference. We certainly would have thought much harder. Especially at primary-school stage. There are lots of posh middle-class families that send their kids to state school at primary level, because they are good at finding ones that are full of families like them – and they work out they can get a free education without really sacrificing the pleasant nature of their lifestyle and social connections. And they can feel terribly virtuous – they can say, "We state-educate our children, don't you know."'

In your circle are there people who do this?

'Yes, loads. But they tend, in my experience, to start tutoring the hell out of them at age nine to get them into private schools. Or they move somewhere – they do the grammar-school trick – they move to an area where they can get a free education, provided they tutor the hell out of them.'

This is why grammar schools, despite supposedly being open to children from poorer backgrounds, have tiny proportions of students who have free school meals. And there are many 'outstanding' schools across the country that have become exclusive because, as wealthy families pay higher prices for the houses in their catchment areas, it becomes only wealthy families who can afford to inhabit them.

Is Thirlpool a privileged school? I ask a bunch of sixth formers in a Berkshire comprehensive.

'Yes.'

The answer is definite from some, a little hesitant from others. Some of them are clearly more comfortable with it than others. Some have been here since Year 7, others arrived for Year 12. In our conversation I have heard that some have parents who are teachers, some who are journalists, some in the film industry or running factories. I've looked at the cost of houses in the vicinity of this school – and I think it would be fair to say that a significant proportion of the kids here are certainly privileged.

Of course that's not the same as saying they *all* are. But the experience of those who aren't reveals quite how divided the classroom can feel, even in a comprehensive.

John, for example, doesn't feel privileged. He was one of the ones who came in Year 12. After the others have gone, he describes himself as having 'A council background. My mum came here from Africa. All of the schools I've been to have been . . . lower-class-background schools. People like me. I came here because the grades were good. I came here, and then I felt like a whole different atmosphere. I felt surrounded by middle-class people that had aspirations to go to Oxbridge and get good grades and go on to do great things – and I just felt . . . outclassed.'

John is burly, with an impressively established beard for an eighteen-year-old. He was quiet in the group discussion, but then opens up one-on-one. He's very clear on the function of school – he used to love Physics, but didn't get a good enough grade at GCSE, so he switched to Business and Management. I ask him if he'd rather follow his passion but have no career out of it, or compromise like he has and get a good job.

'Compromise,' he says instantly.

Of those in the group, he is far the most focused on the idea of a job as the endpoint of school. The others have a lot of ideas – often pretty sophisticated – about how school works, but seem far less focused on the transactional nature of education. It is the same when I talked to younger students: a striking lack of the standard answer 'to get a good job'.

They combine this with a strong sense of social justice. 'I think it's as simple as if something's not fair, it's not right and it should be changed.' And yet the presence of privilege, and the way it distorts, persists. In the words of Poppy, 'I know I come from a middle-class background – I'm aware of it, but I don't know if everyone is.'

Interestingly, one of the other sixth formers I speak to on her own, Angie, has a very clear sense of herself as disadvantaged – as the child of a single mother, not from the immediate area – and sees herself in sharp contrast to her peers. You wouldn't necessarily pick this up from speaking to her. She even refers to this, saying that she 'speaks differently' since she came to the school in Year 7. There is an unmistakeable hint of anger, a resentment of the privilege around her. And yet like Keiran her mother is a teacher, which would in itself suggest that Angie benefits from typically middle-class advantages.

Is it relative? I ask. Is your sense of disadvantage a product of how privileged those around you are? The conversation has become awkward. But, to her credit, she thinks carefully and says, 'Yes, I guess so.'

There is one more twist to the landscape of privilege in schools – even aside from the deprivation of your postcode or your family, there is the simple luck of the draw in being one of those poor families who nevertheless have access to a good school and, within that, the luck of finding the teacher who speaks to your experience. We don't normally think of privilege like this, but it can be as profound an advantage as how much money you are born with, or how little dysfunction you find in your family environment. In some ways it's all simply another roll of the dice – and, like much of what we see in education, there is a bewildering unfairness about who gets what.

But just because the landscape of privilege is so fractured and complex, that doesn't mean we should throw up our hands and ignore the basic structural inequalities that underlie it. And while there is much to commend educators in all sectors, a conversation that I had with the Head of an independent school at a conference has stuck with me. For all of the positives I took from those I met in the private sector, I was left with an abiding sense of the hypocrisy behind any defence of the charitable status of fee-paying schools. We were discussing the ways in which charitable status worked. We talked about all the impressive things his school did – including running a Multi-Academy Trust of state schools in the area. Like many others in the independent sector, this Head was clear that removing its charitable status would simply raise fees and render the school more exclusive.

But then we started to discuss the 'opportunities' presented by overseas schools branded with the corporate identities of the English public-school system. It's a big thing, this – dozens of private schools do it, setting up overseas branches that operate 'independently' and, crucially, not bound by any regulation to be non-profit-making. That profit-making body then makes regular 'donations' back to the schools – or should I say charities? – that give them their names and reputations.[3] 'Donations' of several million pounds a year.

As I talked to someone who was clearly profoundly moral and dedicated to education, I couldn't escape the sense that living within the system had made him blind to the ways in which it is, on a basic level, wrong. If private schools are charities, they need to start behaving like charities, which means genuinely *designing* their existence around a charitable aim – not simply retrofitting charitable add-ons while leveraging reputation for profit.[4]

But we also need to acknowledge that all of this is not just about grades. While private schools do appear to get their students better results and into better universities,[5] as we've already seen there is evidence to suggest that their students make less progress once they get to those universities.[6] Private school doesn't simply make you cleverer or even necessarily better qualified in the long run.

I don't know that this would change the calculation for many parents, though. Because, alongside the baldly divisive desire of parents like Jackson to keep their children 'safe' from malign state-school environments, elements of private education can be surprisingly soft-edged in their framing. The counter-intuitive truth about private schools is that many of them sell themselves not only on the core business of getting students good grades, but on their nurturing pastoral atmosphere and the wider opportunities they open up, and on the cultivation of rounded, responsible adults. Whether or not they achieve this, there's no doubt that wealthy parents choose private-school education for their children for reasons that often go beyond academic achievement.

Paying for an education is in obvious ways a more transactional approach to school, but look beneath the surface and it is the free state-school education that is structured in a far more nakedly utilitarian fashion.

11. Personal development

No matter how transactional the structures of education are, or how utilitarian the language we use to describe it, the reality is that much of a teacher's daily life is occupied by the dozens or hundreds of interactions with young people that are not to do with teaching in any formal sense. Instead they are to do with guiding and supporting them, modelling desirable behaviour or offering advice as they face the myriad dilemmas of being young.

When you talk to teachers, these are the moments they value. They talk about the quiet conversation, the moment a student opened up. The resolution after two friends have fallen out. The support given, in the face of loss. Even in the most content-heavy times at school, in the midst of the most intense exam preparation, there are still moments when students seek more than just knowledge, when they need reassurance, and direction, and motivation. Because the process of growing up is not simply about learning *things*, and adding *capacity*, as if bolting them on to a pre-existing personality. It is a process of fundamental change and development.

For me, this is why the study of literature can be so profound. When we read, we see characters defining themselves and being defined by a narrative. We see selves coming into being as a story unfolds, finding themselves in key events. This enables us to see more clearly and think about our own stories, and how we are defined by narratives, too. Life might be more complicated than in storybooks, but we still try to fit it into the shapes we know from them – telling stories about ourselves of success or failure, of self-definition or sacrifice. The stories we read, and borrow from, give us a pattern that can make sense of the incomprehensible complexity of our own lives. They give us something we never find anywhere else: a beginning and an end, and a path from one to the other. It doesn't matter how simplified they are. A map works not by showing everything, but by highlighting the most significant and unchanging landmarks – and stories are a map to regions of the human heart that are otherwise unnavigable.

Teaching is, in a very real sense, storytelling. The most profound hinge of any story is anagnorisis – Aristotle's term for the moment of transformative realisation – and there is a rare and transcendent wonder that you can sometimes feel, as an English teacher, when you guide a class through a moment like that and you sense their realisation alongside that of the character. In those moments you know that at least some of them – perhaps only one of them – have fundamentally changed in front of your eyes.

Forgive me; I know that was a bit gushing. But teaching gives you a ringside seat at the drama of the creation of self. Sometimes only gushing will do. You meet them as children, and they become adults – you meet them as malleable, and they become fixed. The author Philip Pullman came up with the most elegant metaphor I've encountered for the process of growing up. In *Northern Lights* and its sequels, he describes a world in which every person has a daemon, a spiritual sibling in animal form. For children these constantly change shape, only to settle into one form on entering adulthood. I don't think it's a coincidence that Pullman was a teacher.

This process of helping students to begin to know who they are and what they believe to be right is a continuous and all-pervasive aspect of a teacher's work. But at moments it is also formalised: in Personal Development lessons, in assemblies, in the need for SMSC (Social, Moral, Spiritual and Cultural education) to be present in lessons, and in the ways schools describe their ethos. There is an entitlement to this in the National Curriculum, and a whole separate grade for it from Ofsted, as well as an explicit list of 'British values' that schools are required to promote – listed as Democracy, the Rule of Law, Respect and Tolerance, and Individual Liberty. The tricky thing is knowing when you've succeeded.

To check someone's maths skills, you give them a Maths test. But what test can you give someone to check their values? Drop a tenner in the yard and see if they hand it in? This wouldn't necessarily be a problem if it weren't the case that every other subject is built around assessment and grades. The fact that Personal Development is not can give the impression it is an afterthought – a chance to doze off in class. And yet, if it's done well, this part of schooling can be genuinely valuable and important. If students are given a forum where things that matter to them are raised, and are given the language they need to discuss them, they can begin to formulate their own sense of identity and morality. Lessons can knit to form a consistent set of tools with which to interpret the moral world. And assemblies can bring those values into visible life.

A word about assemblies. They can be dry and turgid explanations of why you should work hard, or cockeyed explanations of how you bloody well should have a growth mindset. But when they are done well, they offer a collective experience that can be genuinely transformative. The collective aspect of them is key – 200 or 300 kids in a room together, silently listening, creates a quasi-religious atmosphere, which is exactly their intent: schools have a requirement to carry out collective worship, and in most non-religious schools this is done through values-based assemblies.

Designing an assembly is not like planning a lesson. It has more in common with political campaigning. It is all about the short, direct metaphor and a consistent, repeated message – the best way to embed something deeply. When I was head of sixth form, I repeated again and again the metaphor of education as an apple tree: that exams were the fruit and were good to have, but they would only be produced by looking after the whole tree. I must have used the same set of images – a series of comic pictures of weird-looking apples and then of a hippy hugging a tree – twenty or thirty times. It became a joke amongst staff, and amongst students. And then in one of those moments in teaching that if it happened in a film you'd scoff at it, when they left the school the kids bought and planted an apple tree outside it with a label saying 'Sammy's apple tree'. We stood around and they laughed at my obsession, even as they also told me how much that simple message meant. I still pass the tree on my way in, and I think about what it means that if you want kids to believe in your values, you'd better say them again and again and again.

But for all the impact that Personal Development lessons and assemblies can have, they are far from being a panacea. In recent years mental health has become something of a buzzword and thus the subject of many assemblies and Personal Development lessons. This is, I'm sure, better than not addressing the subject in these forums (although it is surely no substitute for having a humane social structure, comprehensive family support and a functioning Health Service). But there can be a tick-box quality – whereby we 'raise awareness' of a problem and think that's the same as solving it. Where so long as something is 'in the curriculum', it is being purposefully addressed. And where we close our eyes to the difference between what is said and how it is received. I remember one assembly given by a colleague about the ideas expressed in Professor Steve Peters' book *The Chimp Paradox* – a thoughtful, impassioned and valuable fifteen minutes of advice on how to manage your emotional reaction to events. The kid I spoke to afterwards told me it was all about how the teacher had 'a monkey in her heid'.

What's worse, sometimes we draw attention to questions of ethics and morality in exactly the wrong way: if we speak without credibility, or with obvious hypocrisy, the message received can be the reverse of what we intend. High-flown ideals are worse than useless if the pupils' day-to-day interactions with staff do not match the values expressed. If you are told to 'be kind', by people who are not, it simply seems like a con trick.

It is those moments, those personal touches – as simple as a smile and a 'good morning', or as complex as mentoring a student through a long-term family crisis – that really count. When you're an adolescent busily working out who you are, it's all too easy for negative narratives to take hold: narratives that say you are worthless, that you are failing, that you are unlovable. But if somewhere you can find who you are reflected back at you with considered, careful, unconditional positive regard – with the kind of care that a trusted adult, unconnected with the dramas of your family and friends, can provide – then a better story can be told.

For some students, the process of self-realisation and becoming is more challenging than for others. And for teachers there are increasing dangers as one negotiates the fraught public debates around 'identity'. Whether through gender, race, sexuality or disability, there are many ways in which our school system (designed, as it is, to function at scale) struggles to accommodate the individual identities of students. And yet there are also ways in which teachers – operating on a simple moral calculus of doing right by the child in front of you – can point the way forward for the rest of society.

Jenna is in Year 10 at a school in Cheshire. She wears her own clothes today – the school is having a non-uniform day. Amongst other things, we talk about her twin sister, who has obsessive-compulsive disorder.

'She is two minutes older. She is *incredibly* smart,' says Jenna. She smiles self-deprecatingly as she returns to talking about herself. 'I'm not the smartest in the family.'

Are you identical? I ask.

'No.' She hesitates. 'I was born a boy. I'm trans actually.' She says this with total self-confidence. Her hesitation isn't nervousness – throughout, she gives the impression of someone perfectly poised, unsurprised by anything. Rather, she seems almost sorry for me not knowing.

When I started teaching, no children at my school were out as trans. In fact no children that I was aware of were out as gay. Now I expect some kids to be publicly in same-sex relationships by the age of sixteen, as a matter of course. Meanwhile trans identity has become a flashpoint for the latest iteration of the culture wars and, in many people's view, a tricky issue for schools. In August 2022 Suella Braverman, then Attorney-General, made it clear that in her view schools – and pupils – should not feel any pressure to use children's preferred pronouns[1] or to let them change to a differently gendered name, and should not teach that people can 'change' gender. At the same time, the Cass Review into concerns about the approach and procedures of the pioneering Gender Identity Development Service at the Tavistock Clinic in London precipitated a rolling scandal around the provision of hormone therapy to trans teenagers,[2] and the Scottish government passed (and was then blocked from implementing) the Gender Recognition Act, designed to make it easier for people from sixteen upwards to acquire a Gender Recognition Certificate. And as I write, the DfE has published the long-deferred official government guidance for schools on 'gender-questioning children', authored by Education Secretary Gillian Keegan and then Minister for Equalities Kemi Badenoch[3] – guidance that is highly contested, not least because it is explicitly based on the premise that being trans is an 'ideology' and a 'belief'.[4]

How long have you been living as a girl? I ask Jenna.

'Since Year Five' – which is when pupils are nine to ten years old.

Is it something that's accepted at school?

Another hesitation, this time with more behind it. 'Yeah,' she says. 'By teachers, yes, perfectly fine. Some people are a bit transphobic, but my friends – no, perfectly fine.'

If you've been living as a girl for so long, since Year Five, presumably the other students just know you as a girl?

'No. They knew me as a boy. I came out in Year Nine' – which is when children are thirteen to fourteen years old.

How was that process for you?

'Easy. A bit scary. I walked into a classroom one day wearing a skirt – and I'd always worn pants [I presume she means trousers] and everyone looked at us – and I may have heard someone call us a tranny. But overall, it was quite accepting.'

I'd describe Jenna as exceptionally self-possessed. The phrase seems more accurate than for most: her self is something she has taken full possession of, a mantle she has consciously adopted.

Other kids that I talk to in the process of transition are less so. My conversation with Peter back up in Carlisle feels very different from the one with Jenna. He moves as he speaks, shifting restlessly. His eyes move too, and while his words are verbose and confident, he often jokes at his own expense and laughs at things that seem serious to me. Our conversation has a lot of laughter – it's like speaking to a stand-up – but I end it with a sense that this is someone who has not found school a happy place. Not that Peter says so.

When I ask him about social status in school, he says, 'I drift around at the bottom – but I'm having the time of my life, man!' He speaks with an Americanised inflection, though he is not American. 'I'm allowed to have fun – they aren't!' We laugh, and he adds, 'There isn't even a way for me to climb up there, because none of them like me.'

Do you ever get any sense of threat?

'Well, yeah, I've been bullied before, obviously. I mean, I kind of do look like a massive target to them sometimes – I'm a very bully-able person.'

What makes you bully-able?

'The fact that I'm a massive dork! I mean, I cannot hold a conversation sometimes. Also the fact that in Year Seven I was an utter cry-baby. I still kinda am, but not as bad. I remember in Year Seven I was basically tret like a little chihuahua – like sometimes they'd drag me around, and if they didn't want to hear me they'd shove me in things: like when a girl has a little chihuahua in a bag, only I wasn't the girl, I was the chihuahua.'

Did you ever feel there was anything to do with race? Peter is dark-skinned.

'No, not really. Actually I did get called the N-word. Nine times, by one kid. He sucks.'

Do you think the school is more accepting in terms of race or LGBT?

'With race it's more "Hey, don't be racist or you're getting a consequence." With homophobia they kind of acknowledge it – they sometimes do education on it – but I kind of feel I'm getting talked down to. Like, for example, I remember my form tutor did a presentation on bisexuality. Which is something I'm very familiar with; so is my best friend. We kind of gave each other a little look throughout it, going, "Is this about us?" And it kind of just felt like she herself did not know much about it, so even then it felt like a very surface-level presentation.'

We talk about being trans. What Peter describes – misgendering, teasing comments – feels like a continuum of the bullying he experienced when younger. This is one of the things that seems missing from the comments by Braverman: an awareness of the fact that any difference is weaponised in the intense world of being a teenager, and that children who are struggling with their identity may already be highly vulnerable – making hard-and-fast rules on how to respond highly problematic. Peter's reaction to the ways people pick on him is defiant, though, even if that defiance makes me worry for what it hides. 'Why would I care about someone I don't even like?' he says.

I cannot decide about Peter. His presentation is so relentlessly upbeat, it's hard not to be persuaded that he is simply a happy-go-lucky fifteen-year-old, and yet his experience of school and the abuse he has met would seem, in many ways, to have been traumatic. I ask about the role of school in supporting his transition. And suddenly he says something direct. 'School gives me a place where I actually have a small chance of being called my name.'

As we talk, he opens up about how difficult he finds it with his parents, who don't accept his identification as a boy. I listen, and later I will talk to the safeguarding officer at the school, just to be certain they are aware. They are – and as we talk, we come to no firm conclusion about how best to move forward.

Because that's the messy reality: schools are the front line in this increasingly contentious debate – and it can sometimes feel like we are being given instructions by generals so far from the action that they have no concept of the human cost of their strategies. But this is a fundamental part of the true function of schools, and the skill of those working in them is to respond to the nuances of adolescence with humanity and professionalism, finding the way forward that suits the child in front of you.

One of the common phrases used by conservative educationalists is 'Keep politics out of schools.' But the attempt to screen off what is perceived as 'political' has an unpleasant history. In the eighties and nineties, teachers were subject to Section 28 – a law against the 'promotion' of homosexuality. Disturbingly, there are similar laws making it onto the statute books of certain states in America as I write: for example, the state of Florida has banned the teaching of African-American studies on the grounds that it promotes a narrative of white guilt. And there is an increasing visibility in Britain of a demand that the curriculum ought to be defended from 'woke' ideas about the history of race and gender. What all these movements have in common is an assumption that what they are keeping out is 'political' while what they are leaving in is not. The absurdity of this is hard to avoid: a quick glance at the basics of the SMSC curriculum, and the prescribed British values, shows a list that is quite literally political itself, resting on concepts like democracy and the rule of law.

And it is quite right that politics is part of SMSC.[5] How could it not be? Political choices, in the best sense, are guided by moral considerations. In practice what this means is that teaching respect for the rule of law *demands* that we teach respect for equality legislation that enshrines 'Gender Reassignment' as a protected characteristic.

The real question, then, is not *whether* schools ought to teach certain subjects, it's *how* they teach them. And this is what the public discourse ignores. Many of the attacks on social and moral topics in education focus on straw men – absurd, extreme positions used to discredit far more nuanced ideas. One can teach the history of slavery in the British Empire without telling a specific child that it is their personal fault. One can teach pupils that individuals have the right to assert their own gender identity without telling a child that they can just choose if they are a boy or a girl. These wilful distortions – blunt statements that, if they did appear in a lesson in the form they are reported, would be basic professional incompetence – are weaponised to stir up a backlash and steer us towards normative positions from a generation ago.

But just because the arguments are often made in such bad faith doesn't mean we can ignore the challenge they lay down. Whatever we teach, the way we teach it will imply certain moral values. We are not, and can never be, in the business of neutrally programming minds with objective facts. Whether we like it or not, we inculcate the values of the wider society in the next generation. Those values may be disparate, confused, contradictory, contested, but even so the challenge and the duty of a school are to replicate them – not by flattening their complexity, or ironing out ambiguity, but by presenting them with moral clarity.

It's not easy, but consider for a moment what happens if we duck that challenge. If schools keep the 'politics' out of it, if they stick to 'neutral' facts without making moral judgements, then the moral judgements are going to come from somewhere else. They will come from families, each in a very different space and under different pressures. They will come from the media, with its increased fragmentation. And they'll come from social media, with its divisive algorithms and curated bubbles. Without a central, normative forum that can bring together and discuss what is *right* and what is *true* – and without the moderation of a skilled teacher who understands the complexity of those terms and can challenge simplistic narratives – quite simply, in the words of W. B. Yeats, *things fall apart*.

And yet there are limits. One of the patterns of recent years is that whenever something difficult or complex crops up in public discourse, there are cries for it to become 'part of the curriculum', as if that is a magic bullet. Schools are made to carry the can, then blamed for not carrying it well enough. The gender debate throws the problems of this tendency into sharp relief – when we, as a society, are not sure what we think, then we cannot expect schools to fix it with a ten-minute discussion in registration.

12. Bad kids

In my career as a teacher I have been called a fat cunt, a stupid cunt, a beardy cunt and a black cunt (I am white). Also a faggot, a prick, an idiot and a fucking idiot. At other points a divvy, a wally, a beanbag and (weirdly) 'Homo sapiens'. I've had a door slammed on me, kids push me out of the way, balls thrown at me, snowballs thrown at me, pencils thrown at me and food thrown at me.

I've seen kids fight, threaten, punch through windows. I've seen them sobbing with rage and fury because they've been asked to sit down. I've seen their social-media accounts, a tickertape of obscenity. I've seen them climb the fence and leg it, and then at other times I've seen them try to break into school. I've seen them steal items from the restaurant, from classrooms and from each other.

I've had to explain to one parent that their child was in trouble because he'd been sharing a picture of a man having sex with a chicken. I've had to break into the police liaison office to release two kids who trapped themselves inside. I've suspended a lot of kids, and I've been part of the decision to permanently exclude a few.

None of this is pleasant, but all of it is par for the course and you get used to it (just about). But if there is one thing that might make me give up teaching, it is the conversations with kids where they simply say 'no'.

'You need to do your detention.'

'I'm not doing it.'

'You need to.'

'No.'

'You'll end up in isolation.'

'I won't go.'

'I'll have to exclude you.'

'I don't care.'

Then you call the parents.

'She'll need to do the detention.'

'I can't make her.'

'She needs to do it.'

'You'll not exclude her for that. It's only a detention.'

'But she needs to do it.'

'Well, she's not.'

At this point I clench my hands silently and pray for patience.

Dealing with difficult behaviour is the single most problematic task in schools. It is the thing that breaks teachers, and that breaks students. You cannot teach effectively with poor behaviour, nor can you learn. And for all the sympathy I have with the variety of viewpoints and approaches to managing behaviour in schools, there is a hard truth: a school is nothing if the kids do not feel safe. And yet the tools one has in managing behaviour are surprisingly flimsy.

In my current school there are 1,500 students and 120-odd staff. If all the students decided to do something, we couldn't stop them. If half the students decided to do something, we couldn't stop them. To be honest, if fifty students decided to do something, we couldn't stop them. When three students decide to wander around the site, as happens very occasionally, one key strategy is that you do not chase them. Because once you start to chase them, it's a game, and they are faster. Even if you catch them, the damage is already done. Your time is already wasted, the other students have already seen it, the classes are already distracted. The only real way to manage bad behaviour is to stop it happening in the first place.

How one achieves that, though, is the subject of much debate, not dissimilar to the one between 'progressive' and 'traditional' ways of building the curriculum. The latter, epitomised by the way Michaela is run and championed by Tom Bennett[1] – the government's so-called Behaviour Tsar, which as a concept is oddly appropriate – is that a school is an unavoidably authoritarian set-up and we should lean into this. Adults are adults, and they know best. What's more, the way to secure a safe and productive environment is by having clear, consistent and prescriptive rules, in the more extreme cases ranging to every aspect of how kids should conduct themselves.

There is of course a difference between the way a rule is phrased and how it is actually policed, which leaves plenty of room for it to be reported luridly in the press, usually as a 'zero-tolerance' approach[2] in which teachers are channelling *RoboCop*. Recent rules that I've seen in outraged articles include:

- Silent corridors
- Smiling at all times
- Sitting up and looking at the teacher during lessons
- Walking using a 'university walk' – hands one in the other, held behind the back
- Having the correct branded socks
- Using the word 'Miss' or 'sir' at the end of every sentence.

Enforcing this approach usually means a set of escalating sanctions, starting with detention, then involving isolation rooms and ending up with exclusion.

The alternative approach is often characterised as a philosophy that 'all behaviour is communication'. In this paradigm, the key to resolving a behavioural issue is to understand the way it expresses the 'unmet needs' of the student: that Bobby is marauding round the school, kicking doors, because he has been rejected by his father. You need to dig down to root causes and solve *them*. Again, this can be misrepresented horribly – often by people who take the other approach – as providing no boundaries and no safety for students or staff.

One guru of this method is Paul Dix,[3] whose book has the unfortunate title *When the Adults Change, Everything Changes* – which is true, but also freighted with an unhelpful suggestion that it is therefore the adults' *fault* if everything doesn't change. The caricature of this is one of a woolly touchy-feely approach, exemplified by the idea of restorative justice, which involves getting the misbehaving child to face the person they have wronged and engage in a process that resolves it. If you search Twitter/X, you'll find plenty of teachers complaining that instead of being punished, some miscreant was merely asked to say sorry and then let off.

I have been a pastoral deputy, the person ultimately responsible for pupils' behaviour, and I have tried a bit of both. As ever, the truth about what works and what doesn't is not clear-cut. 'Zero-tolerance' rules can work, but only when they are applied with kindness and consistency. There is a world of difference between screaming at someone, 'Silence in the corridor!' while glaring furiously, and calmly reiterating with a smile that we should be quiet and respectful as we walk. And if someone struggles to comply, it would probably be best to consider why and then talk it through with them – almost as if acknowledging that 'behaviour is communication'. Equally, if you actually *read* Paul Dix's book, you will see that he presents five 'pillars' to his approach – and these include 'relentless routines' and 'calm, consistent adult behaviour'. Almost like he's saying you *do* need clear rules, and you *do* need to hold pupils to them.

What both approaches agree on, though, is the way in which 'behaviour management' is not an addendum to the academic – the process of guiding and socialising students, day in, day out, is a core part of the moral education that schools provide, both in facing out towards society and building responsible and law-abiding citizens, and in facing inwards by providing individuals with the self-knowledge and self-control that keep them from harm.

But let's leave the theory to one side for a moment and look at the question from a different angle. Let's meet some of these 'bad kids'.

The Blue Sky School is hard to find. It's somewhere north of Ashington, on the edge of an estate, at the back of a leisure centre. I drive past several times. Eventually I find a small door in a blank wall labelled 'pupil entrance'. But it's locked and I can't see how to get in, so I walk round to the leisure centre and find the reception to Blue Sky tucked behind a fitness studio.

Harry is the first pupil I meet. We talk in a small room next to the Head's office. Harry is black-haired, in Year 10, with a cautious smile and what your nanna might call 'a twinkle in his eye'. He looks cheeky, but not malicious. Blue Sky is an Alternative Provision (AP), a school that takes children who have been excluded from mainstream, either temporarily or permanently. Harry's here on respite, although currently he's attempting to reintegrate back into his mainstream school. This means three days at Blue Sky, two at his school.

I ask how he feels about school.

'Fine. It's nice here, because it's smaller classrooms and it's easier. When I was at Kirby Duncan, it was bigger classrooms and it was all rushed, cos the corridors were packed full, so even though I had loads of mates there, I was still pretty anxious. And then when you were in class – I'm not saying Kirby Duncan is bad, but . . . it's, like, very rushed. Like in and out. Like they don't have time just to be messing about. Whereas here, you get taught more. You have time. So when I come here I don't get so anxious.'

How long have you been out of mainstream?

'About a year.'

And why was it that you came to Blue Sky? Why did your time at Kirby Duncan break down?

'I never went. I wasn't as naughty as some kids there, but I just didn't follow the instructions. So they brought me here.'

We talk a bit about social media. Harry wishes we could turn all phones off. He says he likes a kickabout, and he likes walking about, listening to music. He has the kind of neat, old-fashioned hair that I often see in the North-East, with gel and side-parting. He wouldn't look out of place in my grandfather's generation. He even says he likes 'old music' – although, depressingly, that seems to mean Oasis. He tells me about his family and they sound lovely, supportive and motivated. He likes reading books on archaeology.

Are you clever? I ask.

'I don't know,' he says, but he smiles. His voice is warm and low.

We dig into what happened with him at school.

'In primary school I was quiet, I'd just sit there. I had all my friend-group, but I'd just sit back and do me work. But when I got into Year Seven – I think it's cos you go through hormones and all that – I became rebellious.'

Spell it out, I say. What do you mean, 'rebellious'?

'Walking off.'

And was there a trigger?

'The first time I walked out was in Maths in Year Seven. It sounds stupid, but I needed the toilet and I was desperate and I was putting me hand up. Then there was a group of girls who all went at the same time. They're not going to all be needing it – they're going to be going and talking, and that. She lets four girls go, and I'm like: this isn't fair. They're going to go and probably vape and sit down and chat, like most girls in that school do. So I just said, "I'm walking out."'

So did you get an exclusion?

'Yeah.'

How did it feel getting the punishment?

'I didn't care.'

Why not?

'I don't think most people in that school cared.'

But surely the whole point of a punishment is that you should care about it? I suggest.

'But they're too soft. They're like "Oh, you can go home." It's just . . .'

What should they have done?

Harry smiles. 'What do *you* think they should have done?'

I tell him they should have been fair about who went to the toilet.

I find Harry charming. He has a gentleness of manner and a real spark underneath. And his experience tells us so much about how disruptive behaviour can start, and escalate, in school. One aspect to managing pupils' behaviour that's really simple, and pretty universally agreed on, is that they need consistency. If the story is as Harry says it is, then he's not wrong to feel hard done by – and for a Year 7 pupil there are few things more terrifying than the thought of potentially pissing yourself in class.

But what's revealing is how little the sanction he was given seems to mean to him. It points to one of the most basic challenges of keeping discipline in schools, which is that the punishments available to the school can very quickly lose their power. And if the worst punishment of all – the threat of which underpins the others – is suspension, then you face a basic problem: suspension is not a punishment for many pupils. If they don't want to be in school, it gives them what they want.

The way around this is not to think in terms of 'punishment' at all. The aim of a sanction is ultimately the same as the aim of a reward:

to motivate and to teach. All that matters is whether it works; if a sanction has no effect, it is useless. And for it to work, the students need above all to see the point of it, which means understanding the legitimacy of school rules in the first place.

Getting them to see the point means being honest. I tell my students explicitly that there are some rules that are functional, and some that are moral. Rules on uniform, for example, exist not because you are a bad person if your tie is squint, but because having a uniform and policing it helps the smooth running of the school. Whereas rules on not breaking people's noses are fundamental moral principles.

Those functional rules might seem petty, but they can be really important for behaviour management. This is where my honesty reaches its limit. What we tell the students is that we have uniform because it's fairer (true) and smarter (true), and once you have decided to have it, you need to keep it consistent (also true). What I don't say is that, as a natural slob, policing the uniform is my least favourite job – but I do it, because experience genuinely tells me that enforcing that uniformity and collective identity pays dividends in stopping more significant behavioural issues. It also aids individual teacher control. If you can be sure that the whole school is consistently telling kids to tuck their shirts in, then it is easier for you to tell a difficult pupil to tuck his shirt in – and once he has done so, then he is more inclined to follow your next instruction, too. These little things become a test ground, a way of building the habit of compliance, which then supports the way you deal with the bigger things.

I'm aware, as I write this, that this technique – enforcing compliance in relation to minor rules in order to create a climate of general obedience – is one also deployed by the secret police in your average repressive state. But the truth is that behaviour management in schools is fundamentally illiberal. You target dissidents – don't allow them air time, move them into situations where they are isolated. If you're anything like me, when faced with a plot, you separate the instigators and offer them deals if they cooperate, and say, for instance, 'Of course we could check the CCTV . . . but it would be much better for you if you told me now.' And, ultimately, you may get to the point where you think that for the benefit of the majority you need to make the difficult cases disappear.

To be clear: that is not, and never has been, my *real* attitude to any of the children in my care. I will work tirelessly – to a fault – to keep kids onside, to understand and accommodate them. But teaching is performance as well. I challenge anyone who has been a pastoral deputy to deny that they have ever said something along the lines of 'Other students decided the rules didn't apply to them. And they are *no longer at this school.*' So there is a delicate balance to be struck: kids need to understand the legitimacy of rules, but also that those rules are not open for negotiation, and that ultimately they are answerable for whether or not they follow them.

In the end, though, all sanctions in a school environment ultimately rest on the threat of isolation or exclusion – and in some cases that can be a problem.

Harry and I have returned to talking about his anxiety, which is brought about, he says again, because 'It's a bit crowded, at school.'

Why did that have such an impact on you? I ask.

'Because I was away for a long time, and I reckon if you don't do something for a long time, and if you go back into it, it can be nervous, can't it?'

Were you away because of lockdown?

'No, I just never went in.' Harry explains that he had been put in the Bridge, an internal suspension room, as a punishment. 'And I was, like, I'm not sitting in the Bridge. You sit in this room. I went in there once, and no one gives you any work, and I sat all day reading this book, and I was, like, I'm not going in there again. I had a week to do, but I just didn't complete me days.' And so he simply stopped going into school altogether.

He tells me that around this time there was some upheaval at home. His mother was ill with cancer, and his stepfather had moved out. The Head of the school later tells me that when Harry arrived at Blue Sky, he had to be lifted bodily out of the car by his uncle.

What were you doing when you were off?

'I just sat in my room and deteriorated. I didn't care. I don't know why I did it – I look back and it just seems stupid.'

I think of our 'Bridge' – a room we call 'RESET'. Kids are taken out of lessons when they are disruptive and spend an hour or two there. Sometimes they are there all day. They hate it. But we do it rather than external exclusion for two reasons. First, because we can guarantee they do some work. And second, well, because they hate it.

The problem – and this is the most difficult thing about schools – is that no matter what you do, kids *learn*. The only question is *what* they learn. If you put them in the Bridge, they don't stop learning. They merely learn something different, shaped by that experience. For Harry, a combination of a badly managed classroom at school, a school culture that seemed to excuse his behaviour, and a home life that was (albeit temporarily) lacking in attention and support taught him that school was not fair, that punishment was soul-destroying, but that both could be avoided by simply not turning up.

Blue Sky is hopeful about Harry's prospects, though. He seems a winnable case – someone in whom what has gone wrong is identifiable, and an effort can be made to rectify it. But for Joey, the disengagement with school seems to run much deeper. When I ask Joey my opening question – What did you feel about school when you got up this morning? – he replies in a low, slow drawl.

'I dunno – I just thought it was going to be like every other day, really.'

He slouches back in his seat. He's small, blond, with a blunt, childish face and half-closed eyes. He looks stoned. Like Harry, he's supposed to be reintegrating back into mainstream. I ask if he knows what this means.

'I don't really know, to be honest.' And when I ask why he was put on this programme, Joey says, 'Behaviour, really.'

I wait. Was there a particular incident? I ask eventually.

'No, like behaviour built up.'

I try a few approaches to get him to say the kind of things he might have done. Joey pauses for so long that he forgets the question. Eventually I ask it differently. In a lesson, would you normally get the work done?

'Sometimes. I wasn't really bothered, like. They'd just try and say loads of things, and I'd be like, "I don't really care." I was a very refusing kind of person. If I didn't want to do something, I just wouldn't.'

Sounds like you couldn't see the point.

'No, I could. I'm just laid-back, like.'

The next few minutes are like getting blood out of the proverbial stone. Not because Joey is unwilling, but he seems barely to remember where he is. He tells me his mum was a bus driver, but she no longer works. I ask what his mum thinks of his behaviour.

'She likes me a lot better here. I'm better-behaved here. In the other school, every day I'd have done something wrong.'

As he talks, his words are halting, but he's more awake now.

'It's a lot harder to be naughty here. I see worse behaviour in mainstream than here.' He's talking more quickly. 'Most people don't try and be naughty, but in mainstream there are certain things that just make you react, but here it never normally happens.'

What kind of things make you react?

'Like when the teachers are being cocky with you. That's just like a-asking for a reaction, really.'

As Joey says this, for the first time I can see that he has a stammer beneath his hesitations. It breaks the slow surface of his speech and I imagine him in school, losing his temper, storming off.

'Being cocky is like them knowing you have to do what they say, and just like abusing being a teacher. Here it doesn't really happen.'

But what if I was to say teachers do have power?

'Yeah, but if you act like that, with most people it just won't work.'

But is that right? I point out to Joey that with the number of kids in a school, if a teacher can't tell you what to do, it can get quite unsafe.

He shrugs.

We talk more. It's hard transcribing what Joey says, because there are so many pauses and repetitions. His hands rest on the table, surprisingly thick and calloused for a fifteen-year-old. He tells me he likes hard work. He likes working with his hands. He'd rather do that than anything he does at school.

'Teachers in mainstream – it sounds weird – but they'll just try and make you kick off, and I'll always do it. I'll just treat them how they're treating me, and then I'll be in the wrong for it. They've got more power than me.'

What's amazing about this conversation is how simple it is. Everything that Joey has described is about power and authority – who holds it, and how they wield it. It reminds me of some of the observations in *Schooling the Smash Street Kids*, a sociological account of kids in Sunderland in the seventies. The author, Paul Corrigan, embedded himself in two secondaries. He expected to see some kind of reaction against the *values* of school from the naughty kids – some sense that this was a world they didn't buy into. Instead he noted that the kids took no issue with the way the school operated, apart from the simple fact that it had power over them at all. In fact they didn't even take issue with that; they accepted it as the natural order. But by that same natural order, they saw it as their role to push back. Not for a *reason* – just because . . .

It reminds me of *Mad Max* or other post-apocalyptic stories, where the original use of things – the purpose of school and of teaching, the rationale behind teacher authority – has been lost or forgotten and all that remains is the basic game of status and conflict. Talking to kids like Joey is a window into a world so restricted that it operates by different rules.

In reading about other countries,[4] particularly the East Asian countries that score so highly on PISA tests (the international system for comparing educational outcomes), I often come across comments about how children feel pressure from their families to succeed, and how parents – mothers – feel pressure to support school, to help with homework, to encourage extracurricular studies. Amy Chua, in her book *Battle Hymn of the Tiger Mother*, talks about how this is a form of love: the love that says you need to build the habits and routines of hard work and the pursuit of excellence, even if it seems at the expense of short term pleasure, because long-term happiness is only built on the feeling of mastery. This is often explicitly set against a 'Western' mindset that is flabbily focused on the 'choices' and 'autonomy' of children – when the reality is that children are not autonomous, and compliance and hard work are essential for growth.

I can't comment on how prevalent this stereotypical mindset actually *is* in East Asian cultures, but there's no doubt that in England we have a huge diversity of cultural attitudes to school and to study, and amongst the kids I've taught there have been plenty who were 'tiger-mothered' – East Asian or not. But what we certainly do have in England is a deep class divide, and on either side of it education and school are seen very differently.

Lynsey Hanley talks about this in her memoir, *Respectable: Crossing the Class Divide*. She explores the ways in which there is a real distinction between 'working-class' attitudes to childhood and 'middle-class' ones.[5] To generalise wildly, the middle-class attitude is that education is central to childhood, and that childhood is a process of 'optimisation'. This can happen in many ways – developing a reading habit, having 'a sport', getting good grades or simply nurturing healthy attitudes – but, fundamentally, childhood is seen as a process with adulthood at the end, and the function of much of what we do for our children is about developing them as adults. The 'working-class' attitude – to generalise even more wildly – is that adult life is hard, so when you're a kid you'd better enjoy it.

We could label these two perspectives differently. Differentiating between them as a matter of class is fairly useless in identifying who actually has these attitudes – because, apart from anything else, far more people identify as working class than actually fit the common definition of 'employed in unskilled or semi-skilled manual or industrial work'.[6] Even so it's useful because it helps to explain one of the key points of friction between students and school, when it comes to behaviour.

If you grew up in a town like Sunderland, before the era of industrial decline, when being working class meant very simply that you would go on to a job in the shipyards or in the mines, then those 'working-class' kids would have gone to school in the knowledge that it wouldn't fundamentally change anything about the opportunities or career they might have as adults. The jobs they could get would not ask for grades or degrees. And while social mobility was of course possible, even desirable for some, it came with extra baggage: of leaving your context, of changing your identity. For the middle-class kid and their family, meanwhile, school was (and is) very different. It is what defines you as being separate from the working class; it is what success means. Your place in the world is less certain, more precarious, so your education becomes the foundation of your middle-class status. These two views foster entirely different attitudes to school and engagement. For the working-class child, school is a phase of life, a formative experience, but the end result is not so important. For the middle-class child, success at school is paramount.

As society has changed, the old, secure industrial jobs have been replaced with precarious, low-status service work, and the middle-class attitude has come to dominate what education should be. No matter what your background, you are there to optimise your chances. Only, if you are from one of the culturally working-class communities at the blunt edge of this, the changing attitudes of your parents are likely to lag behind the changing world around you. If they grew up in a world where university wasn't for people like them, it is a hard ask for them to accept that this is suddenly different. And while in many, many instances this acceptance does occur, in aggregate there is still a cultural inertia that maintains older ways of thinking.

What does this all mean for behaviour? It means that working-class kids exist in school in opposition to the dominant narrative – subordinated to values that are not culturally embedded in their lives, and vulnerable to falling into Joey's way of thinking: that school is merely the power-play of class writ large, with no deeper purpose of self-development.

But it isn't only the long tail of industrial class relations that keeps class division alive in schools. Even in the changed landscape of post-industrial Britain there is the hard fact that the kind of career opportunities available to middle-class kids are usually either invisible or non-existent for their working-class counterparts. And for those working-class kids who do make the leap into higher education, they become, by definition, class emigrants to some degree. The net result: little visible evidence in deprived, historically working-class communities that school has much impact on your later life. For the teachers and schools trying to make working-class kids behave, both the carrot of social mobility and the stick of school exclusion can very quickly lose all impact.

Near the end of the GCSE season I pick out a couple of the kids that I've spent the last few years telling off and chasing down and ask to interview them. I've chosen to do this now because the disciplinary relationship changes when the end is in sight. The sting is taken out of it. You become a little more reflective.

Candace is one of them. She is leaving in two days. She tells me she likes school. She also says she's naughty. I ask her what this means. 'My attitude, and my temper. I can lose it easily.'

She is slight, and bounces around the school with a spiky energy. For several years I've chased her from her favoured smoking spots, but there's always been something charming and good-humoured about her – even as I've also seen her erupt into fury.

Do other people not lose their temper? I ask.

'Yeah. But at the same time no. I look at some people that are the quiet ones in class, and I think that the reason they're quiet and sit by themselves is because that's how they want to be.'

She looks at me in the way that little children can sometimes, when they're trying to figure you out – wide eyes and unblinking. Only Candace also has the faintest of smiles. When I told her I wanted to speak to her for my book, she was with her friends and she shrieked and pranced, shouting that she was going to be famous. I said I'd anonymise her, and for the next five minutes she ran around, striking poses and saying, 'I'm going to be *anoninonus*!' But now, in my office, there's something serious and almost sad about her.

So it's a choice that they're quiet? I ask. Do you choose as well? To be the opposite of quiet, I mean.

'No,' she says. 'It just happens. I get bored, and if I get bored I get irritated.'

Has that always been the case?

'No!' She sounds surprised at how vehement she is. Almost like she's forgotten how she was. 'In Year Seven and Eight I was perfectly quiet. But there was . . . new friends. And just the way people look at you. If I was in Year Eight and I was quiet, they'd say something. But now I'm loud, they don't say anything.'

So it was self-protection?

'Yes.'

So was that the right thing to do?

'No. I feel like it was completely wrong.'

I smile. Are you saying that because it's me asking?

But Candace doesn't smile back. Her face is serious, and sad. 'No. It's genuinely wrong. I really regret the way I acted in Year Nine and Ten.'

What kind of things do you regret?

'Dolling. Not going to lessons. Not listening to teachers – just carrying on. I really regret that.' She laughs for the first time, but not her normal cackle, an oddly shy laugh instead. 'Because now I know nothing.'

But it did give you a status that meant people didn't mess with you?

'Yes.'

Should the school have done something differently?

'No – it's nothing the school can do to stop it, I think, it's just the way people are – they're horrible sometimes.'

She looks so vulnerable as we speak. She's normally so vivid and excitable. I can't think of when I've seen Candace so still. Her eyes are still on mine. It feels like she agreed to this because it sounded exciting, but that the conversation is more disorientating than she expected.

I remind her of the word *naughty* and that she agreed she was, and ask her if she thinks she is *bad* as well.

'No.' She's sure of this as well.

What is bad then?

'Not turning up to school at all. Or threatening people, fighting, or proper arguing with teachers – going too far with it.'

We have seen how class can lead to the kind of alienation or lack of motivation on which bad behaviour feeds, but there is a wider, cultural factor at work as well, which is bigger than class. Candace's naughtiness is a social strategy, a response to the values of her peer group and the pressures they exert, but I'd argue that it isn't only her peer group who think like this. 'Going too far' is such a revealing phrase. It suggests that *some* bad behaviour is the norm, expected and accepted, and it encapsulates the strong thread of ambivalence about school and behaviour in British culture. Think of Dennis the Menace, and Just William, and St Trinian's – all about naughty children and how heroic they are. Think of Harry Potter, in fact. (My own children are in a *Harry Potter* phase, and have been pretty heavily for a while. This means I listen to the audiobooks a *lot* on long car journeys.) It's a world of lessons being boring, of the important stuff being in between and around them. It's a world where Hermione is faintly ridiculous for working hard, and where Ron and Harry always squeeze through by the skin of their teeth – despite the obvious fact that Harry is kind of brilliant at this whole magic thing. And where Fred and George Weasley are heroes for doing some pranks that, as a Head, would leave me absolutely fucking livid. We have a long tradition of writing about school and study like this, which makes it absurd, a ritualistic game of pranks and detentions and gurning teachers. Even the good teachers are the ones who fundamentally rebel against school.

Reading the education consultant Lucy Crehan on East Asian school systems, it is really striking how this is not the norm elsewhere. She describes the way in which Chinese students look up to the 'heroic' Confucian scholars of the past, struggling to study in the face of poverty and adversity.[7] I think of Jeremy Clarkson, ritually tweeting every exam season about how he failed his A levels and he's done all right.

This is more than simply an oddity. There is a deep-seated problem in the way we think about behaviour in schools in Britain, and I don't know the answer to it. Culturally, our values are aligned towards individualism, towards mild rebellion, towards cheekiness and irreverence. We are liberal, not in a political sense, but in that deep-in-the-bones sense. It's what Orwell touched on in his descriptions of why Fascism wouldn't take hold in the UK – although maybe he'd think again if he witnessed the recent rise of the comic politician, the fascist-as-decent-bloke-down-the-pub trope that has smuggled in extremism under the banner of common sense.

Is it any wonder, then, that we feel conflicted about discipline or 'behaviour management' in schools? The attitudes that I hold while trying to get 1,500 kids to toe the line are not the attitudes I would vote for. And this tension is, I think, hard-wired into how we think and talk about schools as a whole. For every comment about how kids should behave better, there's another comment about the absurdity of uniform rules. For every story about success in exams, there's another one about schools overreaching their authority, or about kids protesting. And we have to be honest with ourselves: from the way we talk about this stuff, it's clear that we *like* the naughty kids. Listen to what people say about their school days. They look back and say, 'I was no angel.' They say, 'I was a lazy little sod.' They describe the times they got in trouble, and the ways in which they didn't comply. Think about the total scorn poured on Theresa May when she admitted that the worst thing she'd ever done was run through a corn field. And then we kicked her out and voted in Boris.

This is what schools are up against, day in, day out: a culture that purports to value the rule of law and the rewarding of hard work, but does not actually celebrate the discipline and aspiration that make either of those possible. If anything, it mocks them, and elevates the sloppy and populist over sober expertise. This dovetails destructively with the false meritocracy that we explored in Part One, and it can leave kids reading the opposite message from the one we think we're giving them. We think schools offer hope, possibility and an inculcation into adult, middle-class norms – but for some kids they present a game where the supposed goal is a mirage and the only way to really win the status they crave is to break all the rules.

13. Outside the mainstream

There are some kids whose bad behaviour goes way beyond cheeky. Matt is also at Blue Sky. He's in Year 8. He tells me how he ended up there.

'Nibthwaite, I just like . . . I didn't like it, so I was playing up, and I got permo'ed [permanently excluded] from there. And then I went to Kenny [Kennerlea Farm Academy]. And one day I was just in a mood, cos the teacher said something, so I smashed the computers and that, and then the police came. The teacher said something to me and I just flipped.'

And you were permanently excluded again?

'Yes.'

Two permanent exclusions in a year is pretty extreme. Like much else in schools, exclusions have become greatly politicised of late, but the fact is that permanent exclusions are relatively rare and closely monitored. If a school moves to permanently exclude a pupil, this has to be submitted through the local authority, to go to a panel of governors and is subject to appeal. To give a sense of frequency, at my current school there tend to be around four exclusions in a year – on or below the national average for secondary schools (adjusted for the pupil population of the school – in our case, 1,500). Ofsted monitor these numbers closely, and there are various checks and balances to make sure that students are not simply excluded to get them off the books before they take their exams – one facet of a practice known as 'off-rolling'.

In my experience, the decisions that lead to a permanent exclusion tend to be relatively clear-cut. If there is any doubt about its necessity or justification, schools generally don't go this far. For us, they come either at the end of a very long process, where we've tried all we can, but are ultimately faced with nowhere else to go – or they are in response to one-off extreme events, often connected to weapons or assault.

So while exclusions are drastic and to be avoided if possible, and understandably they occupy much attention, they are something of a distraction when it comes to comprehending behaviour management in schools. What is more useful is to look at the steps that lead towards them. If we do this, we can begin to really see what schools have to contend with in order to create the safe environments that are a pre-condition for education, and the troubling lack of resources they face.

When dealing with really problematic behaviour in a pupil, there are two considerations. One is how to help that pupil get a better deal out of school, modify their behaviour, learn how to cope. In most extreme cases, part of this lies in referrals to outside agencies, to tackle the impact of trauma, to look at undiagnosed special educational needs. The other consideration is how to safeguard the rest of the school. The hard truth is that sometimes you have to choose between the two. The presence of a child who is seriously disruptive has a massive impact – but even more, the fact that the other students see no meaningful consequence of the disruption is corrosive to everything that school is about.

As we've seen, detentions, isolation and suspensions of a couple of days can all become empty threats pretty quickly. Once experienced, they diminish in the eyes of children and can become instead a goal, or a badge of honour. More importantly, if there is no support from home, no parental voice backing the school, they are worse than useless – with suspensions in particular simply disengaging the child from school even more.

I have a vivid memory of one parental meeting where we told the mother of a pupil that, as a result of a serious fight, we would be sending him for two days' respite at another school. We stressed that the reason we were doing this, rather than suspending him, was so that he wouldn't lose out on learning.

She just said 'no'. 'He won't be going there.'

But he needs to be in school, I said.

'He doesn't.' Her son sat there beside her, impassive. 'I don't care about school. I didn't get an education. My daughters didn't get an education.' She glared. 'I don't see the point of it.'

I remembered her daughters with a shudder. Her son looked at me blankly. It was one of those moments where you genuinely hit a brick wall.

In the end, all the efforts made towards reducing bad behaviour by controlling the school environment need backing up, if they aren't to be seen by the pupils as empty threats. Even in the best-behaved schools you will get outliers, and if they are allowed to be visible and unchecked, then the school will quickly stop being well behaved. So sometimes there are unavoidable situations where the behavioural contract between school and student breaks down, and at that point there are really only two solutions. Either option one: a reset is engineered whereby the student begins to behave differently; or option two: they go elsewhere. Unfortunately, I think most teachers would agree that option one only happens when somewhere in the system there is the threat of option two.

However, the crucial point about this measure of last resort is that excluding a pupil need not be the same as washing your hands of them or giving up on them. It might even be the best option for them. When you permanently exclude, the local authority is obliged to provide a placement, either at another school or at an AP, like Blue Sky. Equally, it often happens that the moment a pupil leaves a school for ever isn't actually a permanent exclusion – it's a recognition that they are better off elsewhere. If, as a school, you can find a placement for a short time that will genuinely allow them to reflect and change before reintegrating, or if you can manage a transfer to another school where they can start again without the toxic weight of everyone else's negative expectations, then you may well be changing their lives for the better.

This is particularly true for some of the most complex behavioural situations, which are inevitably those where students are struggling with trauma, mental ill-health or other specific needs. As we know, the very definition of insanity is doing the same thing again and again and expecting different results. If a student cannot cope in the classroom environment, then we cannot simply keep setting them up to fail – we need to do something different. And if their trauma or complex need makes them, for example, repeatedly bully and intimidate other students, then we have to do something different as a matter of urgency.

To me, the real problem with permanent exclusion is that, in the majority of cases, it could be avoided if we had better options for supporting students who cannot deal with mainstream schools, through personalised part-time arrangements or through dedicated and intensive therapeutic practice. But we don't. And we cannot risk the safety and well-being of other students.

So we end up with counter-intuitive situations where, for example, a student is assessed by the Vulnerable Pupil Panel and granted a place at Alternative Provision. We all celebrate. But the place doesn't become available for six months. So for six months we hang on, desperately trying to manage a student who is already disengaged from school and now knows they are going elsewhere. We have no levers left. And after five months a serious incident happens, resulting in that student and another being permanently excluded. Time has been wasted. Staff effort has been wasted. Other students have suffered. Two students have left instead of one. And the irony is that the pupil's long-deferred place will now be made instantly available because of their permanent exclusion.

Were you like this in primary? I ask Matt.

'No. It was fine. But then at secondary the work started getting harder, and then just difficult. Make you stressed more – but in primary it was easy.'

Do you feel clever?

'No.'

Tell me again why you were excluded the first time.

'I was in normal class, and then it was like RE, and that's the most lesson I hated, and every time I'd get excluded, or I'd end up chucking pens at the teacher or summat. I done that and then I was in Bridge for half of Year Seven, and then I just walked out, so I got permo'ed.'

Why were you throwing pens at the teacher?

'She kept on shouting at me, saying, "Go on, get your work done." People were talking, and then I'd talk and she'd tell me to get my head down, so I threw pens at her.'

And was that the right thing to do?

'No.'

Have you ever thrown a pen at a teacher here?

'No.' Matt seems definite.

I ask him why he's so sure he wouldn't do it here at Blue Sky. He says it's because they're not strict. Is strict bad?

'No. It's just horrible.'

But should teachers ever be strict?

'Sometimes. But not if they're just pure getting in your face and like . . . In Nibthwaite, one of them got in me face and then I was like, "Get out me face", and she was like, "Well, no, you need to do your work." '

Did that upset you?

'No.' Like Joey, Matt speaks with hesitations, but he is far more fluent, with a quickfire delivery and nervous eyes. 'It's just, like, they're here to teach us, not to shout at us. When I was doing my maths or summat, she'd get in my face and start screaming.'

Are there any situations like that where you think, 'This teacher's got a point, and maybe I shouldn't have done that?'

'I don't know. I had like a drink on my table and I chucked it, and the teacher was like, "Go and pick it up", and I just went, "No", and then I was in detention. I should have just gone and picked it up.'

We talk for a bit, about holidays, and what Matt wants to do. He doesn't know, but he does like to travel. He's been to Spain and France. I look at him – his thin face, his wide eyes. There is something very dark here. Later the Head will confirm it. He has not had an easy life, this boy. I think of all the kids I've known, the traumas that sit behind their blank faces. The times when someone's taken me to one side and quietly filled me in on details, and I've felt sick to the pit of my stomach.

We return to the circumstances of Matt's last exclusion. How did you feel when you smashed up the computers?

'Angry. All my mates were in one room, and then they started locking the doors.' He means that the teachers locked the doors of the room that the rest of the class was in, to prevent them from entering the room that Matt and another boy were in. His face is still, but his eyes move to the side. His hands are bony and pale. 'We just sat there, me and Lucas.' His voice is deep and worn, too heavy for his slight body. He sounds artificially aged at the same time as he looks so terrifyingly young. 'We put all the windows through. Broke the boards. Snapped the doors. Then, when the police came, we went on the roof.'

I picture the scene. I've seen mayhem in schools, but never on that scale. The level of rage that Matt must have felt is staggering. I wonder how he can have any hope of a life that isn't defined by his trauma. But since he's been at Blue Sky, the Head tells me, Matt hasn't been suspended once.

One of the most commonly cited factors in exclusions is SEND: special educational needs and disabilities. This includes SEMH: Social, Emotional and Mental Health. It's clear that Matt, like many of the children I spoke to at Blue Sky, falls into this category. If they are lucky, children with these particular needs will end up at a Special Education school, a setting specifically designed to meet those needs.

South Hope Academy is on the edge of a mid-sized town in the South-West, on a rise above the floodplain of the River Severn. From the playground you look out to green fields scattered with industrial buildings, with the huge white complex of the Amazon warehouse in full view. The building is purpose-built – with a planted green roof and curved walls that swoop up to it. Eighty primary-age kids go here, all of them with ASD (Autism Spectrum Disorder) or SEMH.

Doodle, the school dog, is first at the door to greet me. Actually Doodle is one of two school dogs – the other, Freya, is in a classroom, looking after some Year 6s. There is a sense of space and of quiet, unlike most schools I have visited, which tend towards the bustling and overcrowded. In the classrooms between one and nine kids sit behind conventional rows of desks, in neat pale-blue polo shirts, with up to three adults teaching and supporting them. Sometimes you might notice a trait that suggests autism – a child making flapping motions with their hands, or holding themselves in a way that seems subtly out of kilter – but there is little on the surface to distinguish these classrooms from any other school, beyond the simple numbers and staff ratios.

When I talk to Craig, the Head, he describes how the kids come to him. 'There's about a sixty–forty ratio,' he says; 60 per cent exhibit such behavioural issues that they are either permanently excluded or in danger of permanent exclusion, while the other 40 per cent are identified directly through an EHCP.

An EHCP is an Education, Health and Care Plan and, however they have arrived here, all children in this school will have one. It is the document that itemises the specific needs of a child and unlocks the additional funding needed to support them, in ways that go beyond the capacity of the normal funding arrangements. Craig says he gets about £10,000 per pupil per year, with an additional top-up based on what band of need they are in. If that sounds like a lot, consider the potential costs involved in providing a typical level of care for a child at South Hope. If a child requires one-to-one support, for example, that means a full-time salary, which (even at a low wage of £19,000 a year) – once you include pension, National Insurance and other 'on-costs' – comes out at around £26,000 for the school. And that is just staffing.

Kids in mainstream have EHCPs, too. Sometimes the decision is that mainstream schooling, with support, is the best place. But wherever they are educated, there is the same burden of cost. And like everything else in our system, there is a gulf between what is measured and what is actually there. Getting an EHCP is a challenging process – and the numbers of applications have soared in recent years. Given that the costs are statutory and cannot be trimmed, this has led to a reported drive to achieve 'at least a 20 per cent reduction in new EHCPs issued'[1] – something that sits at odds with the reality that schools are experiencing of kids with specific needs, often exacerbated by home circumstance, that cannot be met within the constraints of normal funding. When you add in the fact that many children in the most deprived areas experience the worst trauma and are liable to have the greatest need – and yet often lack the social capital to push for an EHCP, and can end up instead in the more punitive world of exclusions and PRUs – it's easy to see how, like elsewhere in our system, inequality can become baked in.

But at South Hope the kids they deal with are only here because their needs are more than the mainstream can cope with – and the approaches needed vary from child to child.

Craig tells me that they have a lot of information about the children that come through the assessment route, 'but it's still not enough. Strategies for different kids are never-ending, because you can use one strategy one day, and it might not work the next day.'

This is a flexibility of approach that mainstream cannot provide, and in fact it runs directly contrary to the ways schools built on a larger scale have to approach SEND.

He agrees. 'A lot of the mainstream schools are not set up for that – they're hit with a rod from DfE and Ofsted, your SATs scores, your exam results – and sometimes that takes precedence over what individual kids need.' But just like a mainstream institution, South Hope can struggle with those whose needs are too complex for them. 'I've got some kids coming to me where sometimes maybe they shouldn't be coming to me, they should be going to a different type of provision, but because of the cost difference they come to me – and we can't offer what they need.'

I ask what proportion of his kids have specific needs, like ASD, and what proportion are there because of SEMH, resulting perhaps from childhood trauma. The answer is both simple and hugely complex – no one has one need. There are primary and secondary needs, and pretty universally ASD and SEMH are intertwined. You have kids here who are struggling with trauma, but their ability to process and respond is affected by their ASD – and kids who have experienced such disruption and abuse that their normal development has frayed into multiple other needs.

Take Alex, who has ASD. He's in Year 6 now and is sharp, articulate, well regulated. He tells me about how he was in a mainstream primary until the end of Year 3, but that he was then referred to a PRU (like the Blue Sky School we first met in Chapter 12) before being given a place here. Although Alex himself doesn't seem clear on the process, Craig tells me that the PRU was only a temporary placement while the EHCP was submitted, and that South Hope was always the plan. Now school is a positive place for Alex – although, like everyone, he does get a bit of the Monday-morning blues.

'If it's a Monday, I feel a bit tired because I'm just finished the weekend and I wake up early. Let's say it's a Friday, I wake up in an energetic mood; and if it's a normal Wednesday I still feel good because I'm meeting my friends at school and I'm learning stuff.'

I ask about his experience of mainstream.

'I was kicked out of Farnsworth Juniors,' he says.

I ask if he remembers why.

'I think it's cos I didn't do my work, and I didn't value school back then, and I was kicking off all the time. I remember once it was a trip day, and they just basically said to me you're not allowed to go on this trip, and that just hit me – the realisation that I'm not allowed to go on this trip – and that made me really angry. And that's probably why I got kicked out.'

Alex speaks so carefully and calmly. He's the same age as my youngest son and, based on this conversation, I'd say they were developmentally very similar. There is a reflectiveness about how he speaks that I notice in a few of the kids at South Hope. I ask what 'kicking off' means.

'Normally I'd start punching walls, and I'd get a desk and just throw the desk around and start shouting, and I'd basically start disrupting the class, and I'd just start causing chaos.'

He describes this in a way that is at once detached, aware and without shame. I ask about the work. Did he not do the work because it was difficult, or because he didn't want to?

'I didn't find it difficult, I think work was pretty easy, I just couldn't be bothered doing it.'

Why?

'I just didn't really value school back then. Normally it was because the work was boring and I didn't really want to participate.'

You can hear the echoes and effects of conversations that he has had with teachers since – the vocabulary of 'valuing' school and 'participating'. But these are not just buzzwords to Alex – he uses them correctly and reflectively.

Craig tells me that Alex was unmanageable at Farnsworth. He tells me that when Alex goes off, he goes off big. He isn't violent towards people – it isn't intentional and directed – but the intensity of it can be frightening. He tells me that these incidents were happening all the time, but that in the last year there have only been two.

Alex tells me about the PRU he went to, before coming here. 'I was the same as I was in Farnsworth. I felt really – you know, I don't really enjoy school any more. I kept on kicking off in the PRU too. And in the PRU they don't have a calm room.'

The calm room at South Hope is a room with nothing in it besides a shiny plastic bench – a blobby shape with no corners. Students are brought there when 'kicking off', and members of staff will sit with them and wait. Craig says they will often talk to each other, casual conversations loaded with little hooks to catch the attention of the student and bring them back down.

With Kenny, the hook is always *Star Wars*. In my own conversation with him we cover a lot of ground, and I find myself having to nod along as he mentions increasingly esoteric facts about the films. Apparently there is a mismatch between the side of the face that Anakin has a scar on in two of the episodes, and Kenny is convinced this has a hidden meaning.

Kenny is in Year 5. I ask how it felt getting ready for school this morning.

'It felt good, because I can do my work, and I want to finish it off, because when I finish it off I feel better.' He goes on to talk about what he likes in particular. 'I like to do football when it's playtime. I like to write. In literacy we've been doing about World War One, and I've been doing about Spanish Flu.' He pauses. 'I might need to cough,' he says shyly. 'I have hay fever.'

He is a delicate child, with big eyes and a fragile look. He moves cautiously. Craig tells me that sometimes Kenny can clam up, but in our conversation – perhaps because of my interest in *Star Wars* – he is often animated and engaged. Every now and then, though, there is a kind of retreat in his eyes, a blink back into himself. His speech is precise, with a warm smile sometimes creeping in between his words. He's been at South Hope for two years.

'It was kind of frustrating. One of my teachers, she was nice, but she also, well, she used to shout a lot. So I had two special teachers – the first one I didn't like, but the second one I really liked. He came in every Friday and every Wednesday and he used to talk to me, and read with me, but when he left I was really sad.' Kenny looks sad still. 'He gave us some things so I could remember him – he gave us his pen, he gave us a notebook.'

So then you left that school?

'It wasn't really that nice. I had to help design this little sheet, which said what I need to do to last all week, but it was just a little bit *hard*.'

When he says 'hard', he draws out the word. I notice this with a lot of children – there are certain words that become their go-to words for describing a feeling, and they acquire a greater significance than simply what they say. I can hear a whole lot of other issues behind what Kenny says.

'It was really *hard*. I couldn't handle it, so I decided to come here. I had thirty people in my class, but here I have eight or seven. I had three people on my desk – because there wasn't enough desks and chairs. It made me feel a bit nervous. I didn't like it, because I don't like it when there's loads of people around.'

He pauses. Smiles.

'Unless you're going to a football match. That's fine. But in the classroom, with tons of people, that's not okay.'

Kenny is lovely. But I can see how much he would struggle in a more conventional environment. I find this school both heartbreaking and uplifting. The kids here get such an amazing deal, but I feel for the other students who could benefit and don't get this. And when I meet some of them – like Josh, sitting in the corridor, refusing to move – there seems such a deep well of pain inside them.

Craig tells me of great successes here, but he also tells me of the list of children who have passed through his school, only to be returned to mainstream schooling without appropriate support, or whose home lives have deteriorated further. He's been Head since 2006, and working in Special Education for twenty-five years, and there are too many tragedies. Suicide, violence, prison. It's easy to think of stories of abuse and suffering as extreme, or as outliers, or as the work of a few bad people who can be prevented from causing harm through police intervention and the justice system. But here, and everywhere

I've visited, and in my own work at school, I hear of the same problems again and again, and none of them fit into nice neat boxes that can be separated off from 'normal life' and locked away. Inevitably, schools have to pick up the pieces. And the plain fact is that for all the great work that can be done in an institution like South Hope, most children with complex needs do not make it to a Special Education school. However good the work that South Hope and mainstream schools are able to do, it is nothing without an overarching system of social care and early intervention, which can successfully address the problems these children and their families face at home and in society at large – a system that currently does not exist.

Imagine this: you love your parents. But your father hits your mother. Sometimes he hits you. Your sister is annoying, so you hit her. But to lose any of them would be to lose the only home you have.

Or this: your mother is an addict. You were severely neglected and taken into foster care. But your ASD means you cannot process the trauma, and the foster care available is unable to cope. You have had five placements break down in six months.

Or this: you were taken from your mother at the age of ten after your school found you scavenging for food in the bins. In eight years of foster care you stabilise and are cared for, but you cannot stop yourself stealing. The school finds you exhibiting worrying sexual behaviour and has to ask you to leave. Your mother offers you a home when you leave care at eighteen and you return to the person who abused you.

All of these children – real children that I've taught and remember and think about still – were in mainstream provision.

It's so easy to think that most people are 'normal'. That most kids have home lives that are 'normal'. That those who are 'special' can be put to one side and treated for their needs. But their needs arise from the world in which they live, and so the solutions have to lie in that, too. The model that we have feels at times akin to responding to rising sea levels by giving people towels.

We cannot have a world in which none of these things happen. That has never been the case, and never will be. But we can have a world in which we pay attention to children: where we address their needs on the *basis* of need, not on the basis of availability. Where we pick up the can early, before the damage is irrevocable, not kick it down the road until there are no other options – and no hope. Where we think carefully about where they go next, so that kids who've been in specialist provision at primary don't just get dumped into mainstream in secondary, or so that kids leaving care are supported into adulthood. And where we let the different parts of the system talk to each other better, so that when needs are identified, they are shared and acted upon consistently by professionals who are given the time and space to do the job they are trained to do. None of these responses are easy – and they are resistant to simple metrics of success or failure. They involve labour-intensive, expensive, long-term attention; but in the very long term, if we can care for our most vulnerable children better, then we reduce the monetary cost in benefits, and prison places and mental-health wards. More importantly, though, we reduce the burden of misery that can weigh our society down.

Even then, we won't fix everything.

In Kent, six months after meeting Kenny, I find myself in the gym of an Alternative Provision, standing awkwardly while two members of staff discuss a situation they are dealing with. Abdi, an Eritrean boy, is standing outside the gym, through the open fire doors. He is lost in mute fury. The teachers cannot get through to him – both because his anger is beyond the bounds of communication and because he speaks no English. He has been in the school for a few weeks. Before that, he came to Britain over the Channel. Before that, he spent a year in the camps in Calais. Before that, he travelled from Sudan on his own. He is thirteen.

The teachers turn to a colleague who speaks Arabic. But the colleague shakes his head.

'Abdi does not like me right now,' he says. 'I tried to tell him about why we had to be in school.'

More people join the conversation. I am taken away, to look elsewhere in the school. We walk around a bright building, radiating out from an octagonal room in the centre. Children in small groups in lessons are alert and engaged, sometimes with the kind of slightly feverish attention that speaks of the possibility of wild swings, sometimes with a quieter inward focus. You can tell this is a good school, just as you can tell how easy it would be for it not to be.

I think of Abdi. I think of the brief outline I was given of his time in Calais. Sometimes I find myself wondering if we are coming to the end of a period of unnatural stability. If the world I grew up in will seem a golden age in years to come. I think of my Jewish grandmother, who fled Nazi Germany, and the stories her generation told. I think of the Ukrainian family who are staying with us at the moment. I think of their cat, Stepan – seventeen years old, a ghostlike little ginger wraith, which they drove with out of Kharkiv, holding him on their lap for thirty-six hours.

When the Ukraine war broke, and the pictures of refugees were all over the news, I heard people ask with incredulity why there were so many pets. If people were really fleeing, would they take their pets? And because I'm an English teacher, I thought of King Lear crying out, 'reason not the need!' We want because we're human. We need love, and kindness, and meaning, in these times most of all. Bare survival is not enough. Only sometimes the world really *is* cruel enough to take everything away.

Later, before I leave, I see Abdi walking past with one of the teachers. He looks like any other boy – a little slower, a little more detached from himself. He walks as if in a dream, moving because he is moving, not because he wants anything or is going anywhere.

Beside him is a teacher, talking slowly, kindly, in a language Abdi doesn't understand.

14.   How to succeed in life

Back in my Year 13 class on Milton, we are debating free will.

'So God already knows that Adam and Eve are going to eat the fruit?' asks Jacqui.

'Yes,' I reply.

'So why did he put the tree there?'

'To test them.'

'But he knows they're going to fail, right?'

'Yes.'

'And he made everything about them?'

'Yes.'

'He made how strong their willpower was, and how clever they were?'

'Yes.'

'And he knew what Satan was going to do, so he could have just said, "Watch out for the snake, it's lying"?'

'Yes.'

'But all of this doesn't matter because he made it, so they could have said no, even though he knew they wouldn't?'

'Yes.'

'No offence, sir, but that's dumb.'

I love Milton, but the kid has a point. It's hard to make sense of the mess of cause and effect that produces human destiny – whether you're attempting to 'justify the ways of God to men', or attempting to justify the ways of Milton to seventeen-year-olds.

We make decisions for complex reasons: to do with character, home and circumstance. In fact we rarely can isolate exactly which of these is the key influence – if there is one. Sometimes it's the chance of fine weather on the day of an interview. But the temptation is always to simplify: to boil life down to transactions – do this, and get that. And, as we've seen, for all that goes on in schools, everything at some point becomes haunted by the spectre of 'What next?'

The answer that our academically focused system inevitably points towards is 'university, if you've got the grades'. This was my default throughout the first part of my career – partly because, like many teachers, it was what I knew best. But I'm less confident in this answer than I used to be. University is costing students more each year – because even if fees don't rise, the loans needed to live do, and the interest rates and terms of those loans become ever less favourable.[1] Meanwhile the government penalises university courses if fewer than 60 per cent of their students are in professional jobs or studying for a further degree within fifteen months of graduating. It's a reflection of how many are not. We used to try to persuade kids to go to university by emphasising the benefits to their income over a lifetime. But having created a situation in which the value of university is now primarily understood to be a monetary one, even that value seems dubious. The conversations that I have with kids these days are less about 'Will I fit in?' and more about 'Will it be worth it?'

And this is true right through the education system. Although we might be obsessing to an unhealthy degree about the precise ranking of our students, and assigning them sometimes spurious 'worth' through our exams system, the students are doing the same right back at us – ranking and ascribing value to schools and courses and subjects according to a highly literal, careers-focused mindset.

As we saw at the end of Part One, from the hundreds of kids I've now asked that simple question 'What is school for?', by far the most common answer I've received is some variation on 'To get a good job': 'To get GCSEs and a good job', 'To get a good career', 'To do well and get ahead.' The word that interests me most here is not 'job' or 'career', it's 'get'. It's as if the education they are going to 'get' is somehow separate from who they 'are' or will 'become'. Indeed, many of them also say the opposite, but with the same basic assumption. They say that something is pointless because, 'I'm never going to use it.' They say that they 'don't need History', or 'Who needs to know about cells?' They tell me they don't care about school because they've 'already got a job', or their uncle/father/grandad is a plasterer/joiner/used-car salesman and 'he's already promised me'.

Politicians are at it, too. Robert Halfon, once Chair of the Education Select Committee and then Minister for Skills in the DfE, wrote in 2021 that 'the keystone to education must be about providing young people with a ladder of opportunity so that they can go on to gain fulfilling employment'.[2] This kind of rhetoric is pretty universal nowadays. I should know; I was on the Social Mobility Commission, and our publications were so full of ladders that I'm surprised we didn't have to pass a health-and-safety check. It reflects the deep values of our system – a system that is structured around the idea that education is a tool for transporting the right candidate into the right job.

Despite my unease around the ways that education is so often framed as transactional, I have to admit that the clarity of a pragmatic, careers-focused approach can indeed be immensely powerful. Many of the students I speak to tell me that understanding the ways in which their learning can lead to a career is a game-changer in terms of their motivation and their drive to achieve.

'I'm not that bright, so I struggled in school,' says Hannah, who studies at an FE (further education) college. 'But I tried to ignore the fact of that, and try. That's all you can do, really.'

Do you feel brighter here, in college?

'Yeah, I do, a bit.'

Why's that?

'I'm more passionate about what I'm doing. So at school I was doing English, Maths, Science – that wasn't my thing. But I've come in to college to do the course I want to do [a BTEC in Uniformed Services], and I love that course. So I'm more passionate about it, so I'll try harder at it and get better grades at it.'

Do you think you're doing well?

'Yeah.' She laughs. She seems surprised at herself, pleased at the thought of doing so well. 'Yeah, I'd say.'

I find this again and again. It doesn't matter where students sit in the education system, they seem to function so much better when they understand why they are doing what they are doing, and for many of them that means understanding the career it will lead to.

But the edifice of careers advice – and the motivation it is intended to provide – is dependent on one simple assumption: that the career you follow is a product of the educational qualifications you gain. For Hannah, this may well be the case. But I fear that for some other students I encounter it may not be the full picture.

Maddy, who wears a mask even now, a full year after lockdown, and whose voice is quiet and precise, is at the same college as Hannah. She tells me she hated school.

I ask her to elaborate. What did she hate?

'Everything. The teachers were just horrible. If they felt you couldn't do something, they said fine, you can't do it. I didn't get my GCSEs because my mum moved a lot, and I'm Italian.'

Maddy doesn't sound Italian, but the odd, quiet, precise quality to her voice does speak of being bilingual, and of a roaming childhood.

'I got NOTHING out of going to school except for trauma.'

She laughs, and I do too, despite myself, because the phrase is delivered with such unexpected force and poise. Behind the chair, Maddy's two-year-old son giggles. 'Teachers would just see me as a bad kid,' she continues.

What does that mean? I ask.

She takes a breath. 'To me, it means I'm dumb. Half the time I can't do the work, so I'd get angrier, so I'd walk out of class. And I'd get detention, and so on. And half the time I'd just sit there, kind of "I need help" and not do the work, and I'd get in trouble for that.'

Her son pulls at her sleeve. I ask Maddy if parenting is a challenge.

'I was pregnant when I left school. I went to this college for half a year, but then I couldn't do it any more, the pregnancy was too bad. Came back – yeah, I was terrified. Luckily enough, I still had the teacher from when I was pregnant – she's called Lisa, and she's amazing. She understood everything, and she said if I ever need anything, she'll be here.'

What's your long-term goal?

'I want to be a psychologist, long-term. I want to get my Maths and English, get everything done, maybe go to uni, but obviously with the baby and other stuff going on it's a bit hard. My teacher – she knows that I can do it.'

Maddy's life has not gone to plan. For her, circumstances have interrupted and complicated that straightforward linear model of school: that you do X to get Y. What makes me sad, listening to her, is that even as she struggles on, I fear her goal is already out of reach – not because she can't do it, but because no one has been really honest with her about what it would take. She understands the basic equation – get your GCSEs, go to uni, get a good job – but she doesn't know that for the job she wants, the qualifications and the competition are far beyond where she seems to be. She might be able to get there one day, but the level of commitment it will take is forbidding, and that does not seem to have been spelled out to her, least of all by the teacher who, quite understandably, has tried to motivate her by engaging with this vague goal.

Listening to Maddy, I worry that if the only motivational narrative we can offer is a straightforward transaction, then we open the door to discouragement and disappointment as well. And if we counter that with heedless optimism, we won't be nurturing the grit that might be necessary when life gets tough.

Mostly, teaching is a weird cycle of intense relationships, which then disappear off a cliff. You see someone every day, watch them grow, support them in moments of heartbreaking distress and then, if all goes well, you see them one last time, jumping in excitement at the beginning of the rest of their life. And then . . . nothing. I'm pretty used to it now – an old lag who looks on sympathetically when the newly qualified teachers are in tears at the end of term, because their favourite class is leaving. But that doesn't mean I don't get excited when I bump into an ex-student, or when I hear of their success.

This happened most dramatically a few years ago. I was sitting down to watch *Peaky Blinders* with my wife, only to jump up again, spilling my drink neatly on the cat.

'Fuck me, that's King!' A boy I'd taught when he was sixteen, and I was twenty-four. On the fucking telly.

Since then Kingsley Ben-Adir has been in a number of high-profile roles, all of which I've watched with a combination of wonder and a slight sense of unreality, until eventually I decided to track him down through his agent, fascinated to see what this unexpected trajectory feels like – how he had made this transformation.

Because it *is* a transformation. My memory of Kingsley at school was of a sensitive, bright, charismatic student – someone who stood out, but who also struggled at times. When I speak to him, though, he is in the middle of prepping for the lead in a new biopic of Bob Marley: a proper Hollywood production, the vehicle for someone who is en route to being a genuine star. He really is that kid who followed a dream; who found a passion, and became exactly what he always wanted to be. But it wasn't the simple transaction – grades to uni, to success – that our system leads us to expect.

When we see each other on our computer screens there's a fascinating mismatch – I've been watching Kingsley for the last few years, in acting roles and on chat shows, but he hasn't seen me since he was nineteen. One of the first things he says is, 'You were so young.'

He's right. I was. The man I'm talking to feels like a contemporary, not someone who was once a child in my class. We look at each other. It feels warm, but cautious, like the act of talking here is in itself shifting something. As Kingsley speaks, I recognise and remember how he was. He speaks – spoke, even back then – with a combination of care and precision, and moments where he pauses and hesitates, and looks up and to one side, to really catch exactly what he means.

When I ask him what it was that made the difference for him – that set him on his path to success – Kingsley is unequivocal.

'Most important was Mr Pratt; accidentally getting thrown into his drama class that I had no intention of choosing – that was complete fluke.'

I remember Mr Pratt (Jeremy) as an inspirational figure. I expected Kingsley to say something about this drama class, although it strikes me as revealing that joining the class was an accident. Kids don't always know what is best for them, I think; and maybe there's a limit to careers advice, if we haven't allowed them space and the chance to find a passion first.

Now the story becomes more complicated. 'At the same time, Miss Kenny was probably the biggest influence in a way, in Year Ten.' This was Kingsley's English teacher. 'Her and Mr Harwood did that thing where they mixed up the top set – they were the only department that did it. A bunch of us were in there with the top-set kids. What it did was it just gave us this confidence and belief that we could, and a lot of us got the grades.'

It seems like he's discovering what this meant as he describes it to me. Kingsley shakes his head, almost in disbelief.

'She was just such a wonderful teacher – fucking hell, if I really just think about how good she was to me, and how much she looked after me, it was really kind of incredible; she had so much love and she was such a fucking brilliant teacher. She could be so tough, but she was so fair, and so kind.'

She was. Miss Kenny (Carole) is a good friend, and was a mentor of a kind to me as a young teacher. Hearing Kingsley talk makes me remember the department, and the sense of mission and purpose there was. Not to get the grades necessarily – although that was a part of it – but to transmit a proper love of the texts. It really was that simple: we wanted them to love the topics we taught. And we showed love to them, too; we had an old sofa in the office, and kids would come in and sit and talk.

For Kingsley, that made a difference. The story he tells isn't the straightforward transaction of being good at drama and then wanting to pursue it. He didn't *decide* to become a Hollywood star. He decided to care about school in general because a teacher managed to make it mean something to him – and from that, eventually, he found a sense of vocation. The way he puts it, *seeing* himself was key to finding himself.

'She was meeting us all at a stage where we didn't know that novels have bigger significance about how we behave and about how humans interact with one another. She really introduced me to literature. I'm not a huge reader – I really struggle with it – but she introduced the idea that stories can have a greater meaning than just the surface, that they can actually represent things that you see and understand and can see yourself in.' He goes on, 'Before Year Ten I hated school so much, I felt so lost. It had become a social club. I was *so bored* from

Year Seven to Nine.' He was battling trauma at home, and destructive influences in school.

I tell him that what he describes in Years 7 to 9 is familiar to me – that many of the most troubled kids I speak to say something similar about how boring school is, and how little it means to them. But the difference with the way Kingsley responded later is quite radical. The kind of transformative moment that he experienced is rare.

He passes a hand over his face. It might have been transformative, but it wasn't easy. 'I felt like I worked three or four times harder than other people. It took a lot, and I wasn't able to sustain it after. And I got a lot of help.' He frowns. It seems a strain to think about this. 'I also don't know what any of this *means*. I have friends at school who just . . . got it. And I don't feel like I ever had that ease.'

Kingsley was clearly highly intelligent, intellectual even – I remember that vividly about him, despite his insecurities – but when he started A levels, he dropped out, then came back a year later to finish them. He didn't go to drama school right away, instead staying at William Ellis and working as a teaching assistant. There was both a turning point and then a series of other points where he hesitated, or encountered difficulties, but somehow righted himself again. It's not a straightforward trajectory of improvement and success, of goal and reward. More than anything else, as we talk, I see his success as something that has come from life on a knife-edge – a balancing act between his will to go forward and the traumas holding him back. It's a balancing act that doesn't stop with a sudden revelation of self-worth, with a high grade or a prestigious career.

Every day in schools we see this, and sometimes we fail to see how it echoes and permeates in the way a child reacts and responds to their experience. Because a child 'improves' – because they 'achieve' – that doesn't make the things that held them back disappear. We know this as adults; we know that failure isn't fatal, but that success isn't a panacea, either. But in education we can find ourselves neglecting this. I think of the students I've taught who got the A grades, went to the top universities and then struggled to make sense of their new world. It isn't merely anecdotal, either – research shows clearly the ways in which the educational success of disadvantaged kids does not necessarily translate into the workplace. Sam Friedman and Daniel Laurison's book *The Class Ceiling* even explores Kingsley's own profession, acting, and shows how progression is fundamentally linked to class. Kingsley's beaten the odds, but not without cost.

I tell him this isn't the conversation I was expecting to have. It doesn't feel like the narrative we want: about either triumph over adversity, or brilliant success through inspirational teaching. Both are there, but the story is messier, and harder. Miss Kenny was transformative, but English wasn't simply easy from that point forth. The transformation was in attitude and in will to succeed – in how Kingsley *felt* about school.

We talk again about why acting was what grabbed him.

'You can unknowingly, at that age, express a feeling that you don't know you're feeling or don't know how to express in real life. There are certain parts of yourself you can share. That are a kind of release. You don't have the honesty or the understanding to do that in your real life.'

'Honesty' is a fascinating word here. Because the sense of faking it runs through everything Kingsley says about school. Again and again he repeats how he wasn't good at it, he didn't know what he was doing. He feels like he cheated his way through. The irony is that the one unmistakeable thing about the way he comes across now, as an adult, is the measured, reasoned, intellectual quality of his responses. He does not read on any level as someone who 'struggled' at school – quite the opposite. But the intensity of the way he talks about struggling reveals how the image that we have of ourselves at school grows into the grain of who we are; and how the story you tell of yourself informs the choices you go on to make.

Kingsley still seems to be engaged in the same fight he always was – and I can't help seeing the emotion and control of his performances in the light of that gifted, intellectual child filled with trauma and self-doubt. The parts of himself that he now shares publicly are the same ones he wrestled with privately back then.

Some people's journeys into the world of work look very different from King's.

'I really didn't think about careers much. Everything was very academic and focused on that.'

Jackson, whom we first met in Chapter 10, grew up not so far from King in geographical terms, but in a very different social world. His voice is careful, thoughtful, filled with the gravitas and confidence of the voices one hears on the radio. It is all in keeping with the fact that he went to a top public school and then on to Cambridge – although, as with anyone, the facts of privilege do not always speak to the experience of his life.

'Certainly the assumption was that you would go to university,' he says. 'That was almost a given. All the conversation was about where you go, not whether you go. And the idea that you'd then work out what you want to do – I don't think that was particularly voiced at all.'

What is absent from Jackson is any sense of the kind of direct transactional link between what you study and what you do. Yes, 'a good education' in general would lead to 'a good life' in general – but not that this course would 'get' you this outcome.

What about at university, I ask? Did you think about careers then?

'I think I was incredibly naïve about it all. Maybe other people had more pressure or input from their families, but I didn't. I had maybe an idealistic view of my subject at university, and was interested in it for its own sake. At some point in my final year I had a kind of panic, and grasped at the idea of being an academic.'

Like King, Jackson seems to think as he speaks, but rather than expressing amazement at how hard it had been, his astonishment is with the way he barely seems to have touched the sides in his progress through education.

Jackson studied for a Masters after he finished his degree. He says that the sense of financial stability from his family perhaps cushioned him from needing to think too concretely about the world of work. But then, when he realised academia was not for him, he decided to study for the Bar.

'I think I just literally copied what one of my friends was doing. And also I reached for something, in a slightly extreme way, which would pay me a lot of money. So I went from not thinking about it at all, to thinking, "Right, if I've got to get a job, I'd better earn as much money as possible." '

The Bar is the most socially exclusive of all the professions: 71 per cent of the judiciary are privately educated and there is a persistent imbalance at all levels, partly from the costs of training, partly from the ways the network of influence and connection works. What Jackson says next explains why that route from private school into this career is so seamless. He describes the way in which all the currents of his schooling – the training in analysis and argument, the organisation, the research – equipped him perfectly. And how the social world of the Bar was one where he had exactly the personal qualities, the confidence and the familiarity with the structures of patronage and influence that would let him adapt and thrive. He even mentions the system of Oxbridge tutorials, where you have this one-to-one close dialogue with your tutor, as a perfect preparation for the dialectic of the court. Everything fitted.

'It was like a suit that had already been prepared for me that I didn't even know was there,' he says.

For all Jackson's lack of awareness that education was a route to a career, it nevertheless was. It was a transaction whereby you bought a frictionless ease. Compare this with Kingsley's *un*ease at his own success: his sense that it was contingent and lucky, and that he was faking it. Surely this is an indictment of the spurious confidence of the privately educated, a demonstration of the so-called 'Matthew effect': that those who have shall be given more. But at the same time Kingsley's journey, his surmounting of obstacles, his navigating of circumstance, is part of what made him successful – his skill as an actor *derives* to some extent from his experience. Having to work against the odds necessarily strengthens you in a way that having it easy does not.

Jackson, meanwhile, although he did make a lot of money, gave up the Bar ten years later for a career in the public sector. 'It wasn't right for me,' he says. 'In many ways it wasn't healthy.'

I've taught many students over the years who have wanted to be barristers. I don't know of any who have succeeded. There is a palpable inequality in the distribution of jobs, just as there is in almost any facet of our society that you care to name. But what interests me here is how school can determine who you become, in ways that are both intended and counter-intuitive. Feeling good about education, even without a clear goal to it, was something that, for both Kingsley and Jackson, gave them the chance to build themselves into people who could be successful; while for Maddy, the goal of being a psychologist floated insubstantially just out of reach, and her appalling experience at school meant it was unlikely ever to be achieved. Kingsley's lack of confidence somehow formed a thoughtful and intellectual man, while Jackson's ease with the world in which he found himself eventually led to him rejecting it.

People are complicated, and simply showing them a website with some attractive career paths is rarely enough on its own. In fact what intends to motivate can often do the opposite. I recall a staff training session in which a well-meaning colleague asked us to talk about the application of what we were teaching to possible careers. She told us that, for example, the Maths department, next time they were doing trigonometry, could talk about how essential this was for air-traffic control. My heart sank. All I could think of was the 99 per cent of students who instantly thought, 'Well, I don't want to be an air-traffic controller' and switched off.

And the problem deepens when the market forces of education – the need to recruit, and the need to convert student numbers into student grades – push institutions to be less than honest. It might be motivating to know that your GCSE in Law is going to lead to a career as a top barrister, but it's not necessarily true. What Jackson found out was that spending time familiarising yourself with the social world of elite institutions was far more relevant.

There is an inertia to our lives: we are drawn back towards the orbit we came from. My own parents were a lecturer and a social worker, respectively. My career as a teacher was no real surprise. Again and again we can see this effect – from the astonishingly high rates of the children of doctors going into medicine, to the kids who every year tell me their exams don't matter because their dad is going to give them a job at his building site. In this context, the motivation to go beyond this has to be deep and have an emotional power to match the pull of familiarity. I spent a long time working with sixth-form students to get them to go to university, when they had no family history of it – and often found myself with no answer to the simple objection that they didn't want to leave home.

But change does happen; it's just that it is very hard to predict or scaffold. Moments of inflection catch you in unexpected ways. A reading of *Lord of the Flies* sets off a chain reaction that ends in Hollywood. A crisis leads to an offer of help – or it doesn't.

For all the focus on exams and grades, they're actually the easy part. Perhaps the biggest challenge in education is getting your pupils to feel motivated to learn, not as a transaction, but for its own sake. And when it comes to explaining what they will get out of it, what it means for their future, the true skill lies in somehow working out how to be honest about the uncertainties of it. How to give teenagers the confidence to set off down paths when they don't have a clear idea of the destination. And how to get them to think beyond the world they know – whether that's a world of privilege or the opposite.

School is a miracle. The mechanics of it are staggering – 8.9 million pupils in 24,413 schools in England alone – and, in general, it works. It works because it is filled with care, and commitment, and skill, and love. But for all the miracle of school, there is also a tragedy going on. The shape of it can be glimpsed in the strange change in attendance patterns in the wake of Covid. We've gone from a national average that hovered around 95 per cent to one around 88 per cent. Most significantly, there are large numbers of children whose attendance has dropped below 50 per cent – who are only in school for half the time they should be, or less. There are many factors. Some children are genuinely paralysed by anxiety about school. Others are running round the streets, indulging in minor vandalism. Still others are hiding in the warm embrace of a duvet and an Xbox. But for all of them the fundamental contract – the basic belief that school is what you do, day in, day out – has broken down, so that when faced with the transaction that school offers, they think, 'No – not for me.'[3]

This is only one symptom. It isn't simply those children who are dropping off the attendance figures who are struggling. After twenty-two years of teaching, despite all the successes I've witnessed – the positive change, the increased rigour, the growing body of research – I have a sick fear sitting deep inside me that tells me we are teaching only to the converted. That it is the winners alone to whom our system speaks.

So how do we change this?

In Part One I set out my argument that the way we *think* about schools as a society is all wrong, exemplified by the way we use exams. What ought to be a tool for learning has become a tool for assigning worth. The main principle in the design of exams is not 'Do they teach the right things in the right way?' but 'Are they hard enough and comparable enough?' Effectively, exams become a way to sort kids into winners and losers, and to rank schools, ensuring competition between them. Again, as is inevitable in the market-place, we get winners and losers: concentrations of wealthy middle-class families in areas with good schools, leaving those schools with disadvantaged communities at a further disadvantage.

Everyone agrees that schools should be 'fair', meaning that every child gets a decent education, regardless of background. But the standardised academic approach – by which I mean a curriculum based on discrete subjects, taught and assessed in ways that are reverse-engineered from the academic disciplines of higher education – simply cannot deliver this, and for the most basic of reasons. It is fundamentally not *designed* to do so. We need exams. They are vital. We need knowledge, we need a curriculum, we need the opportunity for specialisation. And we need to assess and measure our schools. But my argument is that to achieve 'fairness', to make schools function for all children, we need to value a whole array of qualities beyond the academic, and beyond exam results.

In Part Two I have tried to show how many functions a school has beyond the acquisition of knowledge: the forming of social relationships, the development of character, the building of identity, the encoding of our moral relationship to authority and society. In other words, the social good that schools provide, and that we need them to provide, is not solely in sorting kids into appropriate jobs according to knowledge base and capacity; rather, it involves equipping them with the attitudes and dispositions that will enable them to thrive. More broadly, it lies in the building of healthy communities around them where people are able to live fulfilled lives, and not merely in providing the mobility for a lucky few to leave their less fortunate peers behind.

To engineer a system that actually values what schools do and provides a good education for all, there are some specific things that I believe we should do – or at least try to do – and in the next and final part of this book I'll lay these out. But before we come to these measures, which will no doubt be fraught with practical challenges, I believe we need a new way of *thinking* about school; and, specifically, a new answer to that initial crucial question 'What is school for?' Without this deeper thinking, without that better answer, we cannot even begin the process of reshaping our schools.

PART THREE

How can we do it differently?

15. Thinking differently about school

The overriding rationale behind the way we measure educational achievement and shape national policy in the UK today – whether through the curriculum, league tables or Ofsted – is that academic success leads to economic success, and that economic success will then make life better. In case you're in any doubt about this, let's remind ourselves once again of the language that kids use ('get a good job', 'have a decent career') as well as the language that teachers use ('progress' and 'aspiration') and of course the language the government uses ('skills for the workplace').

This simple economic argument, whereby the social good of education is understood to be primarily economic, both for individuals and for wider society, is all-pervasive. This is why teachers up and down the country, along with politicians and parents, say (in so many words), 'Do well in your exams and you'll earn more.'[1] Yes, we say other things too, about personal growth and happiness, but those are secondary to the economic argument that states that 'academic achievement equals economic productivity'.

This line of reasoning is false. Even as I write the sentence, I do a mental double-take, because it is so hard-wired into our collective psyche. But it *is* false. Academic achievement may well have a *relationship* to economic productivity, but it is a complex one that is not reflected in the language of straightforward equivalence we use.[2] For a start, as we intuitively know, take any class of kids and you will find that their future earnings will not map neatly onto their grades. Of course there will be a correlation – and, in some instances, there will be some significant causation – but it will not be true to say that if you got that extra grade in Maths you will get that extra promotion in ten years' time. Our destinies are shaped in myriad other ways – not least because of what we choose, which is an expression of our interests, our values and our identities. One straight-A student might choose to be a teacher, for example, while their peer who barely passed an exam sets up his own plumbing business and ends up not only earning more, but also with less debt.

Academic achievement does not even equal *potential* economic worth. While there is a correlation in the aggregate between academic achievement at school and earnings in later life, research has shown that this correlation only holds true in some areas of the country. In other areas, those from poorer backgrounds who achieve equivalent grades end up earning as much as one-third less.[3] Geography, income, familial education and demographics all impact on the way academic achievement is converted into economic worth.

The connection also breaks down when we zoom in to consider different kinds of job. While higher grades might *generally* correlate with higher income, it is absolutely not true to say that jobs with higher academic thresholds for entry are also the highest paid: those who work in the university sector, nursing or teaching are paid far less than those who work in finance or banking, to take the most obvious examples. A lawyer who passes the many levels of qualification to practise at the criminal Bar is likely to earn far less than a solicitor practising commercial law.

There is a deeper problem, too, with thinking of wider economic productivity purely in terms of the income that an individual receives. Some of the occupations on which the overall economic productivity of the country most relies – skilled trades, manufacturing, construction, transport and health and social care – are those with the lowest wages. Equally, some high-wage jobs (tax accountant, for instance) result in a net loss to the Treasury or even (in the case of a hedge-fund manager short-selling the pound) might actively undermine the economy. We often bemoan the scarcity of people willing to take low-wage jobs in the care sector, but if the values of society reflect only economic worth, why would they?

As for the question of whether economic productivity is the same as having a good life, I think most people would instinctively agree that money does not equal happiness. And they would be right. First, while one can say that money supports happiness, there is significant evidence that this has a ceiling – that beyond a level needed for a life with less stress, additional money does not provide additional happiness. Second, the research of behavioural scientist Paul Dolan and others suggests that happiness is most strongly associated with purpose and social relationships – and while the pursuit of money can be a legitimate source of purpose, it is not the only one.[4]

To give the argument its due, many people who say that 'good grades' equal 'better jobs' would no doubt admit this is simply a shorthand. The fact is that we need some way of measuring education, so we need some kind of grade. And we need some way of expressing the worth of that grade – and leaving aside all the caveats above, it is of course true that, in the aggregate, across the whole population, getting more and better grades at GCSE and A level *does* correlate with earning more money, even if the causation is far from direct. The real problem lies in the way of *thinking* that this inculcates in students, parents, teachers and society as a whole: do this and you will get that; learn this and you will achieve that; achieve this and you will earn that; earn this and you will become that.[5]

This is a problem because it completely undermines the value of education, not least amongst the pupils themselves. As I argued in Chapter 14, perhaps the most important challenge any teacher faces is motivating their pupils to learn. As we have seen, most teachers eventually fall back on the transactional or instrumental argument when faced with the question 'But what's the point?' We tell them we are equipping them for a good economic life. In doing so, we walk into a trap. As is often pointed out, a lot of what we learn has nothing to do with the knowledge that we will directly apply to our lives in adulthood or in our jobs. Few of us 'use' trigonometry, or the features of glaciation, or the plot details of *Macbeth*. We have handed students the perfect reason to disengage.

So we find more sophisticated ways to show how such knowledge is 'useful'. Instead, we argue that the curriculum provides, on the one hand, a broad base of cultural literacy in 'powerful' knowledge – a baseline on which more specialised knowledge can later be built – and, on the other, equips us with 'transferable skills'. In this version of education, studying *Macbeth* is important because it provides us with an understanding of an important cultural reference point – Shakespeare – and an ability to decode and analyse political situations, such as a board meeting, through careful dissection of how participants communicate. Trigonometry is a tool in developing logical mental processes (transferable skills), and a way of embedding a deep understanding about physical space and mathematical relationships (powerful knowledge) that may well support any number of complex work-related processes.

The problem with this argument is that it shares the same terms as the first one: school is a route to an economically better life. For a portion of kids this is true, but for too many kids – and for the ones who most need a better life than the one they already have – the evidence all around them suggests that simply *isn't* true.[6] From the point of view of a student who looks around them and, quite rightly, doesn't buy the argument that attending school is going to get them a better job or more money, the people and institutions who make this argument – their teachers, the schools – are idiots, deluded or lying. Whichever it is, you have lost them: education becomes something to be rejected as useless, rather than a fundamental necessity or a profound tool for personal fulfilment.[7]

So what is the alternative?

I have always liked the Buddhist parable of the blind men and the elephant. One man touches the trunk and declares it to be a snake; another its tusk and says it is a spear; the third feels its side and decides it is a wall; the fourth its leg and asserts it is a tree. Focusing on the use of the subjects we teach betrays an equivalent narrowness of vision, in which we mistake the part for the whole. We are fixating on the use of the trunk, or the purpose of the tusks, while ignoring the key fact of there being an elephant standing there. What do I mean by that? I mean that education, knowledge and the experience of learning are not just a means to an end: they amount to a living, breathing creature that enriches us, irrespective of how 'useful' the various parts are.

Right now, as I write, my youngest son is doing an online 'draw-along' – a Zoom based art class with his favourite comic-book artist. He's an emotional kid, and he is highly invested in this. While waiting for the class, his lips moved silently as he counted down with the timer. As he draws, he stares with fierce intensity at the page, then smiles in the pauses. The picture he makes is excellent, for a nine-year-old. He says, 'Yes!' to himself.

This experience is 'flow', according to the psychologist Mihaly Csikszentmihalyi, in his book of the same title,[8] in which he talks about the relationship between how skilled you are in an activity and how challenging it is. He says that happiness comes from being in this state of 'flow' – the state of being engaged with something where the level of difficulty and your own level of skill are calibrated so that it is hard, but you can do it. He describes this as the state common to everyone who is successful in a field – the feeling of an athlete pushing themselves in a race, or a scientist trying to figure out a problem.

We all recognise this feeling. It is why we talk about 'challenges' and 'obstacles' whenever we talk about 'success'. And it's why, as we saw with Kingsley Ben-Adir, the *feeling* of being good at school can be as transformative as the stuff you actually learn. It's a high – a high that, once you understand it, you chase throughout your life by exposing yourself to challenge and attempting to increase your skill. The *process* of learning, when it feels like this, is the template for life-long fulfilment, no matter whether it ends up being through your expertise and engagement with gardening or with nuclear physics. The 'use' of the content pales beside the purpose of the process.

When I was a child I was obsessed by insects. I read about them, searched for them, kept them in boxes and jars. I learned a lot about insects that has been of precisely zero *use* to me in my professional life. But one day, when my own children were very little, I sat at the side of a pond and I saw a large, ugly, bug-like creature crawl up out of the water. Deep in my brain I remembered some of that obsessively gathered knowledge. I told the boys to wait. We watched as it crawled up a leaf, then held fast, then split its back open to reveal a huge yellow-and-black dragonfly. We watched the dragonfly slowly unfurl, pumping its wings full of blood to stiffen them. The boys stared in open-mouthed wonder.

The world is an astonishing place, but our brains see it in ways that all too often flatten and diminish it. We take things for granted unless we know the stories behind them. We see a wrecked castle wall, a pile of rubble, but the knowledge of the battle makes it come alive. We see a grubby-looking bug, but the knowledge of insect lifecycles enables us to wait and watch the miraculous emergence of a dragonfly.

Education enriches by teaching us the joy of skill and challenge. It enriches by opening up the world around us and by showing us that, for the person who is in the process of learning, the world is endlessly full of meaning and interest. And by doing this, it also does the most enriching thing of all. It taps into the deeper search for meaning that provides us with the sense of *purpose* so essential to living well.

School is not the only, or even the most important, source of this. For many people the ultimate purpose they find is through love, through family and friends. But as we've seen, even there school is not separate from love. It's part of the ecosystem within which love thrives or withers. And if done correctly, through the fostering of an open, moral, engaged culture of learning, school can teach us the most vital lesson of all – that if you push at obscurity, it clarifies. That difficulty is subject to explanation. That hard work and empathy, in love as well as in the workplace, lead to joy. That discovery, and revelation, and transformation, *can actually happen*. Without this, the search for meaning will never even begin.

What this boils down to is something very simple that is at the same time very hard. Rather than focusing on that endpoint of school, we need to remember the process. Rather than seeing schools as places that deliver outcomes – that produce skills – that feed destinations – we need to remember that they are places to be, places to live, places to grow in: places that you *experience* and that can enrich.

This is not simply in order to make education fairer and more effective, though it most certainly is a pre-condition for both of those things. It is also beneficial to the learning process itself. In Cordelia Fine's book on gender difference, *Testosterone Rex*, she describes something called 'stereotype threat'. Researchers found that if students were reminded of a negative stereotype about their own group before the test (in this case the negative stereotype that girls are less good at maths than boys), it had a material effect on their performance. What this tells us is something we all know already: the connection you feel to a set of knowledge, the investment you have in it, the sense in which you own it, intimately affects your ability to retain it. Forget the crude dichotomy between 'knowledge-rich' teaching and 'skills-based' teaching. The context of where you learn something, how you learn it, who you are and who you learn it from is an essential part of the particular *quality* of what is learned. The *experience* of learning matters – hence you can 'learn' *Macbeth* but hate it, or get an A in Maths but forget all the content immediately afterwards, because the process was an entirely functional but boring short-term exercise in passing an exam.[9] And that is why we all reach adulthood with a unique and idiosyncratic mental curriculum made up of nuggets of information that stuck, because of reasons as diverse as whether you fancied the girl you sat next to in Geography, whether you tended to have French in the sleepy period after lunch and, of course, how funny your English teacher was.[10]

We need to see the knowledge that pupils acquire not as a neutral substance to be poured into them, but as something that is intimately bound up in the context in which they acquire it. We have to move away from the idea of outcomes, of *results*, and re-centre education around *experience*. Rather than being a factory that turns out a product, we need to see school as the *home* that our children live in for a significant proportion of their lives, and whose values underwrite lifelong happiness, whether or not you 'succeed'. We need to see education as a public good, like clean air and parks, and not a method for individual advancement.

The irony is that the many outstanding schools across the country have shown that this is the best route to good results anyway.

Let's come back to earth again. Let's grant that, as well as enriching through wonder and the search for meaning, knowledge and learning are *also* useful. We shouldn't justify learning solely on the basis of its utility, but it would be perverse not to embrace that utility when it arises. And yet, more perversely still, the problem with our transactional approach is that it has led to a curriculum that seems designed to *obstruct* the use of knowledge, whether in the form of 'powerful knowledge' or 'transferable skills'.

The traditional version of the curriculum especially is composed of discrete, specialised, academicised subjects that are reverse-engineered to fit with later, yet more specialised study: GCSEs are designed to equip students for A level, which are in turn designed to equip them for university. They involve highly domain-specific skills that often don't have obviously transferable qualities. E. D. Hirsch, the key educational thinker behind the reforms of the last decade, would make the point that skills *are* domain-specific and *don't* transfer. This is fair – but it also begs the question: what defines a domain? It's all very well saying that chess doesn't help Maths, when they are clearly different. But where exactly is the boundary between English Literature and History? The best, most original thinkers are those whose ideas range across categories and boundaries – those who expand the boundaries of the domains they are trained in. And the rest of us need to be able to do this, too, because most of life doesn't divide into neat categories.

If the purpose of the curriculum is to provide a base of interconnected general knowledge to understand and enrich the world, that purpose is not reflected in the way we define, assess and teach subjects. Witness the teaching of Maths and English – disciplines that are integral to understanding the world and expressing oneself in every other subject, and yet are taught and assessed in discrete silos. We could easily tie history content in with English, sociology and art, or Maths with graphic design and computing, demonstrating the use of the knowledge as well as the use of the grade, without sacrificing any of the rigour of the content. Instead our curriculum is designed as a series of ladders leading towards the specific disciplines of higher education (but one with few rewards for those who only climb half-way up).

On top of this, it is in the nature of exams to funnel knowledge into narrower and narrower categories. *This* topic is for *this* unit in *this* paper. And the necessity of teaching to exams allows schools to forget that the point of revision is not to pass exams; rather, it is the point of exams to make you revise and fix the knowledge and skills for their own sake. In this way exams can drive a further wedge between children and their understanding of how knowledge genuinely fits into the world around them. And so the potential utility of that knowledge is diminished or even lost. In a very real and self-defeating way, exam grades become the thing that is useful, rather than the knowledge they represent. If we wish to preserve and enhance the utility of what we teach, then once again we need to value it for its own sake and move away from the transactional approach. To do this we need to recognise three things.

School means different things at different ages

Let's not fall into the trap of thinking that one answer will fit all. Any understanding of what school is for also needs to take into account that children are growing and changing and developing at an astonishing rate during their school years. An overly academicised approach at the age of ten might be wrong – but it is entirely appropriate for kids contemplating university. In early years a key priority is muscle tone and fine motor skills, while in sixth-form colleges careers education is essential. Pedagogy that sounds absurd in a GCSE Science class is entirely appropriate in Year 1, and approaches for Drama at KS3 are understandably different from those for Maths at KS5. And so we also need a system that has a basic logic in the way it progresses – a movement between these stages that enables us to build and progress – rather than one reverse-engineered from the endpoint.

There are two ways in which our current system doesn't possess that logic. First is the way in which we are haunted by university as an end-goal of education. The ideal of academic rigour we get from that pushes younger ages towards a concept of study and knowledge that is more appropriate for later years. A levels are, understandably, built around the needs of universities, but while it makes superficial sense that GCSEs are built along the same lines and dovetail neatly with A levels, this doesn't hold up to scrutiny. GCSEs are compulsory and are intended to be general, not specific. To think about them only as a gateway to A levels and university, when 62.5 per cent of students don't attend university and 34 per cent don't even start A levels, is damaging.

This problem goes further than GCSEs, though. The pivot towards a knowledge-rich approach has caused a basic fallacy to permeate our system. The logic is seductive – if knowledge is good, then we should structure the system to provide that foundational knowledge as early as possible. But the implementation of this approach has loaded primary education with a lot of the paraphernalia of secondary – of subject categories and subject leads, and domain-specific planning. At heart, there is a misunderstanding of the value of primary: as a place where universal enthusiasm for learning is fostered, where the things that are taught are taught so well they stick for the rest of a life, and where the boundaries that we use between academic disciplines often have very little relevance, even where ambitious knowledge is being taught.

This brings us to the second way in which the differences between ages cause problems. This lies in the transitions between institutions. In the case of transition at the age of eleven, the very different imperatives of primary and secondary education can mean there is a profound mismatch of values and structures. And this transition has far more impact on the vulnerable student with no counterweight of stable values and parenting at home. Primary schools tend to be more homogenous than secondaries, with smaller, more local intakes of kids, allowing a far more directly interventionist approach with parents – working closely with those in need, and supporting them to parent their children. At secondary, with fourteen different teachers and several hundred kids in a year group, this can fall by the wayside; and the marketisation of the system, whereby the direct connection between a 'feeder' primary and its secondary is broken for the sake of parental choice, and local planning is fragmented due to academisation, makes it much harder to mitigate the fallout.

Another cliff-edge transition exists between GCSE and A level, and again it is the least advantaged who often struggle the most with it. While GCSEs are designed to lead on towards A-level study, that is often not how they are taught. The methods one uses to teach in a school with a majority of students in deep disadvantage, who are perhaps perceived to be unlikely to go on to A level and who lack the deep engagement born of parental support and aspiration, often slip towards the instrumental: you can easily end up cajoling kids with language like 'Just get a couple of marks here and you'll pass', or browbeating them with 'You'll never get on that course without your pass at English.' By contrast, in more advantaged circumstances, where GCSE students are likely to move on to A levels, they are often taught with that in mind: 'You don't need this now, but understanding the Civil War will help in A-level History next year.' This is heightened by the fact that schools in affluent areas are far more likely to be able to sustain sixth forms, teaching students all the way through GCSE and A level – leaving the schools with less well-resourced cohorts more likely to be for the ages of eleven to sixteen,[11] ending at GCSE, and even more vulnerable to a style of teaching that has only the GCSE criteria in view. The effect is a further entrenchment of privilege: disadvantaged kids are taught in a way that can ignore the needs of A level and so even if they pick them, they struggle; advantaged kids are taught in a way that assumes they will continue, and so they are ready for the step up.[12] This is not a criticism of those schools – as with anything, the endpoint you are given determines the methods used to get there. If the measure of success is a grade, then it is logical to do everything you can to get that grade.

But there is a further impact. More students from disadvantaged backgrounds then go on to non-school-based institutions like FE college and, when they get there, they are more likely to choose courses that lead to lower-income careers or go on to lower-tariff universities.[13] Colleges are certainly not a poor relation to school-based sixth forms, but there is an undeniable risk when the very students with the least social capital and the least supportive homes move away from schools that know them and their capacities at a key inflection point in their educational journey.

At each of these transition stages, the idea of choice and a market economy in education actually leads to a narrowing of options for the most vulnerable. Unable to pay to live in the best catchment areas, they cannot choose schools; and funnelled towards colleges by demographics and school type, they cannot choose post-sixteen provision.

What is needed, then, is a coherent view of the journey that children make from age three to age eighteen. A view that looks at primary and secondary and tertiary education not as separate institutions, but as integrated staging posts. This in turn means moving away from a market-based approach founded on parental choice. If education is important for all, it must be planned for all – and that means no longer leaving the links between institutions to be governed by which academy chain happens to run them.

The relationship between school and success is not straightforward

As we've seen, the reasons that people achieve and don't achieve are complicated by race, class, gender, family background and qualities of character. So much that determines a pupil's 'success' happens outside school. The realisation I've come to, in twenty-two years of teaching and during my travels across the country to visit schools and schoolchildren, is this means that achieving 'fairness' through school is a chimera.

Put simply, before we can have a fair education system, we need a fair society. We need to ensure children don't grow up in poverty. We need to protect them from abuse, and exploitation. We need to give them routes to hope and prosperity in adulthood. If we want 'upward' social mobility, we also need 'downward' social mobility – and we need neither of them to be undergone at personal loss, whether of money, status or identity. We need a society that doesn't give undue rewards to some who get lucky, and that doesn't unduly penalise those who don't.

That's a big ask, to say the least. But while we wait for those things to happen, we need to stop thinking that grades are equivalent and comparable – a disadvantaged pupil who gets a B may have done vastly more to achieve that grade, and be far more capable, than an advantaged pupil who gets an A – and we need to stop thinking that those grades reflect merit, meaning what you deserve, and what you are worth, as a person.

Fundamentally, grades tell us very little, not only about what it took to achieve them (a lot for some, little for others), but also about what we are capable of. The ways we learn, the personal circumstances in which we do it, and the culture of the schools we do it in impact not only on the grades we get, but also on the way we are able to use the knowledge gained – whether we can use it creatively and in the service of original thinking, or whether it is learned one year and jettisoned the next.

After all, notions of success and failure in school also ignore one of the most profound ways in which school shapes our lives. It is a social testing ground – a place in which we learn to interact with the world around us. We learn to make friends, to negotiate with enemies and to fall in love. If this part of school goes wrong – if we are bullied or victimised – the impact can be profound and lifelong and, for many of us, the lessons in human interaction that school provides are the ones we use most often in our daily adult lives. When we think of schools and their relationship to success, it is this kind of success that we should be thinking of, every bit as much as exam results.

Success should mean something wider still, in fact. Well into adulthood, the community that school provides continues to be important in nourishing a fuller life. Schools are a rare focal point in a fragmented world – one that people continue to identify with throughout their lives. This has a shadow side as well: the ways in which more privileged school communities can insulate and protect are beneficial for individuals, but often deeply unfair in the system as a whole. But if we lost school as a community, then our cities, towns and villages would be poorer, and the fabric of social cohesion weaker.

Schools help form and maintain moral values and personal identity. It's not for nothing that religion and education have been hand-in-hand for much of human history – and even now, when our state is increasingly secular and multicultural, it is schools that are tasked with teaching 'British values' and 'Citizenship'; with educating on consent and criminality; with combating antisocial behaviour and encouraging charitable fundraising. When schools fail – when students misbehave or underachieve – the reasons are complex and in many cases extend beyond the school gates. Our education system is filled with dedicated professionals, and in many ways is stronger than it has ever been; equally, the challenges it faces seem to grow daily. The more schools do, the more precarious their success seems to be and the greater the cost of their failure.

And yet how often do we recognise that kind of success? Measuring it in any standardised objective way is hard, perhaps impossible, but like most things that money can't buy, this is because it is so valuable. We need somehow to recognise that value, to make it visible, even if it is not quantifiable.

Technology should affect the means of education, but not the ends

There is much discussion at the moment about how one might move schools into the digital age. Part of this is a response to online learning during lockdown and results in techno-utopian thinkpieces about how schools may be redundant in the future. This, to put it bluntly, is rubbish. As we've seen in this book, online learning addresses only a tiny fraction of what schools actually do; and on the most fundamental level, unless we reorganise society to relieve all parents of the need to work, and provide all households with space and resources to learn in, we will still need physical places for children to go during the school day.

But technology does have serious implications for what and how we teach – and in particular how we assess. Many qualifications are already sat online, but the majority still involve writing longhand with pen and paper in an exam hall alongside one's peers. The defenders of the status quo have two key arguments. First, there is educational value in the way that exams work – in the thought processes required in physically writing, in the effectiveness of reading comprehension on the page rather than on the screen. And second, there are obstacles in the difficulty of administering and ensuring the security of digital exams.

The second is a practical problem to which we can, if we wish, find a solution. It is more a matter of figuring out the details. We shouldn't rush, but there may well be a point when we are ready. The first is fundamentally unconvincing. Research supports the argument that written exams are worth doing, but it does not mean that exams done with computers are not worthwhile, too. And if the exams and courses taken towards the end of one's journey through school are supposed to prepare you for things you might do as an adult, then the argument for taking them digitally seems unanswerable. The retention of handwritten exams at this age starts to look like the sabre-toothed curriculum – a domain-specific skill that does not inevitably support other skills. We may be able to certify a pupil's knowledge with a handwritten exam, but it will be far less useful as a measure of that pupil's potential capacity. Put crudely, students who struggle with handwriting but are fluent in typing will be fine in the workplace, but will do badly at school. So on a really basic level, it is insane that we train students to write fast longhand, but we don't train them to touch-type.

This may seem like a minor, technical point, but it's a glimpse of something much larger. Transformative new technologies undoubtedly have further and significant implications for schools. Most obviously, the recent developments in AI have been changing the conversation entirely about what the skills of the future might be. Currently the most significant aspect of AI for schools and jobs is its ability to create convincing written text – if reports and verbal analysis can be created digitally, where do the traditional skills of literacy come in?

The answer to this one is actually a lot simpler. If history has taught us anything, it is that the new rarely completely supersedes the old. Just because we have cars doesn't mean we don't need to walk. And more importantly for the argument I have been making here: just because you don't *need* to do something doesn't mean there is no worth in doing it. In many ways the reason we still need to write essays is the central thesis of this book: process, not outcome, is what matters. You don't write in order to *have* an essay, nice and neat and filed away – you write in order to *have written* an essay, and to have reordered and structured your thoughts along the way. The real difficulty with AI is that it makes coursework and non-examined assessment nightmarish. So the implications are probably that even as exams become digital, there will be a need to ensure that assessment stays largely within (newly modified) exam conditions.

Think about it this way. Over the course of the twentieth century we moved from a world in which the structures of everyday life kept us fit and active – walking, washing clothes, manual labour, food that had to be cooked from scratch – to one where the structures of everyday life enable inactivity and obesity. To counteract that, we have learned the need to teach and embed habits that once came naturally: exercise regimes, healthy-eating strictures. We need to build the same mindset for our mental capacity. If AI begins to read for us and write for us, that doesn't mean we should stop doing it ourselves as well.

The bigger point is this. In the coming decades it is likely that some of the key trends of today will continue: increasing inequality, decreasing wages, low growth. Our young will have to figure out new ways of living and governing in the midst of transformations – technological, environmental and social – that we cannot possibly predict or probably even imagine. While I have been banging the drum for an approach to education that is not transactional, that is not the same as saying that school should not be designed to benefit the wider society and the wider economy. To deal with the uncertainties of the future, we need to create young people who are confident, well informed and happy – only then will they have the attitude and skills necessary to negotiate this future. We need to ensure they are politically and socially engaged – not only those who 'succeed' in school, but also those who don't win the meritocratic race. We need to give them a voice and a sense of their own value, as well as taking the time and care to equip them with the knowledge and skills they need, not just as workers, but as citizens. Moving away from a transactional approach and towards one that values school – and, by extension, young people themselves on their own terms – will be an essential part of achieving this. We need to do this, not only because it's right, but because the times demand it.

16. A better story

On a bright late-summer day I wake early and drive to Cumbria. It's the Friday of the week before I start term. In the negotiation and timetabling of two-car family life I've ended up with the shit one, and winding my way along the narrow roads on the eastern shore of Ullswater is a slightly worrying experience. I have no satnav and am trying to remember how you find places when you don't have a little chequered flag to tell you you're there.

I catch the flash of a sign and make a sharp turn up a steep drive to the Outward Bound centre. As I park, I can hear the kids. I've been on many a school trip and I recognise this moment. As I walk up towards them, I see knots of children milling round in the immediate aftermath of breakfast, and adults herding them into groups. Almost every teacher will have been in this situation at some point. But not necessarily at the start of Year 7.

This is the very first week at secondary school for these children. They are enrolled at XP Gateshead, the third of three XP schools (the first two are in Doncaster). They are organised into 'crews' – tutor groups of thirteen children who bond intensely, both during this preparatory trip and during the forty-five minutes they spend together every day before lessons start. XP refers to 'expeditionary learning', and every year they will go on further 'expeditions', along the way collectively producing 'beautiful work' – presentations, videos, even a book written by them and published by the school.

Right now, though, the kids have to get up a hill. We start in a circle, and they number off. I'm given a number, too. They introduce themselves to me. They are familiar, these kids – at eleven, they are the same age as my own eldest son, with the same accents and experiences as those I've taught for the last eight years. Year 7 is a time of delicate balance on the cusp of knowing – kids who are still kids, but who at times flash glimpses of teenage self-awareness. Here it is mostly the child that comes out, and they move as they talk, bobbing excitedly like tethered balloons as they tell me about putting their heads under a waterfall, or when someone broke their ankle and had to go to hospital at two in the morning. The teachers seem a little less enthused by the latter.

We set off. As we climb, the kids do what kids do: some race forward, others walk as if lead weights are dragging them back. But when the teacher calls to those at the front to not go any further, she uses the language of 'crew' – sticking together, leaving no one behind, being kind. It's a language the kids have already wholeheartedly adopted, only days into their time at XP.

Language is important here. XP is an offshoot of expeditionary learning in the US, itself a product of the ideas of Kurt Hahn – the German educationalist who founded both Outward Bound and Gordonstoun, the private school in Moray – and the central thread of all of them is the sense of the 'expedition' as metaphor. As such, there is much talk of goals as 'climbing the mountain', or resilience in learning being directly equated with resilience in, say, jumping into a cold lake. The idea is that the experience of learning is as important as the content – and it is the language that links the two. The teachers tell me that the times when students overcome challenges here, in the lake or on the hills, will be directly related to their challenges in the classroom over the next year. 'Remember when you helped Jack in the boat?' the teacher might say. 'You need to use that strength here.'

When we reach the top of the hill, sweating in the morning sun, I see this use of metaphorical understanding in action. First, the instructors gather all the children and adults into a circle. Through a question-and-answer session, they recap the key messages from the week.

It's a Year 7 boy who tells us all where the word 'crew' comes from. 'In the war, there were sailors who were shipwrecked and were in lifeboats, and Kurt Hahn saw that some of them survived and some didn't – and it wasn't really the strongest. In fact it was the youngest and strongest who didn't survive, and the older ones with more experience supported each other and managed much better.' The instructor corrects him gently: it was Lawrence Holt who observed this, and Holt and Hahn then set up Outward Bound to provide the experience of challenge and resilience in the outdoors that would build these qualities in young people for the difficulties of later life.

Now it's time for the crews to demonstrate what they've learned. Their theme is to show a moment where they have demonstrated one of the core values of the school. One by one they perform their presentations – a classic, heart-warmingly shonky mishmash of drama, narration and pratfalls that any teacher of eleven-year-olds would recognise in an instant. But there is a strong thread running through them. They vary in skill and execution, but the message is the same and is totally assimilated by all. They say the same thing, again and again: 'we are crew'.

Everything in XP is built around this ideal of tight communality – of service to the collective, whether in your crew or in wider society. Being here, on this bright September day, with the pin-sharp peaks and ridges of the Lake District encircling us, standing in a ring of children, it feels both revolutionary and deeply old-fashioned.

Schools are strange places. I set out in this book to try to pin them down – to describe what is really there. It seems a stupid goal, in many ways. After all, what's really there is . . . everything. Everyone – every life experience you can imagine – cheek-by-jowl in a crappy building from the sixties, trying to assimilate the totality of useful knowledge for adulthood while at the same time coping with the transformation from being fairly likely to soil yourself on any given day to having stubble and/or breasts and the vote.

And yet, for all the grubby reality that schools contain, there is also something oddly elusive about them. 'School', as we talk about it, isn't as simple as a place, or the people in it. It's a kind of dance, choreographed by the rhythms and transitions of the school year, layered over by memory and expectations, in limbo between nostalgia for the past and hope for the future. The way we move through that dance becomes a story we tell ourselves – a narrative of who we are. The learning, the interactions, the moments of anagnorisis – realisation – allow us to construct ourselves, to narrate our adult lives into being. *I am the person who can do these things, the person who climbed that hill, the person who passed that test.* But also *I am the person whom no one likes, the person who cannot do it, the person who failed.*

And we all tell ourselves different stories, even when the raw material is superficially the same. Two kids get the same mark, but it means something different to each. Two kids study the same subject, but it becomes part of the way one of them views the world. Two kids are excluded – for one, it is the start of something better; for the other, the end of everything good.

When we ignore this part of what schools do – if we think of them as mere machines to create outputs, to deliver grades or knowledge – then we lose perhaps our most potent tool in the shaping of our students. Because what strikes me most, about all of the schools I've visited, is that the best of them have one key point in common. They might seem as wildly divergent as XP and Michaela, they might look beyond the boundaries of school, like Reach, but they all tell a story – and help their pupils tell a story – about the need for something that transcends the individual. They are communities. 'Service' might be the socially engaged humanist mantra of XP, or the deep tradition of compassion in Catholic education, or the small-c conservative values of Michaela, but if it is an ideal that enables children to no longer think of education as a transaction, or of school as a marketplace, or of life as a zero-sum game, then it is the crucial ingredient we need.

And the qualities that exceptional teachers and school leaders have share a vital piece of DNA. They are storytellers. A good school is like a piece of performance art that allows children to be the hero of their own narrative. Whether the story is one of discipline and powerful knowledge, or one of freedom and self-actualisation, it enables children to conceptualise their success at the same time as giving them the emotional and cultural tools to enact it.

Watch a great teacher in their classroom. Explicitly or implicitly, they thread each lesson into a narrative arc. They raise the stakes: this is the most important subject of them all, this is the most fascinating moment, the key breakthrough. You are my favourite class, and you – you in the corner, who never speak, and feel like you don't fit, and aren't sure if you understand who you are are seen and are special and are part of that story.

The thing is, it isn't just the exceptional schools that create communities, or the exceptional teachers that tell stories. Like learning, it happens whether we intend it to or not. The only question is what kind of community, and what kind of story. And this is where we need to think very carefully about the structures that shape education, and the principles behind the design of our schools.

Because, wonderful as so many schools and so many teachers are, they exist in an ecosystem that feeds a very different narrative. It tells us – in exam results, and CVs, and UCAS applications, and Ofsted grades – a story about an Exam Nation, where the things worth doing are the things we can measure and compare. It tells us a story where individual success is paramount, where efficiency is all, where schools are for grades and the rest of the stuff is merely a by-product.

No matter how brilliant a storyteller a teacher is, in their room, in their single hour of the day, they cannot change the narrative arc. Changing *that* is not a matter of tinkering around the edges. Teachers can't do it on their own – but nor can schools. It can't be only the outliers, the experimental schools, the outstanding schools that work properly. Education is too big a deal, both in importance and in sheer scale. It is the deep structures that shape it. And so, if we really want to find a better way as a country, we need to pay attention to the story told by the design of the whole system, and the incentives built into it.

What does that mean in practice? Well, it seems to me that there are five new narratives around what school is for, and how it works, that we need to construct. And to do so we have to make some fundamental changes.

Narrative One: Education is not a marketplace

One of the biggest issues we face in schools is marketisation – the introduction of market forces into school choice, and the conceptualising of education as product – and the transactionalism that inevitably follows, whereby our appreciation of the intrinsic value of education is eroded. The market creates winners and losers, and this is not a story we can afford to tell our children, either morally or pragmatically.

Most fundamentally, we need to break the link between outstanding schools and overwhelmingly middle-class catchments. We need to stop the evolutionary process whereby the better a school becomes, the more competitive entry is, the more the demographic immediately around it changes and the more the most disadvantaged are squeezed out.

The academisation programme is the easy thing to blame here – and there is no doubt that organising schools according to a Darwinian principle of survival of the fittest can cause significant problems – as well as a counterproductive mindset in school leaders. The organisation of academy chains can't be left to the particular needs of individual Multi-Academy Trusts, which might or might not choose to take on a particular failing school, and might or might not open a new institution. It needs to be subject to proper local planning – joining up resources in ways that serve communities, rather than leaving it to the market, which by its nature channels academies away from where they are needed most. And yet in many ways the freedoms that academies have provide the answer as well. Ethical academy leadership, within clear parameters of best practice – whereby academies and trusts are incentivised to make choices that serve the wider interest, under the guidance and planning of proper localised control – could begin to unpick the damage done. And it could also address the single biggest driver of the marketisation of schools: admissions policies.

Rather than doing away with academies, the solution that I advocate, which is already in place in many trusts, is that instead of simple proximity, school admissions should be organised around larger catchment areas and made by banded lottery (where there is a random allocation of places within each of five income bands), with Pupil Premium numbers being spread far more evenly between schools.

Reach Academy, as we've seen, has such a policy, which dictates that their number of Pupil Premium students can never fall below the average for the borough. There are areas, of course, where the level of deprivation is so high that even this won't scratch the surface. But those areas are in need of so much more as well. In the rest of the country, however, this measure would stop at a stroke the creeping segregation by class that shields many 'outstanding' schools from the challenges they should be addressing. This would also necessitate the abolition of grammar schools – something widely agreed on by educationalists.

But I'd go further. The reason that schools are the size they are is often a combination of accident, expediency and, in many instances, market forces. The pressures of expansion, the need to negotiate the ever-increasing costs and the ever-decreasing budgets can lead us away from core educational values. But controlling – and limiting – the size of the student body is a very straightforward way of controlling the nature of the school community and reducing the incentive for destructive competition. As a rule, small is better, and all-through is better still.

We should move gradually towards an ideal model of schools that are all-through, or that work in closely linked pairs, and have a maximum of ninety in a year group. Ninety students is a small enough number that a head of year or a subject specialist can meaningfully know them all – and yet it is a large enough number that the school can employ sufficient specialists to cover a broad and balanced curriculum. The Multi-Academy Trust system is ideal for this: we can maintain economies of scale in the back office, but ensure that schools themselves are at a scale whereby leaders can actually know and influence the majority of children.

And private schools need to be addressed as well. They don't need to be abolished. They are a valid part of the landscape. But they do not need the preferential treatment they currently get. Plans from the Labour Party to take away their tax exemption are fair and should be embraced, but I'd go further. Their wealth – the funds they gain from alumni or foreign, non-charitable outposts – should be subject to a tax, the proceeds from which would go directly to a state-school capital-investment fund – one that directs funds to the areas of need and gives the state sector control over how to use it, rather than simply leaving it to private schools to bestow their favours where they see fit.

Narrative Two: School is at the heart of a community

Schools already are vital in their communities – and teachers already live and breathe those values. Time and again I've listened to those in education talk about their sense of vocation, and it always comes back to that sense of proper commitment to community. But this aspect of schools – the pastoral, the outreach, the wraparound – is not recognised as central in our discourse around education. It isn't measured, and it isn't codified as something children should be entitled to. When cuts come, they come to these programmes first – and, in recent years, when have cuts *not* come?

To change this we need to tell the story of the centrality of schools to their local context and explicitly build this into their design. Just as social care is integral to the work of hospitals, so community outreach and engagement must be central to schools. All schools should have fully funded programmes for working with children and families throughout their time at school – but also before the age at which they start, and after they finish (i.e. perinatal – birth till two – and eighteen to twenty-one).

This is not the same as saying that schools need to do more. Schools are stretched enough as they are. But services like these are essential – and must be provided in a joined-up way that can best be achieved by integrating them with the school structure, by, for example, having the head of a perinatal service sit on the senior leadership team of a trust, having a social worker embedded in school or allowing schools to work more directly with Child and Adolescent Mental Health Services.

The idea of a school operating in a vacuum is nonsensical. Anyone who works in one understands the need to engage with wider services. So let's stop the coverage of wider services from being a lottery and tie them closely into the management of the school.

Most importantly, let's take seriously the ways in which the default structures of school – the hours, the holidays – feed an outmoded model of the family, where someone is always available to do the school run, and extracurricular activities are down to haphazard provision in the area or by the parents. Childcare and wider enrichment are not add-ons; they are something that benefit us all.

So all schools should have funded breakfast clubs, holiday clubs and meaningful after-school activities available freely to all students. Again this is not about asking schools to do more – but it is about enabling and funding other agencies to work within school buildings, and to build this into the way we think about school.

Sam Freedman, one of those in the DfE behind the reforms of the 2010s, told me that the key thing he regrets was the change in focus signalled when the Department for Children, Schools and Families became the Department for Education in 2010. Let's reverse that change.

Narrative Three: Knowledge is for everyone

The knowledge-rich revolution in teaching has made huge gains – but it has also reinforced the ways in which education is designed only around the needs of the winners in the game of academic success. We need a story that shifts focus, not by lowering expectations, but by recognising the ways in which our current framing of learning is one-dimensional.

The inflection point that we have to focus on is at the age of sixteen, when children sit their GCSEs. Post-sixteen, the options we have are idiosyncratic, but in most cases they fundamentally work. GCSEs don't. They are the major problem at the heart of our system. They need to change – not because they are 'bad' exams, but because the purpose they serve is so ill defined and contradictory.

We need to properly separate out the two types of knowledge: the stuff we should all have, and the stuff some of us will later need. The perfect example of this issue at the moment is Maths. Much discussion has been given to the need to increase mathematical ability in the population – but the discussion ignores utterly the distinction between general numeracy and specialised maths. The deficit for most people is in the instinctive and automatic understanding of numerical processes – being able to multiply large numbers or visualise easily percentages, being able to interrogate statistics or to understand the geometry of shapes and volumes. These are the competencies rewarded in the 'Foundation' paper of GCSE Maths that will give a maximum of a grade 5 (or 'strong pass'). But the incentives for schools, and for students, is to push towards higher grades – which are accessed by understanding the more abstract maths of trigonometry and simultaneous equations in the

'Higher' paper that will prepare you for A-level study. The horrible irony is that students studying for the 'Higher' paper often find the basic maths tricky because not enough time has been devoted to it. And a sensible approach – of ensuring *everyone* has the basic competencies secured by first sitting 'Foundation' and only then sitting 'Higher' – is disincentivised in the structure and amount of content needed to be covered – as well as being specifically disallowed in performance tables. It is a system explicitly designed to funnel students towards the academic study of maths rather than to provide general competence.

This is not fair. It's not enough simply to say that everyone needs to learn as if they might go on to a university degree, and that those who fail can then try something else. We need to create a proper *general* standard – the stuff we actually want *everyone* to know for its own sake, for the sake of social discourse and cohesion, and for the sake of personal enrichment. A platform of proper knowledge and mastery on which to build further specialised study – but one that we design in ways that allow all students to access it. That would be a true General Certificate of Secondary Education.

A redesign on this scale is a big project and should be as long-term as possible – meaning that by the time it is in place, the expectation would be that it is digitally assessed, but still in exam conditions for much of it. To emphasise the difference between this and the current system I'll call it a 'Passport Qualification'. This would merge multiple domains of learning into a truly general qualification to be sat at the age of fifteen – with no free choice of subjects.

The 'no free choice' requires an explanation. At the moment we say to students that they have a choice at GCSE, which creates the implication that to choose Psychology at GCSE, for example, is the most meaningful and direct way of becoming a psychologist. It suggests a linear progression from GCSE onwards, which is mostly false. And, most of all, any choice is actually undermined by the structure of accountability measures. The description of GCSE options as 'choices' leads to transactional thinking. It leads to the sense that the education you get is defined by what you *want* and can be rejected if you *don't* want it – and takes away from the case that knowledge is worth learning for the way it supports a 'general' understanding of the world. And on the most basic level, if we make the general curriculum a matter of choice, then we are denying children the possibility of truly stepping outside their comfort zone – we are reinforcing existing preference rather than challenging and expanding.

But that doesn't mean there is no space for personal inclination. There would still be opportunity for choice within the new Passport Qualification. But this would be in choosing topics for interest, not courses for specialism. Most importantly, it would be in choosing a topic for an Independent Project – something very similar to the current Extended Project Qualification (EPQ), where the assessment is not of the content, but of the process one goes through. This allows students to genuinely find their own interests *before* making significant choices – including following practical and performance routes – and to develop research and independent learning skills before they become essential to success, post-sixteen. Just like an EPQ, the assessment of this should be via an oral presentation with questioning from a panel.

Creative subjects would be integral, too. Not because the world of work needs some kind of ill-defined skill of 'creativity' to maximise economic potential – but because the act of creation, the act of being able to point to something and say 'I made that', is a profound joy that everyone deserves. And, of course, the ability to plan, self-direct and carry a project to fruition that, for example, Fine Art fosters, is pretty handy to have.

Another component of this qualification would be that students should have their English assessed by writing essays and stories, but the topics of these essays should be content from other subjects. The current approach of the English Language GCSE, where kids are judged on their response to random, anodyne unseen extracts, is nonsense. They should do numeracy – but again linked to actual content and knowledge (within the context of a scientific problem, for example). And they should do the 'twenty-first-century skills' of the use of information and communication technologies (ICT) – but linked to content, requiring them to, for instance, create formulas in Excel to tabulate the results of an experiment.

Requirements for Personal Development (the part of the curriculum that prioritises social, moral and relationship education) and

Work Experience should also be incorporated, and made part of the final assessment. A key failing of current approaches to these is that they become a tick-box exercise, whereby it's enough that kids have been put in a room where something is said – there is no check on whether learning actually happens. If these are to be valued, they need to be assessed. And any new qualification needs to include proper mandatory time for Child Development, a subject that encompasses parenting and childcare, that even has its own full GCSE equivalent in the current model – but which, scandalously, ends up being targeted predominantly at low-achieving girls, rather than forming an integral part of the entitlement of every pupil.

These are all massive changes to the structure of assessment and curriculum. But in themselves they could still end up feeding the old model of success for some and failure for others – a ranking and sort-ing of young people into haves and have-nots, just with a different set of criteria. We can never eliminate failure, of course, nor would we want to. In many ways, in fact, we need to encourage the possibility of it as a learning experience. That may sound like a contradiction – that we both need to disrupt the ranking of people into successes and failures, and yet also allow the possibility of failure – but it really isn't. We need the possibility of failure, but then also the possibility of learning from it and going on to succeed the second time around. We need to break down the cliff-edge nature of our assessment – the high-stakes, one-shot structure of it.

So perhaps the most important – and the most radical – element of the Passport Qualification starts with the fact it should be brought forward by a year. Sitting the Passport Qualification at fifteen rather than sixteen allows a year between the completion of mainstream education and the current range of choices at post-sixteen that include A levels, apprenticeships and vocational courses. This can be used to create a bridge between the two. A 'bridging year' like this lowers the stakes – allowing for teaching that focuses on the student, not on the grade. Those who fail at fifteen can try again without fall-ing behind; while those who don't fail can go further, using a year without high-stakes exams as a chance to explore knowledge and career options creatively.

What exactly happens in that year would be fluid, but roughly speaking you'd have three options: work towards a re-sit of your Passport, undertake some vocational training to prepare for an apprenticeship or embark on a more academic style of learning – or some combination of the three. But the principle would be that, by sixteen, *every* student has had a full opportunity to get to the same level, and all are ready for the next stage, while those with the capacity have not been held back, and have had a year in which they have broken free of the straitjacket of a standardised approach. During that year the absence of high stakes means that children can actually test out different routes without being penalised, if they don't suit. It challenges the absurdity of current practice, where apprenticeships, for example, must be stepped into blind, without having experienced what they might entail; or where changing A-level choices means an extra year at school, which dislocates a child from their peer group and must be explained away on university entrance. It maximises the current virtues of sixteen to eighteen education – the wide range of options – while mitigating the current, not insignificant risk of making the wrong choice.

Above all, this becomes an incentive for both vocationally minded and academic kids to pass their general exams at fifteen, as it will let them start the next specialised phase of their education earlier and with more freedom.

Narrative Four: School is for everyone

Two problems that are deeply intransigent and fundamentally linked are the corrosive effect of bad behaviour in schools and the complexity of the needs of the students who behave in this way. And the ways in which we talk about these problems betray a damaging lack of moral clarity about our purpose as educators, and our responsibility to children.

In the polarised debate on how to tackle disruptive behaviour, the need to exclude dangerous students for the benefit of others is often pitted against the inclusive, therapeutic, 'trauma-informed' approach that says this only does further damage to the excluded pupil. But the two approaches are not mutually exclusive. Most students who are excluded probably do have deeply held traumas that should be addressed; but equally, if this trauma means they are disrupting education for everyone around them, they need to be supported in a different way, and potentially in a different kind of school.

To do this, we need a radical overhaul of Alternative Provision. We need proper, high-quality coverage for every school. This means units designed not simply to contain and remove challenging kids, but also to reintegrate them into the mainstream. It means outreach teams to work *with* schools, as well as decent long-term AP. Without this, schools cannot effectively support the most challenging students – and we cannot claim to care about all children.

Narrative Five: Measurement is about improvement, not ranking

What we measure defines what we do. The twin poles of performance tables and Ofsted have for years distorted the ways in which schools work, again and again telling us that middle-class schools are better than working-class schools. At the same time they have also driven change and improvement in ways that have reached all corners of the country. So we need oversight and accountability. But we also need an understanding that what we value in schools is more complex than a number or a grade.

The answer, for Ofsted, is that it should be split into two functions. First, safeguarding checks, whereby the processes and attitudes that protect children from harm are evaluated. This includes checking that concerns are reported, that bullying is addressed and that special needs are catered for. This should be a binary yes or no, and should be carried out in roughly the same way as current inspections, with little or no notice, on a four-yearly cycle, and with inspectors who are taken from a central pool. Where schools fail, they should simply be given targets to make up, and then be re-inspected at intervals of six weeks until they do so.

Separately there need to be more nuanced, detailed 'school-monitoring inspections', which should be carried out every year by a specifically assigned inspector – who will continue to come back year on year, building on their institutional knowledge. This should be done without grading, but with descriptors of the schools' good and bad qualities. The regularity of this lowers the stakes – if you do badly one year, then you can improve next year, before long-term reputational damage is done – without sacrificing accountability.

If Ofsted is transformed in this way (with no graded judgements, other than the binary safeguarding check), and the marketisation of education is halted by changing admissions, then performance tables become far less pernicious in any case. However, the one key change that would instantly de-fang them is simple: remove KS2 SATs.

SATs are a terrible exam, particularly for reading comprehension. The questions are weirdly difficult even for adults and are designed seemingly in direct opposition to the insights of E. D. Hirsch, while the texts used are often at the wrong level of challenge for the kids sitting them. The fact that SATs are ostensibly not to test the children, but the school, is disingenuous. In practice the data they provide defines what GCSE grade will be judged as positive progress in the Progress 8 measure, and so it follows kids throughout secondary, governing the sets they are in and the attention paid to them. At the same time the stakes for schools are high, and the pressures of accountability push them to devote excessive attention to SATs in ways that then distort the validity of the grades.

We should indeed have some kind of standardised assessment at KS2, but there is no reason for it to be reported in national tables, and there is also no reason why it can't have some modicum of joy in the construction of the test. And while it is sensible to use this data to measure progress, there's no reason for it to be linked to specific children. The data should be held anonymously, and then used to calculate progress at the end of the general qualification at fifteen – short-circuiting all the paraphernalia of labelling and tracking, and forcing schools to look at the child and not the data.

★

Five new stories to tell, and five ways in which we could begin to tell them. Some of them are more straightforward, others very hard indeed. I'm not in the position to put them into action – and if I were, there's no doubt I'd have to modify some of my thinking. But there is a value in stating things as they should be, divorced from political expediency, simply to set out a vision of what is *right*.

A further caveat with these suggestions. Schools have suffered immensely over the years through ill-informed and rushed reforms. I have had a great privilege in writing this book: I've pontificated freely about what we might do, without worrying about how, when or with what money. I recognise this – and everything I say here comes with the proviso that it should be done over a long timeframe, and with plenty of notice and planning. Finland's school system took thirty years of planning before final implementation.[1] I wouldn't want to wait that long, but we do have to break education out of the deadlock of the parliamentary term. The things we need to do have to be part of a new consensus, planned and delivered across political boundaries. This may sound unrealistic, but I cannot see how it will work if it isn't.

If I'm honest, though, in writing this book I have found myself caught up in a kind of dizzying paralysis. Every time I think I see something clearly, my focus shifts and it seems to be part of a bigger pattern and I find myself disorientated again. As a result, if there is one thing I feel even more sure of it is that whatever happens in the coming years in the world of education, it will be inextricable from what happens in society as a whole. And here I need to nail my colours to the mast: there is no doubt at all in my mind that over the next decade there are profound ways in which we need to reshape the way we all live.

That is a pretty big and vague statement, I know. To explain what I mean and how this is relevant, let me take you back to the classroom for the last time.

Epilogue: The bigger picture

Some of my colleagues roll their eyes at my insistence on teaching *Paradise Lost*. It certainly isn't the most accessible of texts. If I'm honest, some of the kids roll their eyes, too. I suppose I take that as a challenge. If I can make them enjoy *this*, I think, then I'm a *proper* teacher. But I also just love the thing. I love the spectacle of an arrogant, entitled, misogynistic old lecher with a delicate, nuanced, humble and egalitarian poetic sensibility engaged in both attack and defence at the same time. I love the sheer specificity of a universe conjured up with relentless focus on every detail to 'justify the ways of God to men' that manages also to argue the opposite. I love the fact that I, a Jewish atheist, can be brought almost to the brink of belief by something so monumentally nonsensical. But more than anything, I love how reading *Paradise Lost* from a twenty-first-century perspective dramatises the ways in which we are prisoners of the paradigms of our own minds — and the ways in which we can free ourselves.

'Milton is a man of his time,' I tell my Year 13s. 'He believes absolutely in the words of the Bible. You can't criticise him for misogyny in saying that Eve is subservient to Adam.'

'But what about Sin?'

The class is a little obsessed with Sin. Not the idea, but the character.

'Yes, that is fair. The representation of Sin as a woman with a vagina filled with barking dogs is legitimately misogynist.'

In the corner a student looks worried. 'Does Milton *actually* believe this stuff?'

I shrug. 'Yes. Sort of.'

'He believes that hell is real, and there's a big skeleton with a spear, and Satan's head split open to give birth to Sin?'

Again I shrug. 'What you've got to understand,' I say, 'is that we all believe in stuff that will seem not only absurd, but possibly mad in the future. There's so much that we simply accept because it's the way things are, or the way we've been told they should be.'

What comes next is something I say again and again to my classes. They might or might not listen, but to me it is the core of why I teach. Yes, there is knowledge to transmit, poetry to love, stories to write. But the biggest lesson I have held on to from my own schooling, and the one I always try to allow my students to glimpse, is the possibility, just out of sight, of a shift in the paradigm – a step outside our own frame of reference to see that maybe, just maybe, life isn't quite what it seems.

So I tell them that when they are old and they look back on their youth, there will be things they see that they find staggering. They will see attitudes they once held, or actions they took, and they will scarcely believe it was possible. I tell them I don't know what it is that will seem like this, but I have my suspicions. And I tell them there may be things that I say, too, that they will look back on with contempt, ways in which I have already been left behind by the tide of history.

And that is why Milton matters, and why the teaching of literature matters. Because in amongst the stuff that is contingent to the world he lived in is the hard little nugget of wisdom, tested and proved by time, visible more clearly now precisely because the contingent silliness is also so obvious. I don't care about his belief, or my belief – because, in reading *Paradise Lost*, I read not about angels and demons, but about free will and destiny, about shaping the world and being shaped by it.

It's not just literature. All education is in search of this. Not only transmitting the insights of the past, but enabling the future to see clearly enough to discard that which is mistaken, and to hold on to that which is true.

I can't know what we will look like to future schoolchildren. But I can make a guess, and I believe that if we could somehow take their perspective and look back on our own time, we'd see something so clearly that we would question the sanity of the people today who ignore it. We cannot claim fairness and choice where there is none.

We cannot all win. We cannot grow for ever. The model we have lived with for the last forty years of constant, ceaseless expansion and cut-throat individualism has given us so much, but it has also taken much away. It cannot go on for ever. At some point we have to remake the way we think about the world we live in. We have to tell a better story.

Schools are only one part of this. But they are the part I know. And I know they can be better.

Notes

Introduction

1 Some people disingenuously argue that low GCSE grades are not the same as failing. But if grade 4 is labelled a pass, then by definition grades 1–3 are fails.
2 The establishment of the Education Endowment Foundation (EEF), an organisation that collates and compares research findings on education, has been touted as one of the great successes of recent years. But Professor of Social Mobility Lee Elliot Major has pointed out the striking fact that almost all of the interventions that were successful on a smaller scale dwindled in significance, when scaled up. The one exception was giving kids breakfast – leading to the insight that most of the time *how* you implement trumps the impact of any fancy new technique: something most classroom teachers instinctively know.

1. 'You just need school'

1 Riordan, Jopling and Starr, 2021
2 It is statistically true that success at school can be correlated with higher income. But higher income is not the same as being 'good at life'. We'll return to this point later.

2. A history lesson

1 Leach, 1915
2 Leach, 1915
3 Orme, 2006
4 Lawson and Silver, 1973

5 Orme, 2006

6 Orme, 2006

7 Simon, 1966

8 Kay-Shuttleworth, 1862

9 Gillard, 2018

10 Three per cent of students in grammar schools in 2019 were in receipt of free school meals. There has been progress since then in some areas, but it remains far from the idealised vision of equality of opportunity.

11 Free school meals are a deeply flawed measure of whether someone is at a disadvantage educationally – see the discussion in Chapter 4.

12 Davies, 1976

13 'How to apply to set up a mainstream free school', DfE: www.gov.uk/government/publications/free-school-application-guide/how-to-apply-to-set-up-a-mainstream-free-school#assessment-criteria

3. The curriculum

1 The content and assessment method for exams are set by the exam boards (with schools choosing from between them) based on guidance from the Joint Council for Qualifications (JCQ) and Ofqual (the qualifications watchdog), which ultimately stems from the Department for Education.

2 Robinson, 2010. A measure of his influence – and perhaps his audience – is the fact that the most viewed TED talk ever is by Robinson.

3 Peddiwell, 1939

4 Thomas, 2021

5 Gimson and Goodman, 2023

6 Matthew Arnold's famous description of the canon.

7 'What are the benefits of learning Latin and Mandarin in school?' (2 August 2021), The Education Hub: educationhub.blog.gov.uk/2021/08/02/what-are-the-benefits-of-learning-latin-and-mandarin-in-school/

8 Hirsch, 2016

9 Thomas, 2021

10 Weale, 2022

11 Jackson, 1968

12 Willingham, 2010

13 Christodoulou, 2014

14 An A-level equivalent course.

15 I know I run the risk of constantly chasing my own tail here, but remember 'the soft bigotry of low expectations'. This is the problem that Gove's reforms were supposed to solve.

4. Rank order

1 What I find fascinating here is the tacit admission that using a piece of knowledge in an unfamiliar context is, by definition, both useful and beneficial to learning. It seems to promote the importance of precisely the kind of cross-domain thinking that our compartmentalised system structurally discourages. If it helps to bring fruit into a Maths exam, surely it also helps to bring Maths into the English exam. Accepting this logic has wider implications, too. We all, I presume, would agree on the need to have some objective standard of literacy and numeracy. At the moment we achieve that through the English Language and Maths GCSEs. But why shouldn't we assess literacy on the basis of the essays that students write in History, or in Geography, or in English Literature? Why can't we check maths alongside physics? Or computing? Why the need to constantly segregate knowledge?

2 Hirsch, 2016

3 There are pedagogical arguments made for this – some of which I agree with (it encourages students to embed learning in long-term memory, for example). But the real reason for the change was clear at the time: modular exams allowed schools to re-sit and improve grades, in an effort to enhance their standing. As a solution, it was entirely back-to-front. After all, it was the league tables and their perverse incentives that motivated the re-sits, not the modularity. From the point of view of the student, what possible benefit is there in insisting that everything has to come down to one final high-stakes, unrepeatable exam?

4 The NRT is designed to spot any variation in 'raw' ability between year groups and correct for it, avoiding the chance that you might be penalised for simply being in a 'bright' year. Given the size of each national year group, the chance of this is small.

5 Yes, you can retake some GCSE courses at college or sixth form. But the structures and incentives are very different at post-sixteen, and in most instances you would do a GCSE-equivalent vocational course rather than the same exam – and would not therefore have the same route forward through A level and university. The exceptions are English and Maths, where if you fail you have to try again between the ages of sixteen and eighteen – but due to a variety of factors the pass rate for these compulsory retakes is a genuinely appalling 16.4 per cent for Maths and 15.9 per cent for English.

6 Woolcock, May 2022

7 Woolcock, August 2022

8 This is essentially what most universities now do. The evidence supports it: a 2014 study from the Higher Education Funding Council for England found that where A-level grades are the same, state-school candidates at university are more likely to get first-class degrees than private-school candidates – although disadvantaged candidates still underachieve compared to their non-disadvantaged peers. 'Differences in degree outcomes: Key findings' (March 2014), HEFCE: dera.ioe.ac.uk/id/eprint/19811/1/HEFCE2014_03.pdf

9 Of course it is not just the quality of the school that confers advantage in the race for merit. The psychologist and behavioural geneticist Kathryn Harden has made a strong case recently for the idea that if we were to be a little more upfront with the genetic component of educational success and acknowledge the randomness of talent, it might help us work for social justice – by removing the damaging narrative of fault and blame. That is probably a tall order. But we shouldn't forget why we even use the word 'talent' in the first place: the famous parable of the talents that encodes in Christian morality the idea that it isn't what we are given that we should be praised for, but what we do with it.

10 Sandel, 2020

11 In 2022, while 49.8 per cent of all students achieved Grade 5 in both English and Maths, only 22.4 per cent of disadvantaged students did. Over ten years of tracking, the government's disadvantage-gap index has varied between 3.66 and 4.07, but has made no significant shift. The Education Policy Institute, in a 2020 report, said, 'The gap in GCSE

grades between students in long-term poverty and their better-off peers has failed to improve over the last ten years.'

12 Calarco, 2018

13 Reay, 2017. Class is a complicated thing in modern Britain. The British Social Attitudes Survey suggests that 47 per cent of people who fall into the conventional definition of middle class – professional, managerial jobs – identify as working class. Sam Friedman, of the London School of Economics, identifies this recasting of 'origin stories' into earthy working-class struggle as 'a means of deflecting and obscuring class privilege'. At the same time as this inflationary pressure upon membership of the prole-tariat, there is significant semantic confusion about what we mean when we use the phrase. For many, there is a legitimate reason why you might claim a status at odds with your lifestyle. They would argue there is such a thing as 'culturally working class' – something often claimed, for example, by some MPs, who by definition have a 'professional, manager-ial job' and yet would also claim, with some justification, that they shouldn't forget their roots just because they have gained political power.

14 In 2022 the North-East's Progress 8 score was -0.27, the lowest of all nine regions, with London a full half-grade higher at 0.23; 'Key Stage 4 2022: The national picture' (20 October 2022), FFT Education Datalab: ffteducationdatalab.org.uk/2022/10/key-stage-4-2022-the-national-picture/. KS2, on the other hand, was second of nine, with 64 per cent meeting the expected standard, beaten only by – you guessed it – London on 67 per cent; Dave Thomson (22 July 2022), 'Key Stage 2 2022: How things have changed for schools and regions', FFT Educa-tion Datalab: ffteducationdatalab.org.uk/2022/07/key-stage-2-2022-how-things-have-changed-for-schools-and-regions/

15 And in the instance of the private schools, whose teacher-assessed grades soared to a far greater degree than their state counterparts, to be dis-torted by inflationary pressure from parents.

16 Sherwood, 2019

17 It's worth saying that both Oxford and Cambridge are well aware of the difficulties of identifying the right students, and use processes of con-siderable nuance to go further than simple grades – but there's no doubt that once you are at this level of scrutiny, it becomes even less

meaningful to ascribe ranking, and talk about 'the best', when really you're looking for subtle indicators of how someone might respond to a very specific learning environment.

18 Education Endowment Foundation, 2018

19 Riordan, Jopling and Starr, 2021

20 Walker, 2023

7. The social world of school

1 For those of you who are not teachers, this really is a thing. You decide on the day. I know, I know, but the nature of school recruitment is that everyone is operating within the same timeframe – we all want to recruit for the start of term, and we all have the same notice periods. So to go, on a whim, to an interview 300 miles away in a city you've never even visited is to commit to a period of twenty-four hours in which you will be slowly eaten alive by the fear that you are about to either fuck everything up or miss the opportunity of a lifetime.

9. Community

1 Boakye, 2022, p. 129

2 Shackle, 2017

10. Privilege

1 'Elitist Britain 2019' (2019), The Sutton Trust / The Social Mobility Commission, www.suttontrust.com/wp-content/uploads/2019/12/Elitist-Britain-2019.pdf

2 'Universities and social mobility: Summary report' (November 2012), The Sutton Trust: www.suttontrust.com/wp-content/uploads/2021/11/Universities-and-Social-Mobility-Summary.pdf

3 Adams, 2023

4 Even aside from anything else, the positioning and relative wealth of

different private schools across the country is massively unequal – so if the solution were simply to partner with a local state school, that would still lead to a replication of current North–South divides and the marginalisation of communities locked in deep deprivation.

5 'Rich resources of private schools give pupils educational advantage, IOE research shows' (5 November 2019), UCL: www.ucl.ac.uk/ioe/news/2019/nov/rich-resources-private-schools-give-pupils-educational-advantage-ioe-research-shows

6 Henry, 2013

11. *Personal development*

1 Whittaker, 2022

2 Cass, 2022

3 Department for Education (December 2023), 'Gender questioning children: draft schools and colleges guidance': www.gov.uk/government/consultations/gender-questioning-children-draft-schools-and-colleges-guidance

4 To state the obvious, I'm not a doctor, nor am I any kind of an expert on gender and identity. Everything I say on this topic is about teaching and schools – and about how schools can respond when teachers pretty universally lack that specialist knowledge, just as I do. It is certainly not about the medical rights and wrongs of different therapies or approaches.

5 Not the promotion of specific party politics, of course – teachers are rightly required to be neutral. But just because the BBC is required to be neutral, that doesn't mean it has no political role, and the same is true of schools. Teachers have an obligation to actively challenge misconceptions, and to respond to world events with care and a strong moral compass – not to ignore them.

12. *Bad kids*

1 Bennett, 2020

2 A phrase Bennett rightly and explicitly repudiates as a distortion of his techniques, which he always caveats with the opposite idea: that there

are some situations that have to be dealt with differently, even if the overall structure is disciplinarian.

3 Dix, 2017

4 Lucy Crehan, in her 2016 book *Cleverlands*, makes a brilliant comparison of all the highest-rated school systems.

5 Please note the scare-quotes. As discussed already, class is complicated and resistant to generalisations. It disappears in front of you as you explore it. But there are two distinct attitudes to childhood in the UK and they do have some correspondence with class, even if it's not exact.

6 Mike Savage gives an excellent overview of class and how we define it in *Social Class in the 21st Century* (2015), showing that original definition around manual or non-manual work to come from the Registrar General's schema (introduced in 1911), which made occupational category, and not wealth per se, the key dividing line.

7 Crehan, 2016

13. *Outside the mainstream*

1 Booth, 2023

14. *How to succeed in life*

1 The most recent change – whereby students will pay back over a maximum of forty years rather than having the debt written off after thirty years – is the most shockingly regressive policy I've seen, even amongst some stiff competition. It means that those who choose lower-paying (but entirely valid and worthwhile) careers, such as nursing or teaching or the Arts, must pay more for their degrees over their lifetime than those who go into highly paid jobs in the City and can save on interest by paying off their loan early.

2 Halfon, November 2021

3 Some of the response to the attendance crisis focuses on non school alternatives: home schooling, self-directed study, and so on. There are some circumstances in which these might work, but think how

significant home circumstance is in the way school works, and how let down some children are by that equation; and then think about how much non-school alternatives are entirely based on the capacity of a family to support their child. And finally think just how few of those 8.9 million children in England can actually expect a good deal out of this.

15. *Thinking differently about school*

1 In 2021 the government published a glowing report showing the link between income and grades in which the Minister of State for Schools, Nick Gibb, said, 'GCSEs equip young people with the knowledge and skills they need to succeed and this data shows how small improvements to grades can have a huge overall impact on people's lives.' I have used this language, too: I spent four years as head of sixth form and every year I used the same slide, showing the increase in lifetime earnings that could result from going to university. I also spent three years on the Social Mobility Commission – and every piece of research on education and outcomes came back to comparing incomes as a measure of educational and social success.

2 In the DfE research quoted above (Gibb, 2021), a direct correlation is established between GCSE grades and later income. But that is a dataset, not destiny. We have turned that basic correlation – something that has a use in looking at the macro-view of educational and industrial policy, but does not mean an instrumental relationship between exam scores and income – into a line of reasoning that says to individual children and parents that education is about economic advantage.

3 Carneiro et al., 2020

4 Dolan, 2019

5 I can guarantee that vanishingly few teachers would describe their jobs in such utilitarian terms. There are plenty of times and places where we talk about the wonder of learning, the passion for a subject, the idea of finding a vocation. Unfortunately, no matter how it feels for the individual teacher, the overall structures and discourse of education – both traditional and progressive – have become overwhelmingly utilitarian and transactional.

6 As Michael Sandel shows in his book *What Money Can't Buy: The Moral Limits of Markets* (2012), there are some things for which market forces don't work, where thinking in terms of transactional rewards undermines, rather than reinforces, what we are trying to achieve. One of his key examples is education. He cites studies where the impact of direct reward on achievement has been measured, where kids were paid to do well, and finds that the impacts are not linear – that extrinsic motivation is brittle and temporary and can lead to long-term demotivation.

7 None of this is to say that all children view education as transactional, or that all children disengage. The point is that the very people our meritocratic myth seeks to empower are disempowered – and that the children most able to engage with the enriching qualities of learning are those already primed to do so by their social context.

8 Csikszentmihalyi, 1990

9 Guy Claxton quotes a study that shows this effect in *The Future of Teaching* (Claxton, 2021).

10 Lucy Foulkes discusses the psychology of adolescence in her book *Coming of Age* (Bodley Head, 2024). In particular, she highlights the ways in which your teens are a period which fundamentally shapes the adult self, saying, 'Like tattoos etched onto fresh skin, the relationships and mistakes and events we go through in adolescence all leave marks that last.' In a very real, empirical sense, the experience of school (alongside the other events of adolescence) shapes us – she cites research that consistently finds a 'reminiscence bump', whereby people's most significant memories all occur in their teens and early twenties, irrespective of the age they are when they are asked to recall them.

11 A quick look at government data (available on gov.uk) shows that in 2021–2, 16.6 per cent of pupils who attended secondary schools with sixth forms were eligible for FSM. The equivalent figure for pupils who attended 11–16 schools was 25.3 per cent. Unsurprisingly, the difference on inspection is also stark: 7.3 per cent of 11–16 schools are Outstanding, compared to 17.5 per cent of 11–18.

12 This effect is not much commented upon, but seems to me very significant. In my own career I managed the addition of a sixth form onto a school that was previously only for eleven- to sixteen-year-olds – and

was deeply shocked by the ways in which the curriculum design and teaching style did not set them up for the challenges of the next stage (for example, by building habits of self-organisation and wider research), seeking instead to maximise grades by the most direct route possible.

13 Parker, 2021

16. A better story

1 Crehan, 2016

Bibliography

Adams, Richard (12 March 2023), 'How UK private schools' overseas satellites can bring in large sums', *The Guardian*: www.theguardian.com/education/2023/mar/12/how-uk-private-schools-overseas-satellites-can-bring-in-large-sums

Benn, Melissa (2018), *Life Lessons: The Case for a National Education Service*, London: Verso

Bennett, Tom (2020), *Running the Room: The Teacher's Guide to Behaviour*, Woodbridge: John Catt

Birbalsingh, Katharine (ed.) (2020), *Michaela: The Power of Culture*, Woodbridge: John Catt

Black, Paul and William, Dylan (2006), *Inside the Black Box*, London: GL Assessment

Blatchford, Roy (ed.) (2019), *The Forgotten Third: Do a Third Have to Fail for Two Thirds to Pass?*, Woodbridge: John Catt

Blishen, Edward (ed.) (1969), *The School That I'd Like*, London: Penguin

Boakye, Jeffrey (2022), *I Heard What You Said*, London: Picador

Booth, Samantha (12 September 2023), 'MPs demand answers from DfE after EHCP cuts target revealed', *Schools Week*: schoolsweek.co.uk/mps-want-explanation-from-dfe-on-ehcp-cuts-contract/

Bourdieu, Pierre (1986), 'The Forms of Capital', in I. Szeman, *Cultural Theory: An Anthology* (pp. 81–94), Hoboken: John Wiley

Brighouse, Tim and Waters, Mick (2022), *About Our Schools: Improving on Previous Best*, Carmarthen: Crown House

Calarco, Jessica McCrory (1 June 2018), 'Why rich kids are so good at the marshmallow test', *The Atlantic*: www.theatlantic.com/family/archive/2018/06/marshmallow-test/561779/

Caplan, Bryan (2018), *The Case Against Education: Why the Education System Is a Waste of Time and Money*, Princeton: Princeton University Press

Carneiro, Pedro, Cattan, Sarah, Dearden, Lorraine, van der Erve, Laura, Krutikova, Sonya and Macmillan, Lindsey (September 2020), 'The long shadow of deprivation: Differences in opportunities across England', gov.uk: assets.publishing.service.gov.uk/media/5f76d4dce90e07 15c9258c18/SMC_Long_shadow_of_deprivation_MAIN_REPORT_ Accessible.pdf

Cass, Hilary (February 2022), 'The Cass Review: Independent review of gender identity services for children and young people: Interim report', cass.independent-review.uk

Christodoulou, Daisy (2014), *Seven Myths about Education*, Oxford: Routledge

Claxton, Guy (2021), *The Future of Teaching: And the Myths That Hold It Back*, Oxford: Routledge

Corrigan, Paul (1979), *Schooling the Smash Street Kids*, London: Red Globe Press

Crehan, Lucy (2016), *Cleverlands*, London: Unbound

Csikszentmihalyi, Mihaly (1990), *Flow: The Psychology of Optimal Experience*, London: Harper Perennial

Davies, Hunter (1976), *The Creighton Report: A Year in the Life of a Comprehensive School*, London: Hamish Hamilton

Dix, Paul (2017), *When the Adults Change, Everything Changes*, Carmarthen: Independent Thinking Press

Dolan, Paul (2019), *Happy Ever After*, London: Penguin

Education Endowment Foundation (2018), 'The Attainment Gap 2017', educationendowmentfoundation.org.uk: d2tic4wvo1iusb.cloudfront. net/production/documents/support-for-schools/bitesize-support/EEF_ Attainment_Gap_Report_2018.pdf?v=1704024805

Elliot Major, Lee and Briant, Emily (2023), *Equity in Education: Levelling the Playing Field of Learning*, Woodbridge: John Catt

Elliot Major, Lee and Higgins, Steve (2019), *What Works?: Research and Evidence for Successful Teaching*, London: Bloomsbury

Ellis, Terry et al. (1976), *William Tyndale: The Teachers' Story*, London: Writers and Readers Ltd

Fine, Cordelia (2017), *Testosterone Rex: Unmaking the Myths of Our Gendered Minds*, London: Icon Books

Foulkes, Lucy (2024), *Coming of Age*, London: Bodley Head

Freire, Paulo (1970), *Pedagogy of the Oppressed*, London: Penguin

Friedman, Sam and Laurison, Daniel (2019), *The Class Ceiling: Why It Pays to Be Privileged*, Bristol: Policy Press

Friedman, Sam, O'Brien, Dave and McDonald, Ian (17 January 2021), 'Deflecting privilege: Class identity and the intergenerational self', *Sociology*, Vol. 55, Issue 4, pp. 716–33

Gibb, Nick (9 July 2021), 'Higher GCSE grades linked to lifetime earnings boost': www.gov.uk/government/news/higher-gcse-grades-linked-to-lifetime-earnings-boost

Gillard, Derek (May 2018), 'Education in the UK: A history': education-uk.org/history/

Gimson, Andrew and Goodman, Paul (8 June 2023), 'Interview: "If you come into politics, you should come in because you believe in ideas." Gibb on delivering better schools', Conservative Home: conservativehome.com/2023/06/08/interview-if-you-come-into-politics-you-should-come-in-because-you-believe-in-ideas-gibb-on-delivering-better-schools/

Green, Francis and Kynaston, David (2019), *Engines of Privilege: Britain's Private School Problem*, London: Bloomsbury

Halfon, Robert (22 June 2021), 'White privilege is just a MYTH to 1 million white, working-class kids', *The Sun*: www.thesun.co.uk/news/15363153/white-privilege-myth-one-million-white-kids/

Halfon, Robert (17 November 2021), 'Skills shortages cost the UK billions a year. Re-setting our education system can change this – and boost pupils' prospects', Conservative Home: conservativehome.com/2021/11/17/robert-halfon-skills-shortages-cost-the-uk-billions-a-year-re-setting-our-education-system-can-change-this-and-boost-pupils-prospects/

Hanley, Lynsey (2016), *Respectable: Crossing the Class Divide*, London: Penguin

Harden, Kathryn Paige (2021), *The Genetic Lottery: Why DNA Matters for Social Equality*, Princeton: Princeton University Press

Hattie, John (2008), *Visible Learning: A Synthesis of Over 800 Meta-Analyses Relating to Achievement*, Oxford: Routledge

Henry, Julie (16 June 2013), 'Comprehensive school pupils do better at university, two new studies confirm', *The Guardian*: www.theguardian.com/education/2013/jun/16/accesstouniversity-private-schools

Hirsch, E. D. (2016), *Why Knowledge Matters: Rescuing Our Children from Failed Educational Theories*, Cambridge, MA: Harvard Education Press

Hudson, Kerry (2019), *Lowborn: Growing Up, Getting Away and Returning to Britain's Poorest Towns*, London: Vintage

Jackson, Philip (1968), *Life in Classrooms*, New York: Holt, Rinehart & Winston

Kay-Shuttleworth, James (1862), *Four Periods of Public Education as Reviewed in 1832, 1839, 1846, 1862 in Papers by Sir James Kay-Shuttleworth, Bart.*, London: Spottiswoode & Co.

Lawson, John and Silver, Harold (1973), *A Social History of Education in England*, London: Methuen & Co.

Leach, A. F. (1915), *The Schools of Medieval England*, London: Methuen & Co.

Lemov, Doug (2015), *Teach Like a Champion 2.0: 62 Techniques That Put Students on the Path to College*, San Francisco: Jossey-Bass

Lupton, Ruth and Hayes, Debra (2021), *Great Mistakes in Education Policy: And How to Avoid Them in the Future*, Bristol: Policy Press

Orme, Nicholas (2006), *Medieval Schools: From Roman Britain to Renaissance England*, New Haven: Yale University Press

Parker, Kate (30 March 2021), 'The impact of course choice at 16: what research says', *Tes Magazine*: www.tes.com/magazine/archived/ impact-course-choice-16-what-research-says

Peddiwell, J. Abner (1939), *The Saber-Tooth Curriculum*, New York: McGraw Hill

Reay, Diane (2017), *Miseducation: Inequality, Education and the Working Classes*, Bristol: Policy Press

Reimer, Everett (1973), *School Is Dead*, London: Penguin

Riordan, Sally, Jopling, Michael and Starr, Sean (2021), 'Against the odds: Achieving greater progress for secondary students facing socio-economic disadvantage', Social Mobility Commission: assets.publishing.service. gov.uk/media/60dc34c88fa8f50aad4ddb0a/Against_the_odds_report.pdf

Robinson, Sir Ken (2010), 'Changing education paradigms', RSA Animate, www.youtube.com/watch?v=zDZFcDGpL4U

Sandel, Michael (2012), *What Money Can't Buy: The Moral Limits of Markets*, London: Penguin

Sandel, Michael (2020), *The Tyranny of Merit: What's Become of the Common Good?*, London: Allen Lane

Savage, Mick (2015), *Social Class in the 21st Century*, London: Pelican

Shackle, Samira (1 September 2017), 'Trojan horse: the real story behind the fake "Islamic plot" to take over schools", *The Guardian*:

www.theguardian.com/world/2017/sep/01/trojan-horse-the-real-story-behind-the-fake-islamic-plot-to-take-over-schools

Sherwood, Dennis (15 January 2019), '1 school exam grade in 4 is wrong. Does this matter?', HEPI: www.hepi.ac.uk/2019/01/15/1-school-exam-grade-in-4-is-wrong-does-this-matter/

Simon, Joan (1966), *Education and Society in Tudor England*, Cambridge: Cambridge University Press

Thomas, Gary (2021), *Education: A Very Short Introduction* (2nd edition), Oxford: Oxford University Press

Tisdall, Laura (2019), *A Progressive Education?: How Childhood Changed in Mid-Twentieth-Century English and Welsh Schools*, Manchester: Manchester University Press

Walker, Amy (17 November 2023), 'Are schools in poorer areas now getting better Ofsted grades?', *Schools Week*: schoolsweek.co.uk/are-schools-in-poorer-areas-now-getting-better-ofsted-grades/

Weale, Sally (22 May 2022), 'UK's "strictest headmistress" fears schools will stop teaching Shakespeare', *The Guardian*: www.theguardian.com/education/2022/may/22/uks-strictest-headmistress-fears-schools-will-stop-teaching-shakespeare

Whittaker, Freddie 'Schools can ignore trans pupils' gender preference, claims attorney general' (10 August 2022), *Schools Week*: schoolsweek.co.uk/schools-can-ignore-trans-pupils-gender-preference-claims-attorney-general/

Williams, Raymond (1961), *The Long Revolution*, London: Chatto & Windus

Willingham, Daniel (2010), *Why Don't Students Like School?: A Cognitive Scientist Answers Questions about How the Mind Works and What It Means for the Classroom*, San Francisco: Jossey-Bass

Woolcock, Nicola (3 May 2022), 'Privately educated pupils to lose places at Oxbridge, vice-chancellor warns', *The Times*: www.thetimes.co.uk/article/privately-educated-pupils-to-lose-places-at-oxbridge-vice-chancellor-warns-7crr2vlgx

Woolcock, Nicola (12 August 2022), 'Private school pupils turn backs on Oxbridge to chase Ivy League places', *The Times*: www.thetimes.co.uk/article/private-school-pupils-turn-backs-on-oxbridge-to-chase-ivy-league-places-zdk83cs7r

Acknowledgements

The writing of this book, more than anything else I've done, has been a communal effort. First thanks go to the people who started it off – Charlotte Seymour and Connor Brown – and to Will Hammond, who then took it on and worked tirelessly to shape it into something that made sense to the world outside my head. Special thanks to Joanne Maw for giving me the time to make my visits, and to the other colleagues at Southmoor who had to take up the slack in my absence.

Thanks also to the academics and experts whose work I've drawn upon. In particular, thanks to all of my fellow commissioners on the SMC who helped form my thinking on this stuff during a difficult and fascinating three years; and equal thanks to the members of the secretariat whose knowledge and professionalism helped me up my game and think beyond the school gates. Specific thanks to Sal Riordan and Laura Tisdall, who gave me expert advice on methodologies and feedback on parts of the text; and thanks to my readers: Mark, Barry, Nick, Jacob and Ali.

But, of course, the substance of this book is all about the schools I've visited. There were many brilliant conversations that didn't make it into the text, but everything I saw and heard informed the way I thought and the conclusions I came to. Thank you to all the Heads who welcomed me – both for welcoming me and for being headteachers; thanks to the teachers and senior leaders who spoke to me; and thanks to all the office staff who organised the details. A good office is the engine room of a school!

And thanks to the kids. What a brilliant, strange, funny and insightful bunch you are. It was transformative for me to have so much time to listen – and embarrassing to realise how little I get to do so in a normal day. In particular two classes helped me, by allowing me to talk to them about all sorts of random stuff: 11A1 (class of

2024) and 13 Lit (class of 2023). Sorry for rambling, and thanks for your patience.

My last two thanks are big ones. On a personal level, I cannot begin to express how grateful I am to my family. To Pip, Kiki and Om for general awesomeness. To my parents, Peter and Cathie, and my brother, Jacob, for my education – not the one at school, but the one they gave me at home, and on holiday, and in the funny spaces in between. To Joel and Dan, love and thanks. You're brilliant and you make life fun. But more than that, the two of you have provided me with that deep sense of purpose that is the engine of living well. And to Clare. Thank you for your patience with me, and for the joy we share. I love you.

And on a professional level, where do I start? Everyone I've taught, or I've taught with, is a part of this book. Thanks to Henry Box, to William Ellis, to Fortismere. But the place that has fostered the way of seeing education that I've tried to express here is the school at which I've worked for a decade now: Southmoor Academy. To all the kids, the teachers and the non-teaching staff who keep the place going, a special thank you – for the work you do, and for the ways in which you've changed me.

Index